The Potential of Africa to Capture Technology-Intensive Global Supply Chains

Economic Development
in **Africa Report**
2023

United
Nations

Geneva, 2023

EDAR 2023

P9-AGO-489

United Nations publication issued by the United Nations Conference on Trade and
Development

UNCTAD/ALDC/AFRICA/2023

ISBN: 978-92-1-300081-6
eISBN: 978-92-1-002851-6
ISSN: 1990-5114
eISSN: 1990-5122
Sales No. E.23.II.D.22

Acknowledgements

The *Economic Development in Africa Report 2023: The Potential of Africa to Capture Technology-intensive Global Supply Chains* was prepared by UNCTAD. The report was written by Habiba Ben Barka (team leader), Christine Awiti, Anja Slany, Sine Tepe and Ali Yedan. The work was carried out under the overall supervision of Paul Akiwumi, Director of the UNCTAD Division for Africa, Least Developed Countries and Special Programmes and Junior Davis, Head of the Policy Analysis and Research Branch. Research support was provided by Shutian Li, Blaire Ng, Stanislas Sanon, and Stefanie West. Evelyn Benítez and Elena Stroganova provided administrative support.

A hybrid meeting was held on 14 March 2023 to conduct a peer review of the report. It brought together specialists in the fields of trade and investments, global value and supply chains, industrial production, enterprise development, financial services and digital technologies. The participants were: Nora Aboushady (German Institute of Development and Sustainability), Adebayo Adeleke (Supply Chain Africa), Tilman Altenburg (German Institute of Development and Sustainability), Antonio Andreoni (SOAS University of London, United Kingdom), Gilberto Antonio (African Continental Free Trade Area, AfCFTA Secretariat), Guendalina Anzolin (Cambridge University, United Kingdom), Elvis Avenyo (University of Johannesburg, South Africa), Karolien De Bruyne (KU Leuven, Belgium), Amirah El-Haddad (German Institute of Development and Sustainability), Romain Houssa (University of Namur, Belgium), Stephen Karingi (United Nations Economic Commission for Africa), David Luke (London School of Economics and Political Science, United Kingdom), Francis Mangeni (AfCFTA Secretariat), Sébastian Miroudot (OECD Trade and Agriculture Directorate), Simon Roberts (University of Johannesburg, South Africa), Konstantin Wacker (University of Groningen, The Netherlands), and Gainmore Zanamwe (Afreximbank).

The following UNCTAD staff members provided helpful inputs and comments during various review processes: Lisa Borgatti, Dimo Calovski, Theresa Carpenter, Stefanie Garry, Federico Manto, Amelia Santos Paulino, Marios Pournaris, Astrit Sulstarova, Giovanni Valensisi and Anida Yupari.

The Documents Management Section of the Intergovernmental Outreach and Support Service of UNCTAD coordinated the production of the report. The Communication and External Relations section of UNCTAD provided support on report branding and publication. Overall layout, graphics and desktop publishing were undertaken by the Division of Conference Management of the United Nations Office at Geneva.

Notes

Billion signifies 1,000 million.

Dollars refers to United States of America dollars.

Metric tons signifies tons.

Use of a dash between years (for example, 2000–2005) signifies the full period involved, including the initial and final years.

Contents

BOXES

FIGURES

TABLES

Foreword

Many companies across the world are rethinking their supply chain strategies in order to address gaps and mitigate risks. The disruption effects on global production and supply chains of recent global shocks and geopolitical dynamics such as the Covid-19 pandemic and the war in Ukraine, have fueled the need for companies to minimize exposure to global distresses and reduce reliance on geographically concentrated suppliers and buyers.

We know that diversified supply chains generate significant economic benefits for the countries they connect, reduce inflationary pressures, contribute to increased stability and prosperity worldwide, and open new domestic and regional markets. We believe that such perspective for supply chain diversification provides new opportunities for African economies to position themselves as geographic alternatives and optimize their strategic value for future leading-edge supply chains.

In this year's *Economic Development in Africa Report: The Potential of Africa to Capture Technology-intensive Global Supply Chains,* we unpack current global supply chain pressures and identify policies necessary for tapping into these opportunities, including creating a reliable African supplier marketplace for global supply chains.

I would like to highlight some of the potential Africa can leverage to contribute to global supply chain diversification, especially in high-knowledge and technology-intensive industries. Africa's growing population, increasingly large consumer markets and expanding business opportunities are major sources of growth and prosperity for the world and key factors that position Africa as a strategic region in the drive for geographically diversified supply chains. Moreover, Africa's large reserves of critical minerals that are vital for global supply chains of high technology-intensive industries can turn African economies into key suppliers of parts and components in the automotive, electronics, renewable energy, and medical devices sectors. For instance, Africa accounts for 48 percent of global cobalt reserves and 47.6 percent of global manganese reserves, which are critical metals required to produce batteries and electrical vehicles.

While the need for Africa to integrate global supply chains is not new, we urge African countries to avoid being locked into the provision of "just" raw materials, which results in very low-value integration into global supply chains. This new opportunity for African countries to participate in high-value global supply chains cannot be realized without equal terms of mining contracts and policies that can catalyze lateral linkages between large-scale mining and local productive industrial development.

Additionally, most African countries can be attractive destination for the diversification of global supply chains if inherent challenges to linking African businesses are addressed. Creating enablers and leveraging incentives to facilitate financing, technology transfer, research and development and access to production knowledge will be critical.

I trust that you will find this publication to be an excellent resource that breaks new ground for a more effective participation of African economies and businesses in high-technology global supply chains.

Rebeca Grynspan
Secretary-General of UNCTAD

Abbreviations

BRICS: Brazil, Russian Federation, India, China, South Africa

e-commerce: electronic commerce

GDP: gross domestic product

GSMA: Global System for Mobile [Communications] Association

HS: Harmonized Commodity Description and Coding System

OECD: Organisation for Economic Co-operation and Development

United Nations Comtrade database: United Nations International Trade Statistics database

UNCTAD: United Nations Conference on Trade and Development

Overview

Global supply chains: Turning disruption into opportunity

The *Economic Development in Africa Report 2023: The Potential of Africa to Capture Technology-intensive Global Supply Chains* provides a unique insight into the potential for increased integration into the supply chains in Africa by bringing together knowledge on how Africa can strengthen supply chain diversification in high-knowledge- and technology-intensive sectors.

In recent years, global supply chains have come under immense pressure as a result of unprecedented trade turbulence, economic uncertainty, geopolitical events and natural disasters. Consequently, these supply chains were severely disrupted. This has led key players, such as the series of manufacturers, distributors, consigners and so on involved in producing goods of a particular kind and bringing them to market, to re-examine ways to strengthen supply chain resilience. Although the integration of African economies into supply chains is relatively low compared with other regions, disruptions to supply chain operations have a more than proportionate adverse impact on their economies.

Key players and stakeholders are looking to strengthen the resilience of existing supply chains by diversifying their sources. This may create an opportunity for African economies to heighten their involvement in global supply chains. For instance, the semiconductor supply chain, which involves hundreds of suppliers and an intricate process of manufacturing microchips and other critical components in the electronics and automotive industries, was negatively affected during the 2008–2009 global financial and economic crisis, as well as the recent coronavirus disease (COVID-19) pandemic. Other industries that came under supply chain pressure during previous global shocks and environmental disasters, with associated difficulties in trade and investment, will be the focus of this report. These include the automotive, electronics, renewable energy and pharmaceutical product and medical device industries, which are strategic, emerging industries that require the use of critical minerals and high-technology metals for manufacturing and services.

Africa, which boasts an abundant supply of raw materials with utility in the energy, automotive and electronics sectors, could provide an opportunity for the diversification and resilience of global supply chains by offering a new regional market for businesses and industries in their quest to further expand their supply chain relationships. The box below provides a definition of supply chain diversification and what it entails for African countries.

As multinational companies seek to extend their supply chains into diverse regions, African countries could become potential sources of high-technology mineral resources along shorter and simpler supply chains, with the added effect of contributing to the stable development of emerging industries on the continent. More equal investor–State agreements, or host government agreements, especially for the critical minerals and metals that are used in high-technology products and supply chains, will be necessary to develop domestic industries successfully and improve the capability of local firms to design, procure or manufacture necessary parts and components in high-technology-intensive supply chains.

The unequal terms of mining contracts and exploration licences has led many Governments in Africa to review their mining laws and regulations to harness business opportunities for domestic enterprises and better reap the benefits of capital-intensive large-scale mining for inclusive and sustained development in their countries. To date, 17 African countries have local content regulations in place, namely Angola, Botswana, Burkina Faso, Cameroon, Côte d'Ivoire, the Democratic Republic of the Congo, Ghana, Guinea, Mali, Mozambique, Namibia, the Niger, Sierra Leone, South Africa, the United Republic of Tanzania, Zambia and Zimbabwe. In Zambia, for example, foreign suppliers account for about 96 per cent of goods and services supplied to mines, whereas domestic suppliers contribute about 1 per cent, mainly in services (catering, security and office maintenance). This is a case that illustrates the importance of sound local content policies in developing local supply chains and facilitating the creation of backward linkages in the mining sector, for example, generating value addition in domestic supply sectors, creating local employment opportunities or transferring technology.

Under such a scenario, the potential upgrading of industrialization, combined with the rapid wealth creation of the rising middle class in Africa, will start to offer opportunities to develop local supplier bases, broaden local production and increase the African workforce and consumer market. As the interest of potential investors and global suppliers to deepen their footprint across the African continent is carved out, incentives to invest in and build partnership with local suppliers and customers will be key.

Nonetheless, venturing into Africa as a supply chain destination will require enormous investment in adequate infrastructure, as well as the availability of human capital and technology. In many African countries, the state of infrastructure development – transport, warehouse and other facilities – which is not yet at a standard and quality comparable to other developing and emerging countries, is one of the main barriers to logistics and supply chains on the continent. However, national and regional initiatives to scale up financing for infrastructure development and improve logistics performance in Africa, such as the African Union Programme for Infrastructure Development in Africa, are promising and can strategically enhance the integration of African economies into regional and global supply chains.

In spite of the current low levels of technology and human capital in many parts of Africa, which can be a hindrance when gains in productivity and value added are considered decisive in furthering supply chains across the continent, opportunities are emerging that can overcome these lingering risk factors. The young and growing population of Africa, projected to reach 2.5 billion by 2050 – a quarter of the world's population – is embracing technology and has many advantages that can entice firms seeking to expand their supplier and consumer relationships in Africa. The advancement of technology and innovation on the continent is being increasingly driven by young entrepreneurs. The Global System for Mobile Association reported 618 active technology hubs in Africa in 2019, compared with 442 such hubs between 2016 and 2018. This growing technology ecosystem will leverage the innovation and entrepreneurial mindset and skills that will eventually attract investors and technology-based supply chain participating companies. By relocating some of their supply chains to Africa or by entering into a partnership with local suppliers, these companies will then contribute to employment creation, especially in digital- and high-technology-intensive industries and, hence, to income growth. As technology-intensive industries tend to offer higher wages and can have a positive job-multiplier effect, the potential of generating more employment in those sectors will have undeniable benefits for the workforce and foster sustainable development in Africa. In the United States of America, for example, workers in high-technology industries earn on average 101.8 per cent more than workers in non-high-technology industries. Facilitating a conducive environment for firms in those industries to establish or build new supplier relationships in African countries can help raise wages in Africa, which are set at a minimum of $220 per month, compared with an average of $668 in the Americas.

Understanding supply chain diversification

In analysing supply chains and the potential for economies in Africa to integrate into supply chains, the report makes a clear distinction between supply chains and value chains. For the purpose of the report, the use of the term supply chains is defined as follows: the system and resources required to move a good or service from a supplier to a customer. In comparison, the value chain concept builds on this to consider the way value is added along the chain, both to the good or service and the actors involved. The report further outlines the following fundamental steps of a supply chain, which are product development, sourcing procurement, manufacturing, logistics, distribution and customer service.

Thus, supply chain diversification takes into account two principal factors, that is, diversification of the direct supplier base and diversification of the customer base. Supply chain diversification is imperative to reinforce supply chain resilience. There are, therefore, plentiful opportunities for Africa to benefit from supply chain diversification through integration into both the supplier and customer bases. The potential benefits of the African Continental Free Trade Area through increased trading facilitated by the removal of tariff and non-tariff barriers, is poised to offer an advantage for supply chain diversification in Africa.

Nonetheless, for African economies to benefit from supply chain diversification, it is important to manage existing supply chain vulnerabilities effectively. For instance, it would be urgent to implement policies to mitigate poor infrastructure (transport, warehouse and other facilities), informality, weak institutions and regulations, fragmented markets, limited sources of capital, low levels of technology and political risks.

Source: UNCTAD.

New opportunities for global supply chain diversity and sustainability: The comparative advantage of Africa

The recent crises have revealed that undiversified economies in Africa remain vulnerable. For instance, the lingering effects of the COVID-19 crisis, compounded by inflationary effects owing in part to the war in Ukraine, saw economic growth in Africa decline by 0.8 percentage points, from 4.5 per cent in 2021 to 3.7 per cent in 2022. Integration into supply chains, and hence the diversification of African economies, would create an economy with better resilience to shocks. The comparative advantage of Africa for integration into global supply chains could be analysed through factors inherent to the supply chain, that is, procurement, production and distribution, with the third factor including consumer demand.

Procurement

As the global economy adapts to climate change, dynamic production processes will require alternative inputs, and low-carbon technologies are expected to flourish. Consequently, there will be a rise in the demand for specific metals with utility in the low-carbon transition and green mobility, for instance, aluminium, cobalt, copper, lithium and manganese. Given the abundance of these minerals, in particular key metals required for the low-carbon transition, the continent can reposition itself as a supplier of raw materials for global supply chains. In fact, 48.1 per cent of global cobalt reserves and 47.6 per cent of global manganese reserves are located in Africa. Other metals and minerals that are important for the low-carbon transition are also produced in Africa: chromium, lithium, natural graphite, nickel, niobium, rare earth metals, silver, tellurium and titanium.

In addition, African countries need not only supply raw materials for the low-carbon transition. They can also strengthen value chains by ensuring that raw materials are converted into intermediate products within the continent. For instance, in 2022, the Democratic Republic of the Congo had the largest production of copper in Africa, 1.8 million tons. But beyond exploration and extraction, the country is a potential destination for refining metal products, which would lower the costs of transporting bulky, low-value initial extracts.

Production

The cost of production is an important factor in the discussion of the integration of Africa into supply chains, and of the possibility for firms to move entire production processes to the region. For example, since distance plays an important role in costs through transportation and other distribution infrastructure, the cost of production essentially must compensate for distance, and vice versa. Thus, a survey of current factor inputs into the production process provides a clear picture of where African countries stand, what gaps exist and what needs to be done to bridge those gaps.

The report analyses factors of production (capital, labour, human capital and total factor productivity) and finds that capital has been a key driver of output growth since 2003. Next comes labour, followed by human capital, whose contribution has remained largely unchanged. By contrast, the contribution of total factor productivity to output growth during that time has been dismal, and in some cases has declined, signalling a gap in productivity and use of technology. Consequently, while labour is abundant, African countries should implement policies that ensure increased skills and the ability to innovate and use technology in the production process, as well as in the overall supply chain system, which can also have a positive effect on wages and income. In addition, a productivity analysis carried out in the report shows that a reallocation of resources between and within sectors has not always been efficient for the African countries in the sample. Thus, policies that encourage efficient allocation of factor inputs should be implemented.

Distribution

Within the supply chain, distribution is perhaps the most prolific and, therefore, dynamic feature. The logistics aspect of distribution is also an important part of procurement and production. In 2018, for example, performance of African countries was considerably lower (2.46) than the global average (2.87), as measured by the World Bank logistics performance index on a scale of one to five, with one being the lowest, and five, the highest. Nonetheless, when compared with past performance, improvement has been marginal. In addition, the best performing categories were timeliness, and tracking and tracing, both an indication of increased investment in soft infrastructure, such as the Internet and mobile telephones. While it is important to invest in information and communications technology infrastructure, it is imperative that African countries maintain investments in hard infrastructure that reduce the cost of logistics in the supply chain.

Hard infrastructure, such as ports, roads and rail, have tended to lag behind. For instance, investment in African ports is often made on an as-needs-basis, which leads to operational inefficiency at the ports. There are less than 70 operational ports, many of which are poorly equipped and uneconomical, with delays two or three times above the global average. It is therefore advisable that African countries encourage investments in hard infrastructure, including from the private sector, to improve efficiency and capacity that would ensure that more value is gained by trading and participating in supply chains in Africa.

Trade policies and incentives

African countries are engaged in various trade agreements aimed at strengthening trade and enhancing productivity and diversification. The African Continental Free Trade Area has the potential to meet these goals and to foster continental and regional integration, stimulate intra-African trade and harmonize the heterogeneity of trade rules across regional economic communities and under regional trade agreements. In addition to the Agreement Establishing the African Continental Free Trade Area, African countries have joined preferential trade agreements with other regions or countries. The African Growth and Opportunity Act, established by the United States, is such an agreement, and it can generate a complex dynamic gain by facilitating opportunities for new factors of production, including capital. Other preferential schemes and economic cooperation partnerships in the context of South–South cooperation, which are contributing to the growth of local industry and improving intra-African trade, can also boost global supply chains. One such cooperation initiative is the Silk Road Economic Belt and 21st Century Maritime Silk Road, also known as the Belt and Road Initiative, which facilitates access to financing for public and regional infrastructure development projects in Africa and contributes to improving skills, innovation and technology through its various training and transfer of technology programmes.

Opportunities for greening supply chains

Within production and distribution processes, Africa offers several opportunities for greening supply chains and shrinking the carbon footprint of companies. For instance, the green hydrogen potential of Africa opens up opportunities for decarbonizing supply chains, which is becoming a requirement for companies to curb their greenhouse gas emissions. A company's emissions can be significantly improved by choosing suppliers of lower-carbon materials or relocating its energy-intensive industries, such as steel and chemical industries, to low-cost countries for renewable and green hydrogen power. Other advantages of supply chain expansion into Africa include opportunities to tap into its renewable energy potential, which can lower production costs and lessen reliance on fuel-based energy. As one of the world's largest untapped sources of solar energy, Africa can, for example, lend advantages in the solar power supply chain, which can promote the development of renewable energy technologies on the continent and facilitate the integration of African economies into global supply chains.

High-technology-intensive supply chains and industries: Resetting African markets and businesses for mobility and scale

While supply chains have come under considerable strain owing to the aforementioned crises, some industries are more exposed to global shocks than others and are thus increasingly relevant for geographic diversification. This section focuses on the integration of Africa into medium- and high-technology-intensive supply chains by taking advantage of its natural endowments, with such global supply chain integration likely to pave the way for the region's industrialization and sustainable development. Emphasis is placed on the automotive, electronics, renewable energy technology and medical device industries and supply chains, as these are sectors that can be vulnerable to global shocks (for example, the COVID-19 pandemic, trade disputes and geophysical events) and which require more diversified geographic footprints to ensure undisrupted access to suppliers and buyers. Africa can provide such alternative access to inputs and components for these technology-intensive supply chains.

Automotive Industry

The automotive industry is particularly vulnerable to supply chain disruptions, as witnessed during the COVID-19 crisis. While the registration of new vehicles remains low, with over 80 per cent of vehicle registrations pertaining to used vehicles, Africa has the potential to raise its vehicle demand nearly tenfold by 2030. Nonetheless, new vehicle production remains low, at about 1.2 per cent of the global total. Vehicle production is dominated by South Africa, Morocco, Algeria and Egypt in that order, while other African countries have relatively small assembly plants with minimal value addition (Angola, Ethiopia, Ghana, Kenya, Lesotho, Mozambique and Namibia). In Morocco, increased vehicle production has been underpinned by investment in infrastructure, proximity to the European market and policies geared towards strengthening the vehicle manufacturing sector.

A supply chain mapping approach shows that while African countries remain largely dependent on the import of automotive parts and components from outside the continent, there is room for greater regional supply chain integration. In particular, the manufacture of non-specific parts and components (so-called tier 2) provides the most viable production options for most African countries. They are less technology and knowledge intensive than tier 1 suppliers (manufacture and supply modules and systems ready for vehicle assembly), and often represent the next processing stage that requires abundant metals as inputs demanded by a range of manufacturing sectors. Hence these are essential components for achieving supply chain diversification. The identification of feasible export diversification opportunities that could fill recent gaps in the regional supply chain suggests that countries with already existing capabilities can take on the production of larger, more complex automotive parts and components. In addition, clustered production in special economic zones could strengthen economies of scale and benefit from joint infrastructure and financing.

Mobile telephones

The electronics industry, especially the mobile telephone supply chain can catch the eye of many potential investors and companies that are pursuing the diversification of their supply chains and exploring Africa as a new or alternative destination. Most of the minerals and metals that go into the production of smartphones can be sourced within African countries. For instance, the continent has large reserves of cobalt, copper, graphite, lithium, manganese and nickel, which are used in the production of telephone batteries, circuit boards and other components. The abundance of these resources also provides vast opportunity for strengthening regional supply chains in mobile phone production from precursor production. The production of cathode precursors (nickel-manganese-cobalt oxides), a main ingredient in the manufacture of battery components, can contribute to higher value capture in the battery industry and integration into the electronics and mobile telephone supply chain. It is estimated that building a 10,000-ton precursor facility in the Democratic Republic of the Congo, for instance, could cost $39 million, which is three times less than what it would cost for a similar plant in a country without the required natural resources or proximity to countries where those metals can be sourced. In addition to its large reserves of cobalt, representing about 70 per cent of global supply, the Democratic Republic of the Congo could develop a precursor plant by procuring nickel from Madagascar and shipping it through Mozambique or the United Republic of Tanzania or procuring additional manganese from neighbouring country Gabon.

These regional procurement and production opportunities will be facilitated under the African Continental Free Trade Area and strengthened by increased infrastructure investment. Several African companies, such as the Mara Group in Rwanda, Onyx in South Africa and VMK in the Republic of the Congo, have emerged in the precursor development market, in addition to Transsion, the leading Chinese mobile manufacturer in Africa. Developing mobile telephone supply chain capacities in Africa can unlock further potential in the electronics supply chain and open up market opportunities towards the production of tablets, laptops and high-performance servers, and data storage solutions. These are key goods and services that are predicted to be in increasing demand by the growing consumer market in Africa, including electronic commerce and other technology-based services.

Solar panels

Solar panel module assembly is a lucrative area for investment, given the high growth of the renewable energy sector on the continent. Between 2000 and 2020, the level of renewables investment in Africa rose at an annual average rate of 96 per cent, owing to the region's vast solar energy potential. Yet, the continent continues to suffer from significant investment gaps, receiving about 2 per cent of global investments in renewable energy. The production of solar photovoltaic panels is limited, with some opportunities materializing in Egypt, Morocco and South Africa. Despite the rapid growth of solar home systems, systems in Africa are tiny compared with their counterparts in developed countries and require batteries and charge controllers to ensure stable output. Assembly of the solar field, which must be performed at the site, offers significant local manufacturing potential. As many component inputs, such as ball joints, bearings and cables, are used by other industries, these parts offer opportunities for already established companies to achieve lateral diversification of customers. Not all countries in Africa might be able to produce solar panels for their market but the additional employment generation through project development and advisory services, installation and repair services can be substantial and should attract greater attention throughout Africa. Local entrepreneurs are keenly aware of specific local needs, including language and culture, that are essential for the implementation of large-scale investment projects in renewable energy.

Pharmaceutical products and medical devices

In Africa, the pharmaceutical industry is concentrated in generic medicines characterized by simple production processes, limited production of intermediates and active product ingredients, and scant upstream research and development. The trade deficit in pharmaceutical products increased from -$2.3 billion in 2000 to -$12.5 billion in 2020. In addition to limited local production and dependence on imports of medicine, poor access to diagnostic equipment in Africa, especially in rural areas, is also a main constraint to public health. Encouragingly, there have been strong advances in Africa in providing health care and diagnostics to people in rural areas through the implementation of technologies and innovative solutions. Nevertheless, despite some progress, African countries recorded a trade deficit of $2.6 billion in the medical device sector between 2018 and 2020.

Apart from collaborating with multinationals to access knowledge and technology to make and supply medical products and devices, it would be important to enhance the local sourcing and manufacture of raw materials. For example, in Egypt, there are major local research initiatives under way to produce the most essential active pharmaceutical ingredients.

Localization of mining equipment and supplying industry inputs

Despite the vast mineral wealth in the region and significant foreign investment that the sector has attracted throughout the years, many resource-rich countries in Africa have not been able to translate their resource wealth into sustainable economic, social and environmental development. Supporting African suppliers to the mining industry has perhaps the most potential among all the benefits countries can derive from mining. This can range from products, such as pick-up trucks, tyres, drills, conveyor belts and specific replacement parts, to services, such as catering, surveying and human resource management. In Zambia, however, foreign suppliers dominate the local market for the supply of goods and services across mining sites, mainly because of various constraints, such as a lack of access to long-term capital, restricted access to production technologies, high costs of production inputs and a lack of full quality control of production. Moreover, the absence of legislative provisions does not encourage domestic production and sourcing. It is important for the mineral-rich countries of Africa to put in place sound local procurement policies based on clear local sourcing and local ownership criteria. Further, to tackle structural transformation in resource-dependent countries and improve the social benefits of mining, there is a need for a new global governance architecture. An example is the sustainable development licence to operate, which is a holistic multilevel and multi-stakeholder governance framework aimed at enhancing the contribution of the mining sector to sustainable development.

Optimizing supply chain opportunities in Africa through enablers and incentives

The global economic crises have emphasized the need for the diversification of suppliers, goods and services to build resilience and better mitigate risks, such as input shortages and soaring product prices. Diversifying and making supply chains more resilient is also associated with digitalization and the adoption of digital technologies through the supply chain. In complex, high-value products and supply chains with shorter lead times, such as medical devices and electrical equipment, the use of digital technologies – advanced automation, machine learning, artificial intelligence and blockchain technologies, to name a few – are a necessity for production, distribution, logistics and procurement efficiency.

For instance, digital platforms and technology-enabled services allow better integration and smooth coordination between different sectors and processes and across distant markets, thus facilitating supply chain diversification. Other technology-enabled services that can enable supply chain resilience and sustainability include supply chain connectivity and logistics; supply chain digitalization; electronic data interchange; supply chain traceability software; and smart services.

Supply chains are complex, spanning multiple interconnected countries. They serve numerous electronic commerce platforms and customers with high demand and involve broad ranges of relationships and collaborations. Such complexity can lead to a race to the bottom for many firms, especially small and medium-sized enterprises.

In Africa, many small and medium-sized enterprises operate outside the global supply chain network because of the limited use of digital technologies. Most local small and medium-sized enterprises rarely use technology due to a lack of skills, informality, infrastructure issues and funding gaps. The main technology-enabled services are almost nonexistent in most African countries. The lack of investment in technology and the low level of human capital are major obstacles to exploiting these potentials.

However, African firms can play a more significant role in supply chain diversification by integrating vertically or horizontally into the supply chain. For instance, by engaging into a business-to-business or business-to-customer collaboration, large firms and small and medium-sized enterprises integrating through mergers and acquisitions can create complementary businesses and expand into upstream or downstream activities. This would enable the integrated companies to streamline their operations and supply chains by acquiring or establishing their own suppliers, manufacturers, distributors, or retail locations instead of outsourcing or importing inputs or other supply chain components. A global supplier can also integrate with an African firm to expand its operations in Africa at similar value or at the supply chain level and within the same industry, thus enabling the integrated companies to expand into new markets and diversify their product offerings. These two types of integration are better facilitated with the use of technology services at all stages, whether transactional or operational.

Countries in Africa should facilitate the adoption and use of these innovative digital technologies that can optimize supply chain practices. Some countries have already embarked on this path. This is the case of Kenya, for example, which has one of the highest adoption rates of digital skills in Africa. Some of the emerging technologies that are increasingly being deployed in that country and which can be leveraged to boost specific industries and supply chains (for example, innovation, product design, manufacturing, logistics and supply chain management) include artificial intelligence, the Internet of things and cloud-computing technologies such as blockchain. This growing technology-oriented ecosystem, also known as the Silicon Savannah, has benefited from sound policies, an enabling regulatory environment and other government-led programmes that favour the upgrading of skills and adoption of digital technology.

Advanced technologies also serve as valuable tools and platforms that can address the financing needs of firms in Africa and potential suppliers or service providers in supply chains. For instance, banks and other credit providers can also use blockchain to improve supply chain financing, as the technology will enable them to make better lending decisions in a fast and cost-efficient manner by having access to real-time and verifiable transactions between the supplier and buyer without having to conduct physical audits or pay for financial reviews. Facilitating supply chain-related investments and finance is particularly important to unleash the potential of small and medium-sized enterprises and their participation in technology-intensive supply chains. Financing solutions, such as supply chain finance, could be opportunities for the integration of these enterprises into supply chains.

Supply chain finance focuses on facilitating access to working capital, bridging the payment time gap between buyers and sellers to efficiently manage cash needs stemming from daily operations and reduce stress to the balance sheet. There are no internationally agreed supply chain finance standards for the following areas: the part of financial supply chain management that is integrated into physical supply chain activities, financing instruments to manage working capital and liquidity in the supply chain and payables finance or reverse factoring.

In general, supply chain finance in Africa faces several barriers, such as know-your-customer or anti-money laundering regulations and buyer performance, which are related to supply chain finance default risk and profitability. In addition, firms in Africa must overcome barriers to conventional bank financing and capital. African countries are often confronted with a disproportionately higher risk perception by major global financial players, which hinders the expected and necessary financial flows into the continent and feeds into their currency risk. Some countries in Africa are constrained by low or nonexistent country risk ratings, weak banking systems, regulatory challenges and a lack of credit information.

Scaling innovative supply chain finance solutions could significantly improve the access of small and medium-sized enterprises to financing and competitiveness in a well-integrated supply chain that could further increase employment, income, quality of life and economic growth in Africa. However, the level of involvement in supply chain finance is low. In 2022, Africa contributed to only 1.9 per cent of global supply chain finance volume ($2.2 trillion) and remains the most underdeveloped supply chain finance market across major regions. However, its growth is picking up speed, at about 40 per cent between 2021 and 2022. The availability of supply chain finance continues to be far less than what is demanded across the continent. African countries should ensure that small and medium-sized enterprises have access to supply chain finance by removing certain barriers. These include the lack of technological infrastructure and technology-enabled services; inadequate legal and regulatory frameworks; high risk perception by local firms, owing to insufficient knowledge and education; a fragmented market; and challenging sustainability criteria applied by banks and other lending institutions. Moreover, women entrepreneurs in Africa face additional hurdles to accessing timely finance, compared with their male counterparts.

Policy options for strengthening global supply chain diversification

The risks of concentrating manufacturing and supply chains in a few markets or sourcing and supplying sector-specific intermediate goods from a few locations can increase exposure to shocks and disruptions in production networks and supply chains. By diversifying or relocating to Africa, supply chain participating companies can source some of the inputs (raw materials and intermediate goods) from the continent, while reducing the costs of transportation and logistics and minimizing risks of supplier delivery delays and other challenges.

African countries offer many advantages that can contribute to or drive the diversification of global supply chains for high-knowledge- and technology-intensive industries. Nonetheless, to attract supply chains, African countries will need to adopt certain policies that strengthen and ensure an attractive environment for businesses to relocate to.

The report provides a list of comprehensive policy options that, if implemented, could provide incentives for supply chains to relocate to African countries. Below is a selection of some of the policy options from the report.

Automotive industry

There is a need for a more coordinated automotive strategy and regional automotive development plan to avoid the duplication of efforts. To facilitate continental vehicle sales and promote the domestic supply of parts and components and aftersales goods and services, harmonized and transparent standards are necessary. The African Continental Free Trade Area can provide a platform to create linkages between automakers (for example, original equipment manufacturers), auto suppliers and local suppliers to access the necessary knowledge and technology to meet car-specific requirements.

Electronics: Mobile telephone supply chain

The enforcement of decent labour laws is paramount in an assembly industry that employs more women than men – women are often more vulnerable to exploitation and health risks. It is necessary to invest in skills development and technical training to create a skilled workforce for the mobile telephone industry. Countries that already have some mobile telephone assembly should develop research facilities to invest in next-generation battery technology.

Renewable energy technology: Solar panel supply chain

There is a need for intensified collaboration to enhance knowledge and technology transfer. This could take the form of mentoring programmes, in which successful, more established companies can exchange information and experience. Moreover, formal and informal intra-industry exchanges are essential to continuous learning.

Health-care industry: Pharmaceutical product and medical device supply chain

To broaden demand and access to medicine, pooled procurement and financing should be further promoted. This can be achieved, for example, by platforms, such as the Africa Medical Supplies Platform, an online portal that enables the delivery of medical supplies to the Governments of Africa. Another important example can be found in a project launched by the Economic Commission for Africa, the African Continental Free Trade Area-based Pharmaceutical Initiative, which contains a centralized pooled procurement mechanism.

Mining industry

Local content requirements or supplier programmes will not sufficiently promote domestic firms if the initial challenges of these firms – lack of electricity and finance – are not tackled at the same time. Supply chain finance and targeted support to these companies can be negotiated ex ante with mining companies before licences are granted.

Localization of supply chains

The future of supply chain transformation in Africa, especially in technology-intensive industries in the automotive, electronics, renewable energy and pharmaceutical sectors, will require viable options for creating domestic supply chains that are reliant and resilient. This can be achieved through localized supply chains, supplier development programmes and the establishment of local procurement requirements.

Regional market opportunities under the African Continental Free Trade Area

The implementation of the African Continental Free Trade Area provides momentum to attract greater attention towards more high-technology sectors that generate local value addition and employment opportunities. As the African Continental Free Trade Area also aims to strengthen national and regional competitiveness by facilitating regional economic performance and industrial innovation, it will help enhance regional supply chain capabilities and contribute to the efforts of supply chain hubs to foster economic development in Africa.

A push for technology and innovation in supply chain transformation

The use of new technologies and digital solutions can provide comprehensive supply chain visibility and transparency and facilitate the ability of supply chain participating companies to respond more effectively to shifting global market dynamics. Identifying the potential of individual countries in high-technology supply chains; assessing the technology and digital readiness of African firms; facilitating technology transfer, reverse engineering and domestic innovation; and developing and increasing the utilization of digitalization and technology in supply chain processes and interactions will be vital for the transformation of supply chains in Africa.

Technology-enabled service providers and supply chain financing for small and medium-sized enterprises

Small and medium-sized enterprises can be strategic sources and key drivers of global supply chain diversification and supply chain transformation in Africa. Adopting digital solutions and models to their business performance, operating in a conducive technology-based supply chain environment or tapping into novel financial tools to increase the participation of these enterprises in supply chains will be necessary for those seeking to expand their markets and integrate into global supply chains. These enterprises could also reinforce their collaboration with larger firms or supply chain participating companies by establishing complementary businesses (vertical integration) or similar businesses in other localities (horizontal integration). Large companies should seek to vertically or horizontally integrate start-ups and small and medium-sized enterprises to diversify and regionalize their supply chain. This is particularly important if regional integration through the African Continental Free Trade Area is to be enhanced.

To benefit from supply chain opportunities arising from global disruptions and emerging challenges, the Governments of African countries can count on the research and policy analysis, technical cooperation and consensus-building support of UNCTAD. Leveraging its expertise and experience in providing on-the-ground technical assistance and innovative capacity-building tools, UNCTAD, in cooperation with the Governments of Africa and other relevant stakeholders, could develop bespoke training programmes and tools that can assist African industry leaders and small and medium-sized enterprises to understand the opportunities to integrate global supply chains through increased access to new technologies, financing solutions and re-skilling programmes. By providing a forum for open and constructive dialogue for policymakers, financiers and development partners, UNCTAD could work with the Governments of Africa, domestic and global industry leaders, and domestic and foreign investors to facilitate, streamline and heighten visibility, transparency and impact in overall supply chain processes. Such collaboration could lead to the adoption of policies and standards that would encourage more local content requirements, as well as to the strengthening of local capabilities that are essential to innovation and the production and delivery of goods and services across regional and global supply chains.

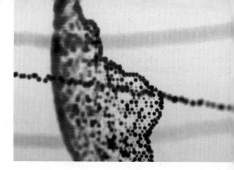

CHAPTER 1

Global supply chains: Turning disruption into opportunity

1.1 Introduction

Global supply chains, complex cross-border organizational structures and industry networks that are necessary to develop, produce, transport and deliver goods or services across the world, can be at high risk in the face of unexpected events and global pressures. In recent years, the global supply chains ecosystem has been disrupted by unprecedented trade turbulence, economic uncertainty, geopolitical events and natural disasters. In many parts of the world, these events have swayed networks of suppliers and buyers that were built over years – if not decades – thus revealing their vulnerability and exposure to unforeseen global shocks. These shocks put businesses at operational and financial risks and triggered systemic volatility and instability within economies. Although African economies are poorly integrated into global supply chains, the disruptive effects of unforeseen global events on supply chains can pose significant challenges to African businesses and traders in their ability to procure, manufacture, sell or export certain goods and services.

This leads to the following key policy questions:

- Is there opportunity in crisis? Can reshoring and nearshoring[1] offer an opportunity to build more diversified and resilient global supply chains?

- What are the prospects for African countries to integrate into and attract higher-value knowledge and technology-intensive supply chain activities?

- Can the bountiful natural resources in Africa, which hold promise for a low-carbon future, abundant labour and green infrastructure, be incentives for creating a cascade of sustainable supply chains?

- How can mineral abundance be better leveraged? What enabling factors are necessary to fulfil these opportunities?

- Which policies (industrial, investment, technology, skills and knowledge) can help strengthen incentives for supply chain diversification and expansion into Africa?

- How can regional integration and initiatives enable the participation of African firms in next-generation regional and global supply chains?

The Economic Development in Africa Report 2023 brings together contemporary knowledge on supply chain resilience and describes how new strategies, policies and technological innovations can enable disruption-proofing of supply chains in Africa, while boosting productivity and manufacturing capacity. This report aims to provide strategic guidance to decision-makers and policymakers in Africa in leveraging the potential of national and regional markets and businesses to foster domestic supply chains and create a trusted and reliable supplier marketplace for global supply chains, thus helping expand the involvement of Africa in global trade and growth. It demonstrates the potential of African countries for integrating technology-intensive supply chains, such as automotive, electronics, machinery and pharmaceuticals, as suppliers of inputs (raw materials and intermediate goods) or sources of other factors that can contribute to making supply chains more resilient to external shocks. As recent supply chain disruptions put enormous pressure on both suppliers and firms, and financial institutions, limiting the scope for debt in financing supply chains, the

---

[1]   Reshoring is when a company transfers part or all of its business operations and supply chains back to its home country. Nearshoring is when a company relocates part or all of its business operations and supply chains to a nearby country, often with a shared border. See www.weforum.org

report explores emerging financial and technology solutions to help address such liquidity constraints, while improving operational efficiency and managing supply chain finance.

The report proposes to bring together current knowledge on supply chain diversification and resilience in some of these high-value and technology-intensive sectors. Reliable transport and utilities infrastructure, as well as adequate water and electricity supply, will contribute to increased production of local components, reduced reliance on imports and better opportunities for foreign businesses to establish or scale up operations on the continent. Further, sophisticated legal and regulatory frameworks that enable digital transactions, combined with the liberalization of trade in services that can allow improved access to technologies and other high-intensity services, will help overcome production and supply chain limitations that prevent many African countries from participating fully in regional and global trade. Enhancing access to supply chain finance and other alternative financing solutions, especially by smaller businesses that can play a leading role in the innovation, manufacturing, packaging, branding and distribution of intermediates, will be essential for Africa to position itself as a strategic region and partner in the restructuring of global supply chains.

Chapter 2 examines the comparative and competitive advantages of African countries to capture strategic business value and position themselves more strategically in key global supply chains. Economic, political, trade, investment, social and environmental factors can help African countries position themselves as an attractive destination in their efforts to achieve supply chain diversification and resilience.

Chapter 3 considers recent global and African trends and the outlook for the principal technology-intensive supply chains, for example, those related to the automotive, electronics, renewable energy and medical devices industries. It analyses the region's potential for higher value capture in global and regional supply chains, including research and product design, components manufacturing, assembly or product integration, distribution, marketing and sales, consumption and buyers, and related services. The chapter concludes with a presentation of case studies on the potential of African countries to integrate such supply chains (for example, as suppliers of inputs – raw materials and intermediate goods, or as a source of other factors that make supply chains resilient) and to leverage growth and social development opportunities under improved contracts and local content requirement policies.

Chapter 4 discusses the enablers and incentives needed to optimize supply chain opportunities for African countries. Designers, manufacturers, distributors, sellers and buyers can have a common constraint when entering and operating in a supply chain: their access to liquidity and working capital. Recent supply chain disruptions and challenges have put pressure on suppliers or companies and financial institutions and have narrowed the scope of supply chain financing. Emerging financial and technology solutions can help address liquidity constraints, while improving operational efficiency and managing supply chain finance. Investing in a growing pool of skills and technologies that can digitize and facilitate smart manufacturing and services will also help achieve resilience and sustainability in supply chains. In conclusion, the report will summarize the contribution of Africa to global growth and its potential for making valuable inputs to global supply chains. It will also provide strategic recommendations for transforming and upgrading African economies, while leveraging the potential of their national and regional markets and businesses. In addition, the successful implementation of the African Continental Free Trade Area will provide a major impetus to the integration of African economies in high-value global supply chains.

Ultimately, the improved integration of Africa into high-value global supply chains will contribute to economic growth and sustainable development through the associated benefits of productivity gains, specialization, knowledge and technology spillovers, value added exports, and employment generation (Research Network Sustainable Global Supply Chains, 2022). The report recommends strategic and actionable policies that various stakeholders in Africa – Governments, the private sector, regional institutions and trading and business partners – can apply to better integrate African countries in the new disruptive landscapes of global trade, business and finance.

1.2 Global supply chains

Given that global supply chains are composed of innovators, companies, suppliers and service providers from around the world that interact through complex dynamic systems and networks, many factors can affect the stability or robustness of these interwoven relationships, thus creating shortages of certain goods, increasing the cost of certain processes or reducing responsiveness to consumers' demand. To counter supply chain risks and vulnerabilities, a holistic approach that involves diversified sourcing and sustainable practices, such as production, distribution, inventory and investment, could be considered. Some of these measures could represent opportunities for African countries to integrate higher-value global supply chains and position themselves to better accommodate the potential impact of unexpected events on global supply chains.

However, showcasing the instrumentality of Africa in global supply chains will require rethinking the continent's position in global trade and examining its potential role in principal industries that could especially benefit from supply chain diversification and resilience. For instance, in their quest to diversify their network of suppliers and thus mitigate supply chain risk, leading companies could begin to target Africa as a new region with supply chain assets in resource-intensive, high-knowledge and technology-enabled industries, for example, in the automotive, electronics, renewable energy and medical devices sectors. Essential goods, such as mobile phones, are used globally on a daily basis. They involve a multitude of inputs and processes that will not work without the participation of Africa, where many of the critical materials are mined and sourced and where a growing consumer market can be delivered the final goods.

Understanding the types of global events that affect these industries and their supply chains and identifying the untapped market opportunities present in many African economies will be prerequisites for devising strategies or measures aimed at diversifying supply chains and building more reliable and resilient networks of suppliers and buyers across regions. The high geographic and sectoral concentration of global supply chains can involve risks, especially when it exposes companies to economic instability, price volatility, trade disputes, natural disasters and other exogenous effects in a specific country or region upon which they rely heavily for their supply chains.

To ensure effective supply chain risk management, companies participating in global supply chains will need to reduce supply chain concentration risks by broadening their geographic footprint and be in a better position to meet supply and demand needs by shifting and tapping into numerous networks across many regions, including Africa.

This report profiles opportunities for African economies and businesses to join global supply chains relating to technology-intensive industries. Therefore, it is important to distinguish between a supply chain and a value chain. Box 1 provides a brief analysis of that distinction.

Box 1
Distinguishing between supply chains and value chains

A value chain is commonly acknowledged as effectively contributing to trade dynamism and competitiveness. The University of Cambridge (2021) defines a supply chain as the system and resources required to move a good or service from a supplier to a customer, while the value chain concept builds on this approach to consider the way value is added along the chain to the good or service and the actors involved. SustainAbility et al. (2008) defines a supply chain in terms of the chain of suppliers making inputs to a final product, while a value chain focuses on the value created by the chain. According to ShipBob (2022) and Wallstreetmojo Team (2021), a supply chain refers to the network of vendors, resources, suppliers, customers, businesses, individuals, activities and technologies involved in every step of the chain, from sourcing raw materials to producing finished goods and ensuring timely delivery of their goods and services to customers. By contrast, a value chain refers to the same steps and network as those of a supply chain but emphasizes value addition or creation at each step. The table below summarizes the key differences between the two chains.

Differences between a supply chain and a value chain

Criteria	Supply chain	Value chain
Definition	Businesses, people and activities involved in the procurement, logistics, transformation and delivery of finished goods	Activities involved in analysing customer needs, planning production and adding value at each step of the process
Goal	To produce and distribute goods so as to increase customer satisfaction	To increase the value of a good so as to create competitive advantage
Process	Operational management	Business management
Main activity	Facilitating production and distribution of a good	Adding value to a good during each step of the process
Stages	Begins with a request from suppliers for a specific good and ends with its delivery	Begins with a customer's request and ends with the development of a specific good

Source: Edrawsoft, 2023; ShipBob, 2022; Tarver, 2022; Wallstreetmojo Team, 2021.

Upon closer examination, a supply chain can be further defined as a network of individuals and companies across various countries and regions. Key steps in a supply chain include the original sourcing by tier 3 suppliers of raw materials, which are refined or manufactured into basic parts by tier 2 suppliers, then assembled into finished products by tier 1 suppliers and sold to end-users or consumers through various delivery and market sale modes. These components are illustrated in the following figure.

Supply chain components

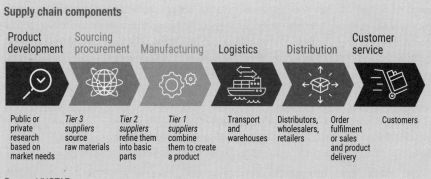

Product development	Sourcing procurement	Manufacturing	Logistics	Distribution	Customer service
Public or private research based on market needs	*Tier 3 suppliers* source raw materials	*Tier 2 suppliers* refine them into basic parts	*Tier 1 suppliers* combine them to create a product	Transport and warehouses	Distributors, wholesalers, retailers	Order fulfilment or sales and product delivery	Customers

Source: UNCTAD.
Note: Tier 1 suppliers are lead or anchor firms.

Sources: UNCTAD, based on Edrawsoft (2023), ShipBob (2022), SustainAbility et al. (2008), Tarver (2022), University of Cambridge (2021), Wallstreetmojo Team (2021).

1.3 The spectre of the impact of global shocks on supply chains

It is important to understand the nature of recent systemic events and their impact on global supply chains (see table 1). The 2008–2009 global financial and economic crisis, which began with the collapse of large investment banks based in the United States (for example, Lehman Brothers) and an unprecedented deterioration of the world economy, resulted in the tightening of credit and a fall in demand for certain goods and services around the world. The contraction in demand was high in industries such as transportation equipment, metals, machinery and electronics and electronic components. In the United States, for instance, consumer orders for transportation equipment, primary metals and machinery dropped respectively by 42.3 per cent, 40.3 per cent and 31.9 per cent between 2008 and 2009 (Hoberg and Alicke, 2014). Many firms operating in those manufacturing sectors found it difficult to consolidate the losses and decreasing margins incurred from the collapsing demand for their goods and services. Also, as suppliers and buyers of the goods and services affected by the fall in demand, many firms found it difficult to access affordable working capital or credit to finance their production, inventories, logistics and receivables. Most suppliers and buyers were heavily dependent on the banks and securities markets that had experienced liquidity problems in 2008 as a result of the global financial and economic crisis (Mefford, 2009). The disturbing effects of the crisis were particularly evident for the semiconductor supply chain, which involves hundreds of suppliers and an intricate process of manufacturing microchips and other critical components in the electronics and automotive industries. Because the interbank funds crisis of 2008–2009 brought deep financial distress for some companies and consumers, their respective investments in information technology and purchases of electronic devices or vehicles plummeted, affecting the demand and supply of memory chips, processor chips and silicon wafers. As original equipment manufacturers of electronic devices and vehicles responded to these demand-and-supply shifts by cutting back their orders and pushing inventory onto the market, the price per bit of semiconductors for computers, such as dynamic random-access memory, decreased by almost 50 per cent (Tech Insights, 2023). In the United States, for example, the financial and economic crisis resulted in an 8 per cent decline in demand for consumer electronics, which led to a 20 per cent fall in the demand for memory chips (Mefford, 2009). In China, the crisis affected various industries and supply chains, with about 67,000 factories declaring bankruptcy (Mefford, 2009).

GLOBAL SUPPLY CHAIN VULNERABILITIES CALL FOR MORE DIVERSIFIED SUPPLIERS AND CONSUMERS

The cost of shipping a 40-foot container from Shangai to New York rose in just three years **5X**

FROM **$2,325** IN SEPTEMBER 2019 TO **$11,778** IN SEPTEMBER 2021

THIS RESULTED IN HIGHER PRICES FOR:
Sourcing inputs and materials
Manufacturing products
Supplying and delivering goods to consumers

The coronavirus disease (COVID-19) pandemic further disrupted the already complex global supply chains, with significant shifts in logistics and supply chain activities affecting the performance and profit margins of many businesses and industries worldwide. The pandemic-related lockdowns and border closings constrained the supply and delivery of raw materials, critical products and other consumables. These pandemic-related implications, combined with a labour shortage (for example, in the manufacturing, transportation and warehouse sectors), resulted in manufacturing inefficiency or shutdowns; congestion on maritime, air and terrestrial routes; and a global shortage of key logistics components, such as shipping containers (Subban, 2022). For instance, the effects of COVID-19 restrictions – massive delays and higher air and ocean freight prices – incited some companies to start looking for other ways to build more resilient supply chains and mitigate the risks of future shocks. According to UNCTAD (2022a), the cost of shipping a 40-foot container from Shanghai, China to New York, United States (Asia–North America East Coast route) rose fivefold from $2,325 in September 2019 to $11,778 in September 2021. On the route Shanghai-Durban (in South Africa), the cost of shipping a 440-foot container also rose, two-and-a-half-fold, from $2,521 to $6,450 between December 2020 and December 2021 (UNCTAD, 2022a). Soaring ocean freight costs, spanning various global supply chain routes, resulted in higher prices of sourcing inputs and materials, manufacturing products, and supplying and delivering goods to consumers. In Europe and the United States, for example, companies in industries mostly affected by the 2021 supply crunch, such as automakers, computer and electronics manufacturers and medical technology innovators, began incurring sales and revenue losses caused by shortages of inputs, high shipping costs and reduced manufacturing capabilities to respond to the backlog of orders from the resurgence of consumer demand for certain products, such as cars, electronics and pharmaceutical goods. Similarly, Apple lost about $6 billion in potential sales of iPhones and other products partly because of semiconductor supply chain disruptions in 2021 (Siripurapu, 2021).

Global supply chains more recently became subject to additional vulnerabilities with the war in Ukraine, reinforcing the need for companies and countries to rapidly build more resilient and diversified supply chains. The effects of the war on the supply and price of crude oil, natural gas, metals and agricultural commodities contributed to further global supply chain disruptions. In an analysis on the effects of the war in Ukraine on maritime trade logistics, UNCTAD (2022b) found that trade restrictions applied to the Russian Federation, the world's third-largest exporter of crude oil, resulted in higher energy costs (a 64 per cent fuel surcharge during the first quarter of 2022). This led to a spike in maritime shipping rates and caused significant inflationary pressures and an additional 1.6 per cent increase in consumer prices globally. Moreover, the destructive effect of the war on the manufacturing and transportation infrastructure in Ukraine upset operations, not only in that country, but also in other countries that traded with or relied on Ukraine for the supply and delivery of key materials and services. For instance, Ukraine accounts for 50 per cent of the global production of neon gas, a chemical element used to produce semiconductor chips. As a result of the threats posed by the war to the ability of Ukraine to supply this noble gas, supply chain constraints have been exacerbated in the global semiconductor and chip-making industries (Simchi-Levi and Haren, 2022).

Innovations and high-knowledge and technology-intensive industries[2] are vulnerable to global shocks, disrupting global supply chains. To illustrate this, table 1 ranks the top 10 industries with a high level of exposure to pandemics, geophysical events and trade disputes.

Table 1
Industry exposure to shocks, selected industries

COVID-19 pandemic		Trade disputes		Geophysical events	
Type of industry	Rank	Type of industry	Rank	Type of industry	Rank
Apparel[a]	1	Semiconductors and components[b]	1	Semiconductors and components[b]	1
Aerospace[b]	2	Communication equipment[b]	2	Communication equipment[b]	2
Furniture[a]	3	Medical devices[b]	3	Mining[c]	3
Petroleum products[c]	4	Pharmaceutical[b]	4	Computers and electronics[b]	4
Transportation equipment[b]	5	Aerospace[b]	5	Glass, cement and ceramics[d]	5
Automotive[b]	6	Automotive[b]	6	Chemical[b]	6
Textiles[a]	7	Machinery and equipment[b]	7	Transportation equipment[b]	7
Rubber and plastics[d]	8	Chemical[b]	8	Basic metal[c]	8
Machinery and equipment[b]	9	Computers and electronics[b]	9	Electrical equipment[b]	9
Mining[c]	10	Electrical equipment[b]	10	Petroleum products[c]	10

Sources: UNCTAD calculations, based on the McKinsey Global Institute shock exposure index and data from the INFORM database, Observatory of Economic Complexity database, United Nations International Trade Statistics (United Nations Comtrade) database, World Input-Output database, World Tourism Organization database.
Note: This ranking is based on an index that measures the forward-looking exposures of value and supply chains in 23 key industries to pandemics, large-scale cyberattacks, geophysical events, heat stress, flooding and trade disputes. For instance, vulnerability exposure to pandemics is measured by the industry or value chain's geographic footprint, which is based on a country's share of exports (United Nations Comtrade database), its exposure to pandemics (INFORM data), and people inflows (World Tourism Organization data).
[a] Labour-intensive industry
[b] Global innovation industry
[c] Resource-intensive industry
[d] Regional-processing industry

The increased exposure to global shocks and a reduced ability to respond effectively to operational problems and supply chain disruptions led many economies and

---

[2] Some high-knowledge and technology-intensive industries will be discussed in this report.

businesses to adopt strategies aimed at stepping up the local manufacturing of certain products to react more quickly to local demand (Simchi-Levi and Haren, 2022). Some Governments responded to global supply chain pressures by supporting their home-based companies' efforts to reshore or improve supply chain resilience. For instance, in the United States Inflation Reduction Act (2022), such supply chain programmes include a $110 billion plan to improve roads and bridges, a $50 billion plan to incentivize domestic semiconductor manufacturing and a $17 billion budget to upgrade port infrastructure in major cities in the United States (Siripurapu, 2021).

Many industry leaders acknowledge the importance of having multiple supply sources across various regions and the capacity to swiftly activate secondary supplier relationships (Kilpatrick, 2022) as effective mechanisms to mitigate the risks of supply shortages and other repercussions of shocks and vulnerabilities on supply chain efficiency. However, the decision to diversify supply chains by reshoring or expanding supply chain operations into other markets and regions depends on a host of factors. These include costs related to wages, transport and production; access to raw materials and intermediates; access or proximity to emerging markets and growing consumer markets; quality, environmental and regulatory standards; technology and innovation capabilities; and the securing of the supply of key strategic products and services. According to UNCTAD (2020a), reshoring may not necessarily build more resilient supply chains, as it can lead to a higher geographical concentration of value added and reduced investment, especially for higher-technology-intensive industries. In some economies, reshoring may require re-industrializing, calling for significant investment (for example, to build manufacturing and logistics infrastructure) and capacity adjustments (for example, reskilling). (See Simchi-Levi and Haren, 2022). Supply chain diversification, which can broaden the distribution of economic activities and provide opportunities for new companies to integrate supply chains (UNCTAD, 2020a), thus becomes a more viable route for building resilience to global supply chain disruptions.

Companies seeking to diversify their supply chains and build relationships with suppliers and customers in various regions will need to invest heavily in fixed costs, for example, by setting up production plants and related infrastructure. They will also need to ensure that the necessary human capital, skills and technologies are present in those regions and markets.

Notwithstanding such costs, the risks of concentrating manufacturing and supply chains in a few markets or sourcing materials and supplying sector-specific intermediate goods from a few locations can increase exposure to shocks and disruptions in production networks and supply chains and can threaten a company's survival.

Although the current globalization of supply chains occurred when companies sought to lower production costs, for example by relocating to lower-cost markets, the heightening risk of global shocks and disruptions that can lead to greater material shortages, raise shipment costs or delay fulfilment and orders, are major concerns for companies that are now aiming to cut costs by shortening their supply chains and sourcing at home or closer to home.

The renewed paths towards supply chain diversification as strategies for building resilience to global shocks can create opportunities for African countries. For example, high value added and capital-intensive supply chains in the automotive and electronics industries can explore broader geographic footprints, including Africa, and restructure their supplier ecosystems to reduce vulnerability and strengthen resilience. By diversifying to or relocating some of their supply chain components to Africa, companies in technology-intensive sectors, for instance, can source some of the inputs (raw materials and intermediate goods) from the continent, while diminishing the costs of transportation and logistics and minimizing the risks related to supplier delivery delays and other challenges.

Moreover, the growing African consumer markets, characterized by a swelling demand for electronics goods and financial technology services, can provide incentives for market proximity. However, to become attractive options for companies seeking to diversify their supply chains, African countries will need to demonstrate reliable manufacturing, transport and logistics capabilities if firms are to relocate some of their supply chain components to the continent. Further, African countries will need to facilitate enabling policy and regulatory incentives to develop regional supply chains that can build the foundation for the full participation of African companies in global supply chains. A first step would be to better understand the importance of supply chain diversification and the potential benefits stemming from the continent's resilience to global shocks and other related disruptions.

1.4 Principles of supply chain diversification

The diversification of supply chains, which is based on diversification in all the components of the supply chain, includes supply base diversification (number of suppliers), customer base diversification (number of customers), supply chain flexibility and diversification of the goods and services produced. The suppliers and customers of a firm represent its relationships. Yin and Ran (2022) divide supply chain diversification into supply base diversification and customer base diversification, while Lin et al. (2021) conceptualize supply chain diversification (concentration) in terms of whether a firm concentrates its sourcing (sales) on a few large suppliers and customers. The first component of supply chain diversification is the firm's supply base diversification. In the supply chain, a supplier is a firm that provides goods and services to other organizations. A supplier can participate in business-to-business or business-to-consumer relationships in a supply chain. Supply base diversification can help firms avoid production shutdowns caused by supply interruptions (Adobor and McMullen, 2007; Yin and Ran, 2022). Firms that participate in non-diversified supply chains are particularly vulnerable to external and internal shocks.

Another important component of supply chain diversification is customer base diversification. As mentioned previously, in a supply chain, customers are firms that purchase goods and services from other organizations. Customers depend on producers, distributors and retailers to meet their needs for goods and services. Customers play an essential role in creating supply chains, as their needs, values and opinions affect the supplier's decisions throughout the supply chain (Achilles, 2014). A supplier of a firm can be a customer of another firm, and vice versa. For example, a customer may be a producer that purchases inputs to make goods and provide services for other customers.

The concept of supply chain diversification also includes supply chain flexibility. This concerns a supply chain's responsiveness to changes in customers' needs (Kaur and Kau, 2022) and the ability to easily adjust production levels, raw material purchases and transport capacity (Wolters Kluwer, 2021). Further, flexibility in the supply chain means a firm can scale to meet the needs of its consumers and adapt to meet the natural ebb and flow of its business, rather than wasting resources due to the inability to make immediate changes (Wolters Kluwer, 2021). Also, supply chain flexibility allows a supply chain to function by accommodating the day-to-day changes that occur naturally. The number of a company's facilities, including manufacturing, distribution, research and administrative facilities, could provide flexibility in a supply chain.

Supply chain flexibility also allows the successful integration of just-in-time and just-in-case supply chain inventory systems to achieve efficient operational processes. A just-in-time supply chain, also called the pull system of a supply chain, is a management strategy that aims to minimize inventory and increase efficiency. When adopting a just-in-time supply chain strategy, a company will order parts or services from suppliers solely on an as-needed basis or will manufacture specific units of products only when it receives an order from a buyer or customer. A just-in-case supply chain, or the push system in a supply chain, is an inventory strategy in which a company orders more goods or services than required from suppliers and produces more goods or services than they are expected to sell (United We Care, 2022). This management strategy aims to minimize the risk for a company to run out of stock of a specific product and be in a position to respond to consumer demand, even during unpredictable times, such as during shocks or supply chain disruptions. As both strategies present advantages and risks, it is important to adopt a balanced approach. For example, in a hybrid push-pull inventory system, some of the supply chain processes employ a just-in-time strategy, while others operate under a just-in-case system. This can be conducive to building a more flexible supply chain and optimizing inventories, that is, having a more accurate demand forecast than a just-in-case system but not aiming to keep standing inventory at zero, as in just-in-case systems (Jenkins, 2021).

Supply chain diversification has proven an effective means of strengthening supply chain resilience while overcoming supply chain disruption and improving company profitability and demand flows. Supply chain resilience can be defined as follows: the ability of a supply chain to return to its original state or move to a more desirable state after being disrupted (Barroso et al., 2010; Brandon-Jones et al., 2014; Carvalho et al., 2011; Christopher and Peck, 2004; Christopher and Rutherford, 2004), the ability of the production and distribution system to meet each customer demand for each product on time and to quantity (Priya Datta et al., 2007) and the ability to quickly adapt and respond to changes (Erol et al., 2010). These definitions and others are recapitulated in Tukamuhabwa et al. (2015).

With regard to supply chain resilience, the diversification of a supply chain allows firms to mitigate supply chain disruption. Diversification, through flexibility in activities, makes it possible to surmount the adverse effects of shocks and thus enable a supply chain to

Figure 1
Features of supply chain diversification

Source: UNCTAD.

return to its original state after a disruptive event. By diversifying suppliers, and goods and services, firms can readily absorb shocks such as the shortage of entrants and soaring prices of a product, overcoming the complete disruption of activities (figure 1).

1.5 What does supply chain diversification mean for Africa?

Global supply chains were designed to operate with high reliability and at the lowest possible cost (Gandhi, 2022). Yet the impact of global shocks and other geopolitical dynamics – the global financial and economic crisis, the pandemic and the war in Ukraine – on the reliability, cost-effectiveness and resilience of supply chains resulted in many companies and Governments adopting measures aimed at securing the supply of components in critical industries and reducing their dependence on a few suppliers and source markets. Some of these measures include support programmes and incentives deployed by the United States and the European Union to reshore the manufacturing supply chains for semiconductors, vaccines and medical equipment to ensure reliability, control and security. The increased interest in bringing back components of supply chains to home or closer to home by switching to or expanding relationships with suppliers closer to the market served or suppliers located in regions and countries with shared values, can open up opportunities for African economies and local firms to participate effectively in global supply chains (Gandhi, 2022). Moreover, some of the emerging trends that are reshaping global supply chains, such as the growing economic power of China and its transition to knowledge-intensive sectors, advances in global technologies and the raising of global environmental sustainability standards and compliance (Research Network Sustainable Global Supply Chains, 2022) can offer new paths for African countries to integrate global supply chains. For example, critical mineral and metal-based supply chains could leverage the potential of technology-enabling domestic firms and suppliers in lower-cost, higher-value and more transparent supply chains, and capitalize on the vast green hydrogen potential of Africa to attract sustainable supply chains to the region.

The potential benefits of regional integration and the African Continental Free Trade Area provide an added advantage for African countries to develop and strengthen regional supply chains, which can help foster their competitive position in global supply chains with enhanced opportunities for higher value capture and specialization. Zhang (2021) showed that the African Continental Free Trade Area had the potential to bolster regional supply chains in Africa and allow them to engage more effectively in global supply chains. The African Continental Free Trade Area will not only help address many of the cross-border trade issues but will also create opportunities to enhance supply chain agility by embracing digitization and enabling innovations in supply chains. A host of other factors – demand, spatial, economic, political, trade, investment, social and environmental – can help African countries position themselves and become attractive destinations and supply partners in the drive to achieve supply chain diversification and resilience.

Addressing supply chain vulnerabilities

However, an important precondition for Africa to play a more impactful role in global supply chains and build resilience to the disruptive nature of shocks will be to address its supply chain vulnerabilities. Key barriers to logistics and supply chains in Africa include poor infrastructure (transport, warehouse and other facilities), informality, weak institutions and regulations, fragmented markets, limited sources of capital, low levels of technology and political risks. These barriers can increase the cost of doing business and trade in many African countries, especially those that rely heavily on foreign imports of goods and services. For example, a country such as Nigeria, which has a population exceeding 200 million, is one of the biggest economies in the region (United Nations, 2022). Yet it remains highly dependent on the import of goods, such as refined petroleum oils, cars, smartphones, cereals and pharmaceuticals, to satisfy its consumers (Observatory of Economic Complexity, 2022; Statista, 2023).

Africa is home to critical minerals and other valuable intermediate goods – refined copper, cobalt oxides and many others – that feed into global value and supply chains. For example, the Democratic Republic of the Congo is the second-largest exporter of copper. According to estimates by the Observatory of Economic Complexity (2022), the country alone holds a share of at least $11 billion in the copper-mining industry. Among other industries, copper mining feeds into the electric vehicles industry, representing a global market value of $246.7 billion (Fortune Business Insights, 2020).

Further, high value added and capital-intensive supply chains, such as communication equipment, transportation equipment, computers and electronics, and semiconductors and components, which are strongly concentrated in Asia, can explore broader geographic footprints, including Africa, and restructure their supply ecosystems to reduce vulnerability and strengthen resilience. According to McKinsey and Company (2020a) and various data sources (see table 1), pharmaceutical goods, transportation equipment, computers and electronics, communication equipment, semiconductors and components, and medical devices ranked among the principal value and supply chains most exposed to shocks and disruptions stemming from the pandemic, geophysical events (for example, earthquakes) and trade disputes. These sectors are categorized as global innovations, meaning that they entail the production of the most intricate and knowledge-intensive goods, and involve highly complex and dynamic commercial, operational, financial, and organizational processes. These are also sectors that are based on high-value, cutting-edge technologies (McKinsey and Company, 2020).

AFRICA OFFERS A UNIQUE OPPORTUNITY FOR GLOBAL SUPPLY CHAIN DIVERSIFICATION

COMPANIES CAN:

- Source some of the inputs like raw materials and intermediate goods from the continent
- Minimize the risk of supplier delivery delays and other challenges
- Reduce the costs of transportation and logistics

RAW MATERIAL · SUPPLIERS · MANUFACTURING · DISTRIBUTION · RETAILERS · CONSUMERS

By diversifying or relocating some of the supply chain components to Africa, companies in some of these high-value and technology-intensive sectors can source some of the inputs (raw materials and intermediate goods) from the continent, while reducing the costs of transportation and logistics and minimizing the risks of supplier delivery delays and other challenges. Moreover, expanding African consumer markets, characterized by a rising demand for electronics goods and financial technology services, can provide incentives for market proximity. It is estimated that the constantly growing population of Africa will reach some 2.5 billion by 2050,[3] its consumer markets, 1.7 billion consumers (one fifth of the world's consumers) by 2030 and consumer expenditure, $2.1 trillion by 2025 and

---

[3] Data from the United Nations Population Division Data Portal. Available at https://population.un.org/dataportal/home (accessed 18 May 2023).

$2.5 trillion by 2030, compared with $1.4 trillion in 2015 (Signé, 2018). These trends point to enhanced business opportunities and growth and prosperity for the world, positioning Africa as a strategic region in the drive for geographically diversified supply chains.

In light of the increasing variations in the global economy and the development dividends that African countries can gain from a deeper integration into high value global supply chains (Research Network Sustainable Global Supply Chains, 2022), opportunities for companies participating in supply chains to expand their reach, improve global competitiveness and become more resilient to shocks or disruptions could chart the path for scaling the sustainable development of African economies. For instance, by sourcing and expanding its procurement activities across multiple suppliers, including in Africa, a supply-chain-participating company can contribute to employment creation through suppliers or by developing business opportunities. It can foster better working conditions by transferring knowledge or observing good labour practices and can also have a positive effect on wages and income, especially in technology-based and high-skilled sectors. As technology-intensive industries tend to offer higher wages and can have a positive job-multiplier effect, facilitating a conducive environment for firms in those industries to establish or build new suppliers' relationships in African countries should be a development target for the Governments of Africa. According to the International Labour Organization (2020), less than 24 per cent of the African workforce (about 32 million employees, one third of which are women) earn the minimum wage. In Africa, this amounts to $220 per month on average, compared with a world average of $486 per month, $668 in the Americas, $381 in Asia and the Pacific, and $1,041 in Europe and Central Asia. In the United States, workers in high-technology industries earn on average 101.8 per cent more than workers in non-high-technology industries (Roberts and Wolf, 2018).

The job-multiplier effect of high-technology industries has been clearly demonstrated in some economies. For instance, Moretti and Thulin (2013) found that in the United States, each additional job generated in the high-technology sector increases labour demand in the non-tradable sector, thus creating between four and five new job opportunities. In the United Kingdom, Lee and Clarke (2019) also demonstrated a significant multiplier from the high-technology sector, where for every new 10 jobs in high technology, 7 new jobs are created in non-tradeable sectors.

CHAPTER 2

New opportunities for global supply chain diversity and sustainability: The comparative advantage of Africa

2.1 Africa: Charting its way through turmoil and crisis

Many factors can influence a company's decision to relocate parts of its supply chain to another country or region, build relationships with new suppliers and gain market advantages for new buyers. A conducive environment for increased productivity, high-growth markets, high-profit entrepreneurship, an active and technology-oriented workforce and a dynamic consumer base will be core factors in making the decision to shift or diversify a firm's supply chain. In many instances, availing of such an environment will depend on a country's stability, its resilience to shocks and its ability to recover sustainably. It is therefore important to understand the current state of African economies and determine whether they can provide opportunities to attract and retain supply chain operations.

A review of the impact of the recent crises on African economies underscores the need for strengthening their resilience to vulnerability and enabling their diversification to achieve greater transformation in line with the Sustainable Development Goals. A recurring theme is the historical overreliance of these economies on commodities and their lack of diversification, as evidenced by good economic performance when commodity prices are high, with consistent reversals of gains when economic shocks occur. The natural resource endowments of Africa, especially of minerals required for the manufacturing and delivery of technology-intensive products and services, continue to be extracted and exported without significant value addition and with limited contribution to resource-based development and industrialization on the continent. Consequently, it is imperative that mining contracts be assessed, and in some cases renegotiated, to ensure maximum revenue for African countries and contribute to a pan-African vision calling for the "transparent, equitable and optimal exploitation of mineral resources to underpin broad-based sustainable growth and socioeconomic development" (African Union, 2009).

This chapter analyses the various economic, market and sustainability dynamics and advantages that countries in Africa can leverage to enhance opportunities for supply chain diversification in the region.

Multiple shocks reverberated across the global economy in 2020–2022: the devastating economic and social impacts of the COVID-19 pandemic; the war in Ukraine, which disrupted the food and fuel supply chain, bringing about inflation; and the ongoing impact of climate change, resulting in a downward trend for gross domestic product (GDP) growth by 2.8 percentage points, from 5.8 per cent in 2021 to 3.0 per cent in 2022 (United Nations, 2023). Africa was not spared, as average GDP growth declined from 4.5 per cent in 2021 to 3.7 per cent in 2022, with subdued output due to weaker demand from developed countries, persistent and lingering effects of the pandemic, high and rising inflation caused by food insecurity and the effects of climate change (figure 2).

However, the average GDP growth rate in Africa masks some variations between regions within the continent. East Africa was the fastest-growing region, attaining 5.1 per cent GDP growth in 2022, with similar forecasts for the medium term (figure 3).

By contrast, growth in the Central Africa region stood at 3.4 per cent, significantly lower than in East Africa. Nevertheless, despite slower growth in Central Africa than in other regions, this was the most rapidly growing region in 2022 compared with 2021,

Figure 2

Yearly gross domestic product growth by world region, 2021–2022

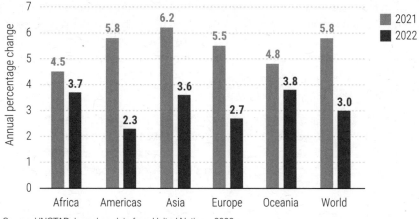

Source: UNCTAD, based on data from United Nations, 2023.

Figure 3

Africa: Gross domestic product growth by region, 2022–2024

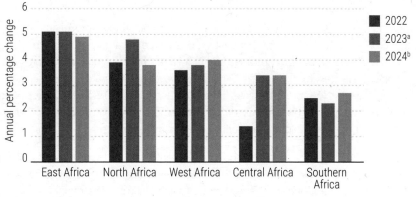

Source: UNCTAD, based on data from United Nations, 2023.
[a] Estimate
[b] Forecast

when GDP growth stood at 1.4 per cent. In 2022, growth in Central Africa was attributable to an increase in oil prices, which boosted oil export-dependent economies.

Growth in North Africa declined to 3.9 per cent in 2022, due to low demand in Egypt, drought in Morocco and a contraction in the economy of Libya. West Africa suffered setbacks, as two of its biggest economies, Côte d'Ivoire and Nigeria, experienced subdued growth. Inflation, power supply challenges and lower-than-expected oil production, despite an increase in demand and price, made for lacklustre economic performance in Nigeria (United Nations, 2023).

Southern Africa was the slowest-growing region on the continent, as its largest economy, South Africa, was held back by structural challenges, such as high and rising unemployment and low demand caused by rising inflation, which eroded household incomes. In addition, the continuing power cuts (load shedding) had adverse effects on productivity in industrial and other sectors.

Inflationary pressure, attributable to food shortages caused by the war in Ukraine, had negative, broad-based effects on African countries. Other than Central Africa, where inflation averaged 4.4 per cent, contained partially by rising commodity prices, inflation in all other regions rose to two digits. North Africa had the highest average inflation (25.6 per cent), driven largely by food and fuel inflation in the Sudan, followed by Southern Africa, which saw average inflation rise to 21.0 per cent, fuelled by inflation in Zimbabwe (United Nations, 2023). Inflation is expected to moderate in the near-to-medium term as commodity prices stabilize and inflation from food prices eases.

On average, the current account balance in Africa deteriorated from minus 4.7 per cent of GDP in 2021 to minus 5.6 per cent in 2022 (figure 4), largely propelled by rising commodity prices and resulting trade deficits for net importers of energy and other commodities affected by the war in Ukraine. However, the average current account balance is expected to improve to minus 5.2 in 2023 and minus 4.9 in 2024, underpinned by an expected narrowing of the trade deficit as commodity prices normalize and export opportunities under the African Continental Free Trade Area expand.

However, the aforementioned crises and trade dynamics, in addition to the beginning of trade under the African Continental Free Trade Area, could provide an opportunity for Africa to become a hub for the reshoring of supply chains. The remainder of this chapter provides an overview of the potential of the region as a hub for supply chain diversification and regionalization.

Figure 4
Africa: Average current account balance, 2014–2024

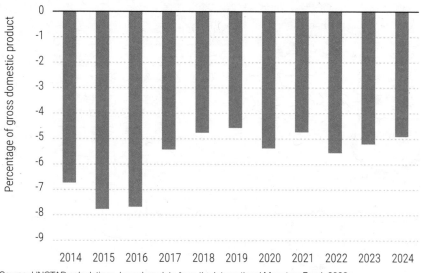

Source: UNCTAD calculations, based on data from the International Monetary Fund, 2022a.
Note: Estimates for 2023 and 2024.

2.2 Opportunities for supply chain diversification: The comparative advantage of Africa

When analysing the opportunities for Africa as an alternative or attractive market for global supply chain diversification, determining the likely outcomes by considering inherent and linkage factors can provide additional insights on the wins and losses companies can expect when making the decision to relocate components of their supply chains to Africa. This chapter will focus on the inherent factors of supply chains, while the linkage factors will be analysed in more detail in chapter 3.

As illustrated in figure 5, the inherent factors of supply chains can be divided into three stages: procurement, production and distribution. Procurement is the process of acquiring raw materials, including sourcing and infrastructure used to acquire the

Figure 5
Inherent and linkage factors of the supply chain

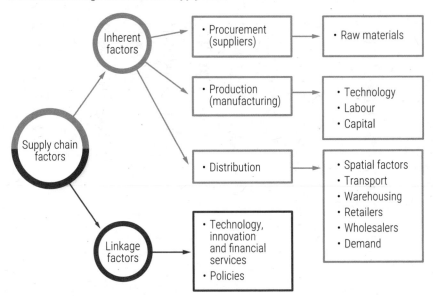

Source: UNCTAD

materials. Production involves the transformation of raw materials into finished products. Distribution is the final stage of the process and involves the movement of goods through a system until they are delivered to the consumer. Distribution is comprehensive and includes transportation, warehousing and retail. It involves the use of soft and hard infrastructure, for instance, and the use of technology in transportation on land, on sea and in the air.

Traditionally, firms sought to manage all three stages of the supply chain from one location. However, over time, supply chains have evolved so that, depending on the industry, different stages can be managed from various parts of the world. For instance, in the automotive industry, it is not unusual for raw materials to be sourced from different suppliers based in different regions. Moreover, some of the global leading car manufacturers have plants on different continents that not only produce different vehicle brands, but also make a variety of car parts (for example, gearboxes and engines) and assemble cars (box 2).

Box 2
Africa: An opportunity to expand the automotive supply chain

Disruptions, the new norm

By mid-2022, motor vehicle manufacturers were debating the effects of the war in Ukraine on the global supply chain. This proved to be a somewhat familiar discussion, after having experienced supply chain disruption as a result of the COVID-19 pandemic. Multinational automotive companies in Europe and North America were no exception, particularly given their heavy footprint in manufacturing cars and car parts and assembling cars in different regions of the world.

There are several opportunities, in particular in the environmental area, for vehicle manufactures to relocate parts of their supply chains to Africa. As part of their cost-cutting strategies, auto manufacturers have sometimes adjusted their energy mix from largely fuel to a mixture of coal and fuel. African countries are in the process of developing energy-generation strategies and can skew their energy sources to a green mix. Further, in keeping with new legislation, such as the regulation stipulating that all new European Union-based registered vehicles and vans must meet zero emission standards by 2035, Africa offers the necessary raw materials required to produce electric vehicles. Another advantage is that Africa is not encumbered with high-carbon-emitting legacy infrastructure, which opens the door to both green and technology-enabled infrastructure.

Given past supply chain disruptions, manufacturers are advised to broaden their supplier relationships to diminish supply chain risks, including those created by trade barriers. Owing to their proximity to European markets, countries in Africa can offer Europe opportunities to diversify its supplier base and build resilience against shocks to global supply chains.

For instance, investments by European car companies, such as Stellantis in Morocco, to provide parts and components, increased the parent company's resilience when wire factories in Ukraine were shut down owing to the war. Kromberg and Schubert stepped in to close the gap in supply. In June 2022, the manufacturer Stahlschmidt inaugurated first-phase operations of a new $11 million plant. Similar dynamics are observed in response to the semiconductor shortage. The leading device manufacturer in Europe – ST Microelectronics – already operates a plant in Morocco and invested in a new production plant in 2021.

Sources: UNCTAD, based on Stellantis, 2023; Tanchum, 2022a; Tanchum, 2022b; The North Africa Post, 2018; Volkswagen Group, 2023.

2.2.1 Procurement: Africa poised to be a supplier of critical inputs for the low-carbon transition

Dynamic and complex supply chain processes will require alternative inputs, with low-carbon technologies expected to develop more and more. A World Bank report (2017) considers various scenarios to determine changes in metal requirements for the green energy transition. The analysis finds that in the most ambitious scenario, achieving a goal of limiting the rise in global temperatures to 2°C would increase renewable energy generation to about 44 per cent in 2050, up from 14 per cent in 2016. The United Nations and the Intergovernmental Panel on Climate Change's (IPCC) also predict better economic outcomes if global temperature is held below 1.5°C. For instance, the Sixth Assessment Report of the IPCC (2022) projects economic growth in Africa to be at least 5 per cent higher by 2050 and 10 to 20 per cent higher by the year 2100 if global temperature is reduced to 1.5°C. Notably, the study indicates that renewable energy is more metal intensive than the current energy production, which uses a substantially large component of hydrocarbons. Consequently, a change in the mix of renewable energy to almost half by 2050 translates into a more than twofold increase in demand for the metals used to produce renewable energy. Similarly, the growth in demand for batteries during the transition to green energy in the automotive industry, for example, will likely raise demand for metals used to make batteries (figure 6(a)). In 2020, demand for battery metals amounted to $12.9 billion. However, such demand is expected to reach $17.8 billion in 2027 (Statista, 2023). Iron ore (1.6 million tons), aluminium (68,000 tons) and magnesium (30,000 tons) had the highest production levels of all battery production metals in 2020 (figure 6(b)).

Consequently, there will be a rise in demand for specific metals and minerals with a utility in the low-carbon transition and green mobility. These include chromium, natural graphite, niobium, lithium, nickel, rare earth metals, silver, tellurium and titanium, as well as aluminium, cobalt, copper and manganese, all of which are produced in Africa (UNCTAD, 2022c). Given their abundance on the continent, African economies can play a key role in the supply chain, particularly in procurement, as suppliers of raw materials and metals. For instance, Africa accounts for 47.5 per cent of global cobalt reserves and 47.6 per cent of global manganese reserves, metals that are used to make electrical vehicles (table 2). In addition to cobalt and manganese, Africa holds over 80 per cent of the world's reserves of phosphate rock and platinum group metals.

The Democratic Republic of the Congo alone accounts for about 46 per cent of world reserves of cobalt, one of the main metals used to make batteries, in particular lithium-ion batteries, which are used in mobile telephones, laptops and electric vehicles (figure

Figure 6
Battery metals production

(a) Market value of battery metals worldwide in billion dollars, 2019 and 2020, forecast for 2027 and

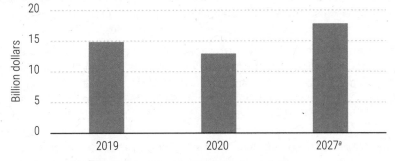

(b) production volume of battery minerals worldwide per 1,000 tons, 2021

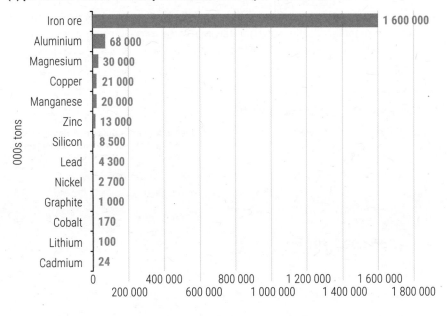

Source: UNCTAD calculations, based on data from the 2022 Statista database.
[a] Forecast.

7(a)). South Africa is another candidate for a resource-based global supply chain, as it holds about 42 per cent of the world's manganese reserves (figure 7(b)). Manganese and copper are the only two minerals required for the manufacture of batteries for both conventional and battery electric vehicles. While the production of and global demand for electric vehicles are growing, the demand for conventional vehicles will continue to outpace electric vehicles in less-advanced economies, as policies and regulations for electric vehicles have yet to be adopted in those countries.

Another critical metal for the energy transition, with a utility in wind and solar energy and the production of batteries for energy storage, is copper. In 2022, it was the most widely mined metal in Africa. The top producers were the Democratic Republic of the Congo (1.8 million tons) and Zambia (830,000 tons) (UNCTAD, 2022c). Cobalt, mined in the Democratic Republic of the Congo, Madagascar, Morocco and Zambia, had the second largest output in Africa. Cobalt is used to make batteries, as previously mentioned, and generate wind energy. Manganese, which like cobalt has a utility in battery manufacture and wind energy, was the third most commonly extracted metal in Africa, with Zambia, its leading producer.

Beyond exploration and extraction, the Democratic Republic of the Congo and Zambia are potential destinations for refining metal products, an opportunity to lower the costs of transporting bulky, low-value initial extracts. Both countries

Table 2

An overview of critical metal reserves in Africa

Minerals and metals for electric vehicles	Reserves in Africa (tons)	Share of Africa in global reserves (percentage)
Cobalt	3,653,000	48.1
Copper	52,000,000	5.9
Graphite	69,000,000	21.6
Iron Ore (Crude Ore & Iron Content)	1,670,000	0.6
Lithium	220,000	1.0
Manganese	714,000,000	47.6
Nickel	5,300,000	5.6

Source: UNCTAD calculations, based on data from the Knoema database, 2023.

Figure 7

Cobalt and manganese reserves in selected African countries

(a) Cobalt reserves

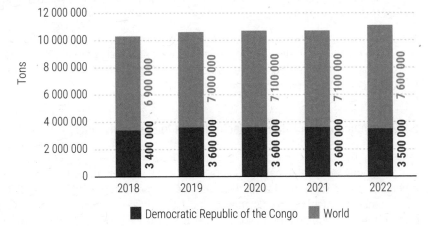

(b) Manganese reserves

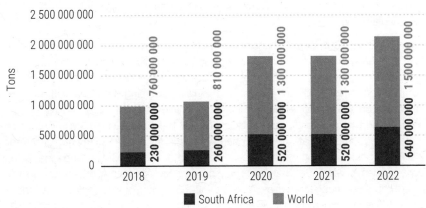

Source: UNCTAD calculations, based on data from the Knoema database, 2023.

make intermediate cobalt products by extraction from copper or nickel ore bodies to minimize shipping costs (UNCTAD, 2020b). For countries such as these, which are vast territories with limited or no access to coast lines, strengthening the metal supply chain to include refining would enhance the supply chain through lower transport costs.

The initial stage of the metals supply chain can be implemented in different locations, depending on how sophisticated the processes are, and whether the capabilities exist domestically. However, proper policies should be in place to ensure ease of operations for supply chains in the production process.

2.2.2 Production: Recalibrating factor inputs for cost efficiency

In general, firms' outsourcing and offshoring decisions are a key determinant for the geography of supply chains. Factors such as distance from domestic markets, production technology and market thickness matter (Grossman and Helpman, 2005). For instance, the farther the distance of the intermediate producer from the home market, the more the cost of outsourcing, with implications for supply chain location. Similarly, production technology (the mix of factors of production – labour, capital and technology) in the intermediate goods market must be similar or more cost efficient than the home market; otherwise it would not make sense to outsource the production of intermediate goods.

After the 2008-2009 global financial and economic crisis, risk became an important factor in outsourcing decisions, resulting in a cathartic shift in the supply chains discourse. Supply risk, demand risk and background risk,[4] either individually or in combination, have significant effects on a firm's outsourcing decisions, with particular emphasis on the quantity outsourced. In an environment of increased risk (supply, demand and background), risk-averse firms will likely order larger quantities of raw materials and intermediate goods to hedge against future risk (Mukherjee and Padhi, 2022). For instance, commodity prices fluctuated during the Covid-19 pandemic and post-pandemic years (2020-2023). This had an effect on output prices, and inflation rose throughout most economies. During the 2008-2099 global financial and economic crisis, however, background risk was heightened as contagion spread across entire sectors, owing to the closely interconnected nature of markets.

---

[4] Background risk is risk arising from external shocks, for example, contagion risk during the 2008-2009 global financial and economic crisis.

As the debate on supply chain resilience progresses, the balance between proximity to supply chains, risks and costs will be important, since resources and finances are finite. In addition, climate-change dynamics will be a central factor, as the type of resources utilized in future production will need to be considered. The following section explores the role economies in Africa could play as intermediate producers.

A macro review of the production process in Africa reveals that capital, followed by labour, human capital[5] and total factor productivity, was the fastest-growing factor input in low-income countries and lower-middle-income countries between 2000 and 2015 (figures 8a and b; box 3). The sample contains 29 countries for which data were available. Ten are low-income countries: Burundi, the Democratic Republic of the Congo, Mali, Mozambique, the Niger, Rwanda, Sierra Leone, the Sudan, Togo and Uganda. Nineteen are lower-middle-income and high-income countries: Algeria, Benin, Botswana, Cameroon, the Congo, Côte d'Ivoire, Egypt, Eswatini, Gabon, Kenya, Lesotho, Mauritania, Mauritius, Morocco, Namibia, Senegal, South Africa, Tunisia and the United Republic of Tanzania.[6]

The higher growth rate in capital can be attributed to increased access to financing, especially after the 2008-2009 global financial and economic crisis, as investors sought higher yields outside the United States and Europe (UNCTAD, 2018a). Consequently, African Governments ramped up spending on infrastructure (World Bank, 2019a), while the private sector increased investment spending on plants and machinery.

Accordingly, capital has been the main contributor to output growth, contributing more than twice as much as labour and human capital in low-income countries between 2000 and 2015. The contribution of human capital remained relatively low, peaking at 0.7 per cent in 2015 (figure 9a). In comparison with low-income countries, capital contributions in lower-middle-income countries only represented twice as much as labour contributions in the decade to 2015 (figure 9b). Importantly, the growth rate and contribution to growth of total factor productivity during that period showed a downward trend in both low-income countries and lower-middle-income countries. The slowdown in growth of total factor productivity in the production process contrasts with an increase in total factor productivity in the services sector (for example, financial technology innovations in finance), and the expansion of the services sectors in African economies.

---

[5] Data on human capital is derived from the Barro–Lee data set and is limited to 2015. Consequently, the analysis, including that of human capital, is limited to 2015. Nonetheless, the analysis is useful in understanding the evolution and drivers of factor inputs into the production process.

[6] For the purposes of this report, the countries covered (where accurate and relevant data are available) are categorized by income as per the World Bank classification, as the analysis looks at factor inputs and their contribution to growth, which is likely to be similar for countries in the same income group across other regions.

Figure 8

Growth rate of factor inputs

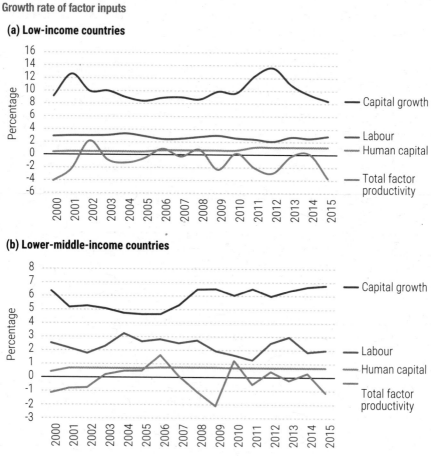

(a) Low-income countries

(b) Lower-middle-income countries

Source: UNCTAD calculations, based on data from the World Development Indicators database (World Bank).

Box 3
Technical note: Calculating capital stock and technology

Capital stock: The perpetual inventory method

In the previous section of the report, the contribution of factors of production to output over a period of 15 years (2000–2015) was examined for 10 low-income countries and 19 lower-middle-income countries for which data were available.

First, the perpetual inventory method is used to construct the capital stock data, capital stock in the initial period being a function of capital stock in the previous period as shown below:

$$K_t = (1 - \delta) K_{t-1} + I_{t-1} \qquad (1)$$

Where: K_t, which equals capital stock in time t, is determined by previous period (t-1) capital stock minus depreciation (δ), and previous period investments I. It is assumed that the depreciation rate is 6 per cent.

Initial capital is calculated from the year 1990. The choice of the year was based on data availability for all countries used in the sample. To estimate the initial capital, the steady state approach is used, that is, it is assumed that capital grows at the growth rate of output. The equation below can thus be estimated as:

$$K_{t-1} = \frac{I_t}{g_{GDP} + \delta} \qquad (2)$$

A weakness of this method is that it assumes that the economy is constantly in a steady state, with output growth and therefore capital growth dependent on a single year, whereby in the event of an investment shock in the first year, the capital stock would be biased. Taking note of this bias, five-year averages are thus used.

Contributions to output growth

Once the capital stock is calculated, the next step is to calculate the contribution to output growth, using the Cobb–Douglas production function. The following assumption is made: Capital contributes 40 per cent or 0.4 to total output. Thus ($\alpha = 0.4$) and ($1-\alpha = 0.6$). The Cobb-Douglas production function can be expressed as follows:

$$Y = AK^{\alpha} (HL)^{(1-\alpha)} \qquad (3)$$

Where: *Y* is total output, *K* is capital (as calculated above), *H* is human capital (years of schooling), *L* is labour, and *A* is total factor productivity. The function assumes that total factor productivity is a given, that is, exogenous.

The next step is to manipulate equation (3) to calculate total factor productivity (*A*). Once this is complete, the growth rates of capital, human capital, labour and total factor productivity, are calculated, then the growth rates of capital and human capital and labour are multiplied with α and $(1-\alpha)$, respectively, to obtain the contributions of human capital, labour and capital to growth. The residual after subtracting the growth rates of labour and capital from the growth rate of output, is the contribution of total factor productivity to output growth.

Limitations

The methodology has two limitations. First, as mentioned above, the initial calculation of capital stock at period t depends on the assumption of steady state growth. Second, assumptions are made with regard to the contribution of capital and labour based on the literature. Nonetheless, the methodology is useful as a starting point, as it gives an idea of the factor contributions to output growth for African countries for which data were available.

Source: UNCTAD, based on Berlemann and Wesselhöft, 2014.
Notes: Data relating to investment, GDP and GDP growth are derived from the World Bank World Development Indicators database (gross fixed capital formation). Employment data are calculated based on population data (percentage of total employed over age 15 multiplied by the population over age 15) from the World Development Indicators database.

The evolution of average labour productivity across the whole economy is determined by the interplay between a within-sector component – stemming from capital deepening, technological change, investment in human capital or reduction of misallocation across plants, such as shifting resources from low-productivity firms to more productive ones – and a structural between-change component resulting from labour reallocation across sectors. When workers move to relatively higher productivity sectors, such as manufacturing and modern services, this reallocation gives rise to structural change that promotes growth. However, if these workers leave the agricultural sector but are forced to work in underemployed or small businesses with low productivity, this potential boost in growth does not occur (UNCTAD, 2021a). Labour productivity growth in manufacturing in selected African countries with sufficient heterogeneity in terms of economic development and industrialization is presented in figure 10; this applies the methodology developed by McMillan and

Rodrik (2011) for the period 2001–2019, which coincides with the growth acceleration episodes on the continent.[7]

[7] The analysis does not include 2020 and 2021, owing to COVID-19-related shocks to these economies.

Figure 9

Contribution to output growth

(a) Lower-income countries

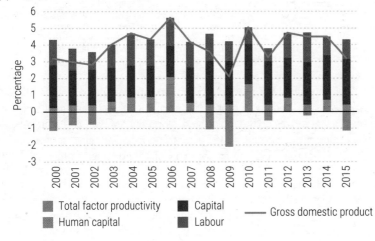

Source: UNCTAD calculations, based on data from the World Development Indicators database (World Bank).

Figure 10

Labour productivity growth in selected African countries, 2001–2019

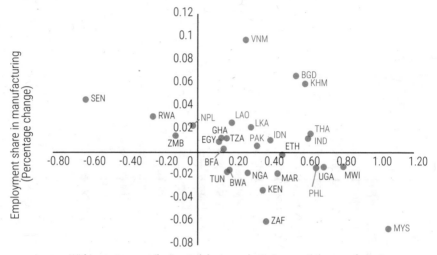

Within-sector contribution to labour productivity growth in manufacturing

Source: UNCTAD calculations, based on data from the International Labour Organization and UNCTADstat databases.
Note: For the sake of readability, countries are identified by standard ISO 3166-1 alpha-3 codes.
Abbreviations: BFA, Burkina Faso; BGD, Bangladesh; BWA, Botswana; EGY, Egypt; ETH, Ethiopia; GHA, Ghana; IDN, Indonesia; IND, India; KEN, Kenya; KHM, Cambodia; LAO, Lao People's Democratic Republic; LKA, Sri Lanka; MAR, Morocco; MWI, Malawi; MYS, Malaysia; NGA, Nigeria; NPL, Nepal; PAK, Pakistan; PHL, Philippines; RWA, Rwanda; SEN, Senegal; THA, Thailand; TON, Tonga; TZA, United Republic of Tanzania; UGA, Uganda; VNM, Viet Nam; ZAF, South Africa; ZMB, Zambia.

Less than 10 per cent of labour productivity growth, on average, comes from gains from the manufacturing sector. This is surprising, given that manufacturing has historically been a key priority on the region's development agenda, and many African countries have carried out reforms to build a strong manufacturing sector, due to its scope for job creation and, above all, for productivity spillovers to the rest of the economy.

Figure 10 shows that despite cross-country heterogeneity, some commonalities are visible: productivity gains from within-sector productivity in the manufacturing sector have been positive for most countries. Negative within-sector productivity growth is especially unexpected in Rwanda and Senegal, where their Governments have striven to nurture the manufacturing sector. Also, the evidence regarding within-sector productivity gains on manufacturing does not appear to follow the observed trend in manufacturing employment shares, which could be a reflection of the following factors:

- Industrial upgrading in the capital- and knowledge-intensive manufacturing industries, especially in larger firms (for example, Ethiopia).

- Absorption of labour by traditional and modern services, as well as the construction sector.

- Data for employment estimates might not fully capture formal and informal dynamics in manufacturing where informal employment is significant for the continent. For example, McMillan and Zeufack (2022) show that the rapid growth of small and informal firms could slow down labour productivity growth in manufacturing. Integrating some of the more productive small firms into value chains could have large payoffs.

The results for Botswana and South Africa are as expected, as they have taken major steps to support industrial development through, for example, financial sector and human capital development, trade agreements and partnerships, and foreign direct investment. In South Africa, the most industrialized country on the continent, manufacturing shed labour partly due to increased offshoring activities in ultra-labour-intensive industries, such as textiles, foods and furniture, and to a shift in employment towards modern services, similarly to Botswana. Figure 10 also shows the comparison with selected Asian countries, including Bangladesh, Cambodia, India, the Lao People's Democratic Republic, Nepal, Sri Lanka and Viet Nam. The results show positive within-sector productivity gains in the manufacturing sector and an increased share in manufacturing employment in nearly all Asian countries.

Despite the limited productivity gains in manufacturing for most of the countries during 2001–2019, there are many areas of comparative advantage that the continent can leverage to foster job creation and growth, enhancing industrialization as the global supply chains undergo transformation. The competitive advantage of Africa in its demographic make-up and resource abundance offers potential for investment in industries seeking new consumer markets and that are labour intensive and/or require inputs of raw materials that can be sourced locally, such as critical minerals, which are central to the manufacture of electric vehicle batteries.[8] Moreover, there is much potential for the African Continental Free Trade Area to facilitate structural transformation in Africa, as the necessary economic and political foundations for the sector are just starting to take hold.

---

[8]   Lithium, graphite, cobalt, nickel, manganese and rare earth metals.

For firms to consider relocating parts of their supply chains to Africa or outsourcing their production of intermediate goods, maximum gains can be made in recalibrating factors of production, thereby enhancing the production technology while lowering costs. A recalibration of factor inputs, such as substituting labour for capital where possible, in addition to utilizing technology services in the production process, could increase productivity, providing employment opportunities for the large population in the region, a key strength for attracting supply chains onto the continent. For instance, in the automotive industry (see chapter 3), the use of labour, not only in car assembly, but also in the manufacture of some tier-2 car products, could benefit the production process by cutting costs, while also increasing job opportunities for the region's growing population.

2.2.3 Distribution and logistics: Growth opportunities in infrastructure

Within the supply chain, logistics have proven to be the most dynamic component in recent years. For instance, logistics have been disrupted by the development of electronic commerce (e-commerce), largely driven by the growth of firms such as Amazon. The pandemic accelerated the growth of e-commerce, with significant changes to order fulfilment,[9] warehousing, transportation and time taken to deliver goods to consumers. The more efficient the distribution system, the shorter the supply chain, that is, efficient supply chains reduce costs, which makes trading across longer distances more viable.

The World Bank logistics performance index provides an overview of logistics performance globally, based on six key areas:

- Customs procedures.
- Infrastructure.
- International shipments.
- Logistics.
- Tracking and tracing.
- Timeliness.

The top 10 performers in the 2018 index were mostly European countries, led by Germany. South Africa was the top performer in Africa, followed by Côte d'Ivoire, Rwanda, Egypt and Kenya (figure 11a). South Africa, followed by the aforementioned countries, also took the lead in all six areas. In addition, South Africa, Côte d'Ivoire and Rwanda scored

---

[9] Order fulfilment is the process an order goes through from the point the order is received by the supplier, to the point it is delivered to the customer.

above the global average of 2.87 in the overall index. In general, the 10 highest-ranked African countries have overall index scores above the African average of 2.46.

Figure 11
Logistics performance index score, 2018

(a) Selected African countries

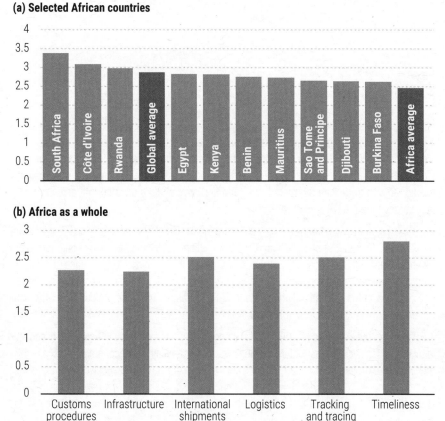

(b) Africa as a whole

Source: UNCTAD calculations, based on the World Bank logistics performance index.
Note (a): Some 160 countries, including 45 from Africa, participated in the 2018 logistics performance index.
Note (b): This figure contains the average for African countries featured in the 2018 logistics performance index.

On average, infrastructure received the lowest score in logistics performance (figure 11b). This area includes information and communications technology, railways and road transportation. Information and communications technology scored higher on average than hard infrastructure in the developing countries. Areas such as customs procedures, and tracking and tracing, which are likely to use information and communications technology services, also scored much higher than logistics, for instance (box 4).

While it is important to invest in information and communications technology, it is imperative that African countries maintain investments in hard infrastructure that reduce the cost of logistics in the supply chain.

Box 4
A review of African ports

Exports

The economy of Africa is largely dependent on the demand for commodities from the rest of the world since an increase in demand and in the price of commodities coincides with periods of high economic growth. Trade is therefore essential to its economy. Ports are the main gateway for the region's trade with the rest of the world and are therefore an important aspect of trade facilitation in the African economy.

Nonetheless, of the 54 countries in Africa, 16 are landlocked (Botswana, Burkina Faso, Burundi, the Central African Republic, Chad, Eswatini, Ethiopia, Lesotho, Malawi, Mali, the Niger, Rwanda, South Sudan, Uganda, Zambia and Zimbabwe). Of these, 11 are considered to be commodity-dependent developing countries. Therefore, these landlocked commodity-dependent developing countries are entirely dependent on the infrastructure of neighbouring countries for the export of their commodities (UNCTAD, 2022d).

A PriceWaterhouseCoopers (2018) analysis on ports in Africa finds that inefficiencies associated with inland logistics, infrastructure bottlenecks, port capacity and economies of scale raise the cost of exports. This, in turn, significantly decreases the value received from exported commodities. Port performance is also hampered by a lack of investments. For instance, UNCTAD (2022a) notes that port calls and turnaround times are hindered by congestion at the ports due to limited capacity. PriceWaterhouseCoopers (2018) finds that investment in African ports is often made on an as-needs-basis, which leads to operational inefficiency at the ports, since port capacity is lower than the actual capacity required to handle shipments.

Imports

While African countries are reliant on exports for their economic performance, recent crises have shown that they are also dependent on imports of essential goods, such as food and medicines, and are thus prone to external shocks. For instance, supply chain disruptions due to the war in Ukraine have led to rising food inflation, as corroborated by Carrière-Swallow et al. (2022), with the underlying effect being a pass-through in the costs of logistics.

In conclusion, increasing port efficiency could be a means to lower directly and significantly the value of imports for African countries, especially during periods of economic shock. Moreover, it is imperative that African countries strengthen investments in ports and encourage private sector investments to improve efficiency and capacity that would ensure that more value is gained in African countries from the import and export of goods.

Sources: UNCTAD, based on various sources.

In recent years, efforts have been made to finance infrastructure development on the continent. A notable example is the Programme for Infrastructure Development in Africa, adopted by the African Heads of State and Government at the eighteenth ordinary session of the African Union in Addis Ababa on 29 and 30 January 2012 (African Union, 2012). The aim of the programme is to craft a vision, policies and strategies for the development of priority regional and continental infrastructure in transport, energy, transboundary water, and information and communications technology over the short and medium terms, up to 2030.

The programme contains priority action plans outlining the steps to be taken in the short and medium terms. Priority action plan I covers a list of regional priority projects to be carried out from 2012 to 2020. Priority action plan II was developed with an implementation horizon of 2021–2030.

The focus of priority action plan II is the creation of ecosystems beyond single projects that include integrated economic corridors; global, regional or local value chains; and linkages of urban and rural economies. This plan aims to better prioritize projects by selecting 50 projects (10 per region) that can strategically enhance regional integration on the continent.

Contribution to output growth

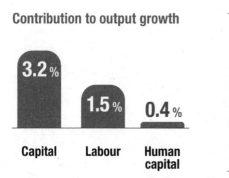

3.2%

1.5% 0.4%

Capital   Labour   Human
                     capital

Africa's growing and
youthful population
provides an opportunity
for job creation

Consumer economy in the making: Opportunities for supply chains

Africa is one of the youngest and fastest-growing consumer markets in the world. Steady population growth and urbanization will continue to be two of its defining megatrends and will continue to have lasting impacts on every segment of the supply chain. First, African countries are poised to embrace their demographic dividend, given their large young working-age population, only if certain preconditions are in place. Second, African cities are expanding rapidly, and urbanization is often cited as a driver of development, manufacturing growth and a transition from the informal to the formal sector.[10] A growing middle class, youth demography and urbanization are factors that should contribute to making the potential of Africa unlimited.

Population growth in Africa will continue to gain momentum in the coming decades. According to United Nations (2022), more than half of the projected increase in global population up to 2050 will be concentrated in eight countries alone: the Democratic Republic of the Congo, Egypt, Ethiopia, India, Nigeria, Pakistan, the Philippines, and the United Republic of Tanzania, five of which are located in Africa. With the population in Africa forecast to double by 2050 and reach 2.5 billion (about a quarter of the worlds' population) (United Nations, 2022), demographic growth could bolster future growth potential for consumer markets in Africa, which are increasingly young, sophisticated, globalized and cost conscious. These are important drivers of consumer trends in emerging markets. Indeed, the comparative advantage of Africa lies in its young and growing population, with the pace of technology adoption among African youths accelerating quickly.

---

[10] While the population in Africa is rising rapidly, economic growth has not kept apace. Consequently, between 2011 and 2022, the average GDP per capita growth in Africa was minus 0.29 per cent (International Monetary Fund, 2022a).

The Global System for Mobile [Communications] Association, commonly known as GSMA, reported 618 technology hubs in Africa in 2019, compared with 442 hubs between 2016 and 2018 (GSM Association, 2019). Nigeria (85 hubs), South Africa (80 hubs), Egypt (56 hubs) and Kenya (48 hubs) recorded the most hubs and are well established as leading technology centres in Africa. The use of technology or high-knowledge-intensive technological services will require active user participation and a feedback loop, with information received from users integrated into services provided (Cunningham, 2021). For instance, according to 2021 figures derived from the 2023 World Development Indicator database, South Africa has a relatively diversified services sector, with a relatively larger share of value added industry to GDP of 24.5 per cent and specialized services in the manufacturing sector (for example, in the automotive industry; see chapter 3).

While some African countries have developed various forms of artificial intelligence (PriceWaterhouseCoopers, 2017), the share of artificial intelligence developed for use in industry and services is still relatively small compared with the rest of the world. Automated intelligence, such as the use of machinery in warehouses to lift, store and assist in order fulfilment, reduces operational costs, while ensuring warehouse safety. The emergence of technology and innovation hubs in Africa may lead to optimal advances in technology adoption, such as artificial intelligence, additive manufacturing (three-dimensional printing), logistics technology and blockchain, and may help lower the cost of supply chains in Africa.

According to the ILOSTAT database of the International Labour Organization,[11] average monthly wages in 2019 for plant and machine labourers are relatively low in Kenya, Nigeria, Senegal and Zambia, compared with Asian countries such as Indonesia, Cambodia, Malaysia and Viet Nam (figure 12a). In Africa, wages for plant and machinery labourers are generally much higher for men than for women in four lower-middle-income countries (Egypt, Kenya, Lesotho and Nigeria) and three upper- middle-income countries (Botswana, Mauritius and South Africa), for which data were available. In some countries (Kenya and Lesotho), men earned approximately twice as much as women (figure 12b). This is likely due to gender-specific roles in the manufacturing sector, where women often take on temporary and administrative roles (International Centre for Research on Women and Kenya Association of Manufacturers, 2020).

---

[11] See wages and working time statistics at https://ilostat.ilo.org/resources/concepts-and-definitions/description-wages-and-working-time-statistics/.

Figure 12

Average monthly earnings in selected African countries and by gender, 2019

(a) By selected countries

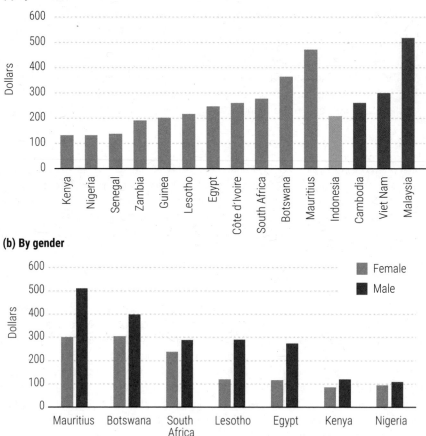

(b) By gender

Source: UNCTAD calculations, based on data from the ILOSTAT database (International Labour Organization).

The middle class in Africa is also expanding. Although there is no uniform measure of the size of the middle class in Africa, the overriding consensus is that it is growing rapidly. To gain a better understanding of this issue, this report provides a compilation of the number of people from the middle classes in Africa from various sources (table 3).

Table 3

Middle-class population in Africa

Author	Year of analysis	Middle class defined by income (Per capita earnings per day)	Estimated middle class population (Millions)
Bhorat et al., 2023	2015	$2–$13 People living on or spending from $2 to over $13 per day	29.27–523.31
Kharas, 2010	2009	$10–100	32
McKinsey and Company, 2010	2008	$55 and above per household	425
African Development Bank, 2011	2010	$2–$20	350
Ravallion, 2009	2005	$2–$13	197

Sources: UNCTAD, based on Bhorat et al., 2023; Kharas, 2010; McKinsey and Company, 2010; African Development Bank, 2011; Ravallion, 2009.

The expansion of the middle class in Africa will be felt through built-up growth impacts on the economy. As more people with higher incomes and purchasing power are lifted out of poverty, consumerism will be stimulated by a growing segment of society, in return fuelling more production for a widening domestic market (Melber, 2022). Further, the concept of a middle class carries with it a sense of financial stability, a developed consumer culture and a clear trajectory of growth (Van Blerk, 2018). Many people of the African middle class buy their goods at local stores and open markets and from street vendors, owing to a lack of formal supermarkets, regimented stock control, brand management (Van Blerk, 2018) and underdeveloped logistic systems.

Although compared with other regions, Africa has been slow to adopt e-commerce, the pandemic has brought a step change in consumer behaviour and e-commerce. Nielsen (2020) reports that a broadening proportion of consumers in Africa will continue to shop online. Additionally, at least 40 per cent of the e-commerce shoppers in each of the four largest economies in Africa plan to reduce the number of trips to physical supermarkets (United Nations, Economic Commission for Africa, 2021) (figure 13).

With the fastest-growing population in the world and the highest concentration of young people, as well as a large potential for e-commerce to their credit, African countries will continue to be magnets for consumer markets and products, with major implications for supply chains in terms of logistics, transportation, warehousing and last-mile distribution. Given the increase in intra-African trading activities, it is expected that African markets

Figure 13

Share of e-commerce users who plan to do less supermarket shopping after COVID-19
(Percentage)

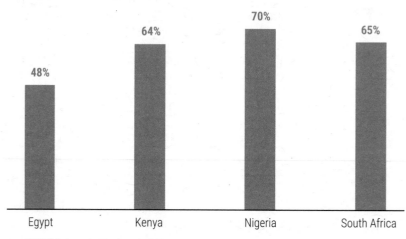

Source: UNCTAD, based on Nielson (2020).

will be reshaped with a greater focus on the creation of new industries and expansion of non-traditional sectors, which will have massive implications for supply chain activities (Oke et al., 2022).

The enlarging consumer market provides room for e-commerce to grow. The fragmented retail and wholesale landscape means that there is no ready-made national—or even regional—network of distributors in most African countries. As mentioned earlier, e-commerce in Africa is at a swiftly developing, yet early stage, with Nigeria, South Africa and Egypt having the most e-commerce traffic. Africa is forecast to surpass half a billion e-commerce users by 2025, which will have shown a steady 17 per cent compound annual growth rate of online consumers in this market. This should indicate a mobile-first approach to any business looking to sell online to the various African markets.

Further, the expansion of the e-commerce market, especially cross-border e-commerce, can transform some areas into regional distribution hubs, as in Mauritius (box 5).

Box 5
Mauritius: A strategic distribution hub for connectivity

Mauritius scored the highest among all the African countries in the DHL global connectedness index 2022 (Altman and Bastian, 2022). With regard to e-commerce, Mauritius not only ranks high in Africa in the 2019 business-to-consumer e-commerce index issued by UNCTAD, but it is also the first African country to sign a free trade agreement with China. (The agreement entered into force on 1 January 2021). As a country that has already ratified the Agreement Establishing the African Continental Free Trade Area, Mauritius could become a gateway to connect China–Africa trade.

Mauritius Freeport serves as the ideal logistics and value addition platform between Africa, Europe and Asia. Set up in 1992 to promote Mauritius as a regional trading and logistics hub, Mauritius Freeport is among the leading hubs worldwide, surpassed only by Dubai Multi Commodities Centre. Moreover, it was named global runner-up and No. 1 in Africa in the Financial Times' fDi's Global Free Zone of the Year 2021 (*fDi Intelligence Magazine*, 2021) (*fDi* [Foreign Direct Investment] *Intelligence*, 2021).

Sources: UNCTAD, based on Altman and Bastian, 2022.

Trade policies and incentives

Despite the well-articulated comparative advantages enjoyed by Africa, without trade, it is unlikely to reap the full benefits of its development. Trade allows countries to specialize in the production of the goods and services that are in alignment with their comparative advantage, while trade policy seeks to foster the establishment of an enabling and favourable environment for countries to do business. Trade policy refers to the tools that a nation may utilize to encourage or discourage imports and exports, including a combination of laws, regulations and agreements.

Preferential trade agreements have become a cornerstone of the international trading system. Owing to the proliferation of these agreements and their enlarged scope, the architecture of the world trading system and the trading environment of developing countries is being swiftly reshaped (Chauffour and Maur, 2011). Preferential trade agreements can generate a complex dynamic gain that operates by changing the rate at which new factors of production, mainly capital, are accumulated (Chauffour and Maur, 2011). Riding on the wave, Africa is engaging in a multitude of such agreements.

The African Growth and Opportunity Act, established by the United States, is a preferential agreement that promotes trade with African countries and the least developed countries. It is a core policy agreement that gives countries in sub-Saharan Africa preferential access to United States markets, allowing them to export products tariff-free. Its aim is to increase trade between the United States and sub-Saharan African countries and more broadly, to foster economic and political development in Africa (see https://agoa.info/about-agoa.html). The Act went into force in the year 2000 and was extended to 2025 by the United States Congress (Office of the United States Trade Representative, 2022; Office of the United States Trade Representative, 2023). As at 2023, 35 sub-Saharan African countries were eligible for benefits set up by the agreement.[12]

According to a report by the Economic Commission for Africa (2015), preferential schemes, such as the African Growth and Opportunity Act, can indeed support trade in Africa, including in manufacturing sectors, if stringent rules of origin are relaxed to fit the limited productive capacity of African economies. For Africa to benefit optimally from trade, it must harness regional integration to the fullest and cash in on the advantages of the multilateral trading system (Karingi et al., 2016).

There are positive developments under way in Africa. These include efforts to foster continental and regional integration, such as the recent creation of the African Continental Free Trade Area. Among others, the initiative is aimed at boosting intra-African trade and harmonizing the heterogeneity of trade rules across regional economic communities and under regional trade agreements (UNCTAD, 2021b). Under the Agreement Establishing the African Continental Free Trade Area, countries engaged to remove tariffs on 90 per cent of goods[13], progressively liberalize trade in services and eliminate other non-tariff barriers.

Beyond the continent, South–South cooperation improved remarkably over a twenty-year period (2003–2023), both in terms of volume and geographic reach (Besherati and MacFeely, 2019). Since 2013, many economies in Africa have become active providers of South–South cooperation. African countries have made significant progress in institutionalizing such cooperation, with the development of national

---

[12] Angola, Benin, Botswana, Cabo Verde, Central African Republic, Chad, Comoros, Republic of the Congo, Democratic Republic of the Congo, Côte d'Ivoire, Djibouti, Eswatini, Gabon, Gambia, Ghana, Guinea-Bissau, Kenya, Lesotho, Liberia, Madagascar, Malawi, Mauritius, Mozambique, Namibia, Niger, Nigeria, Rwanda, Sao Tome and Principe, Senegal, Sierra Leone, South Africa, United Republic of Tanzania, Togo, Uganda and Zambia. (see https://ustr.gov/sites/default/files/files/gsp/2023AGOA.pdf.)

[13] Sensitive Products and Excluded Lists for reasons of food security, fiscal revenue, livelihood, and industrialization will comprise 7 per cent of tariff lines and the remaining 3 per cent may be excluded from liberalization.

South–South cooperation systems and strategies (United Nations, General Assembly, 2022). The example of South Africa and its partners in the grouping of States called BRICS, that is, Brazil, the Russian Federation, India, China and South Africa, is telling. They are significant trading partners of South Africa. More than 17 per cent of the country's exports were destined for other BRICS countries, while over 29 per cent of total imports came from these countries. In 2014, the BRICS countries launched their own development bank, the New Development Bank, as a novel funding model aimed at fostering South–South partnerships. This initiative benefits Africa, as it helps meet the region's enormous intraregional infrastructure needs and facilitates the regional integration of African countries.

South-South trade linkages is vital to boost intra-African trade and global supply chains

Other similar South–South cooperation initiatives include the Silk Road Economic Belt and 21st Century Maritime Silk Road, which includes among its members more than 94 per cent of the countries in Africa. Such initiatives facilitate access to financing for public and regional infrastructure development projects in Africa, but also contribute to improved vocational training and education opportunities, trade and tourism revenues, transfer of technology or expertise to enter into new sectors, as well as overall living standards (Horigoshi et al., 2022). This South–South trade linkage is vital to the growth of local industry so that African countries can improve intra-African trade and boost global import and export supply chains.

At the bilateral level, patterns of trading between Africa and its key partners can influence supply chain diversification factors, such as technology adoption or transfer, industrial policies and trade policies. Prior to the pandemic and its disruptive effect on global supply chains, China was the chief trading partner of Africa for both imports ($134 million on average) and exports ($54 million on average) from 2018 to 2020 (figure 14). India was in second place, after China, with imports from Africa of $25 million and exports to Africa of $50 million on average between 2018 and 2020. Of the leading trading

Figure 14

Top trading partners of Africa, 2018–2020

Average imports

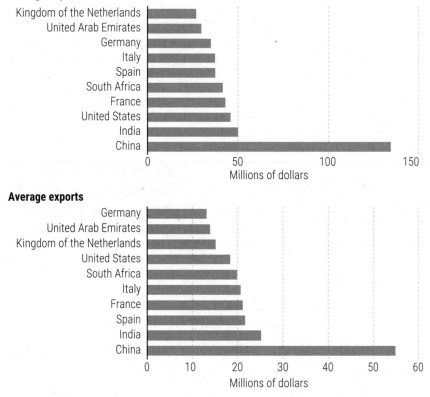

Average exports

Source: UNCTAD calculations, based on data from the United Nations Comtrade and World Integrated Trade Solution databases.

partners of Africa, China and India are located geographically the farthest. Nevertheless, they represent large economies and big markets, with trade volumes making the trade costs worthwhile. Trade between China and India with African countries is an important illustration of South–South cooperation.

Other major trading partners of Africa are France, Germany, Italy and Spain. Given that the four countries belong to the European Union, this makes the European Union, as a bloc, a key trading partner. The United States exports more to Africa ($45 million), than it imports ($18 million).

Similarly, South Africa, which trades mostly with southern African countries, which are part of the Southern African Development Community trading bloc, imported on average $41 million worth from African countries, while exporting $19 million on average between 2018 and 2020. The trading bloc, a regional economic community, has entrenched the removal of both tariff and non-tariff barriers, with extensive freedom of movement of goods and people.

Trade policy can greatly facilitate business activities, but used in isolation will not ensure the advancement of an economy or supply chain integration. Heterogeneous trade agreements among countries in Africa could undermine the efficiency of rules under the African Continental Free Trade Area. Low utilization rates of trade agreements will also hamper the establishment of regional supply chains and stifle commerce (UNCTAD and Common Market for Eastern and Southern Africa, 2023). Therefore, the careful implementation of trade agreements and supportive polices to make sure that trade and economic goals are met (UNCTAD and Common Market for Eastern and Southern Africa, 2023), and dedicated efforts and cooperation among countries and across regional economic and trading blocs, are necessary to reduce the complexity of the regulatory landscape of regional trade, promoting synergies among the various trade arrangements and achieving integration (UNCTAD, 2021b).

Low-income countries in Africa are increasingly utilizing Generalized System of Preference schemes. Their utilization rate rose from 4.9 per cent in 2002 to 63.2 per cent in 2021. By contrast, the utilization of other preference schemes declined from 63.6 per cent in 2002 to about 26.1 per cent in 2021.[14] Often different trade agreements unintentionally cover the same products, therefore the decline in utilization of other preference rates could be a result of a shift to the widening use of the Generalized System of Preference scheme. This is unsurprising, since it is likely better established, with low-income countries in Africa being much more familiar with the Generalized System of Preference scheme than other preference rates based on more recent trade agreements. In addition, low-income countries in Africa continue to benefit from most-favoured-nation-status.

---

[14] See UNCTAD database on Generalized System of Preferences utilization (https://gsp.unctad.org); preference utilization is calculated from all preference-giving countries.

2.3 Opportunities for greening supply chains: Africa as a premium destination

Clearly, production processes can no longer persist on the current path – an alternative production path that will result in lower emissions will need to be adopted. This is evidenced in the signature of 195 countries to the Paris Agreement under the United Nations Framework Convention on Climate Change (United Nations, 2015). The analysis in this chapter so far discusses an alternative production process that would utilize supply sources for a low-carbon future. In addition, the production process offers access to a growing and dynamic labour supply, as well as an advantage in building green infrastructure without the encumberment of existing legacy infrastructure characterized by high emissions.

In this section, it is argued that in addition to the comparative advantages Africa offers as an alternative to global supply chain diversification, Africa also enjoys a green advantage; that is, it is a relatively low emitter compared with other regions. Nonetheless, African countries are committed to reducing emissions, with 53 countries not only signatories to the Paris Agreement, but also having ratified it (see https://treaties.un.org/).

In addition, African countries have committed to cutting carbon emissions through their nationally determined contributions. Some countries, for example, Angola and Burkina Faso, have committed conditionally and unconditionally to reducing carbon emissions by more than one third of business-as-usual emissions by 2030. The main greenhouse gas emissions in Africa are produced by changes in agriculture, forestry and other land use, which makes up more than 65 per cent of current emissions. Major sources of greenhouse gases are carbon dioxide (CO_2) from burning fossil fuels (coal, oil, and natural gas), land use, forestry and other human-based activities that contribute to CO_2 emissions.

While CO_2 emissions from Africa more than doubled in 2019 (1,403,000 kilotons) compared with emissions in 1990 (615,320 kilotons), emissions were still much lower than in other regions (figure 15). East Asia and the Pacific was not only the region with the largest increase in emissions, but also the one with the highest emissions starting in 2019. Emissions in South-East Asia surged after 2000, an indication of greater production activity coinciding with an increase in outsourcing production processes from the West towards the East. Other regions with high emissions were Europe, Central Asia and North America.

Despite the large and growing population in Africa, CO_2 emission per capita contributions (1.2 kilotons in 2019) remain well below the global level of per capita contributions, which averaged 4.4 kilotons in 2019 (figure 16). African countries have committed to

Figure 15
Global increase in CO2 emissions, 1990–2019

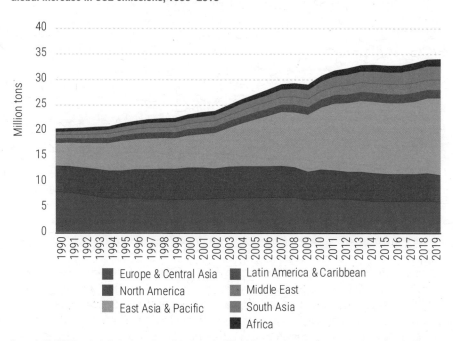

Source: UNCTAD calculations, based on data from the World Development Indicators database (World Bank).

further curb their low greenhouse gas emissions levels, which offers an advantage for companies seeking to diversify their supply chains, with the potential to produce in a sustainable manner, thereby ensuring the fulfilment of Sustainable Development Goal 13 on climate action. For example, with over 60 per cent of its greenhouse gas emissions deriving from electricity production and about 65 per cent of its electricity generated from the production of coal and over 15 per cent from crude oil, the Government of South Africa is taking steps, through its commitments to nationally determined contributions, to recalibrate the energy production mix with a shift towards renewable energy and more energy-efficient lighting.

The green hydrogen potential of Africa also offers opportunities for decarbonizing supply chains, which is becoming a requirement for companies to reduce their greenhouse gas emissions, tackle climate change and in some cases, to operate. A company can

Figure 16

Africa: Average CO2 emissions per capita compared with world average

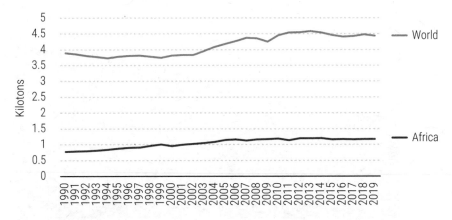

Source: UNCTAD calculations, based on data from the World Development Indicators database (World Bank).

commit to reducing or achieving net zero carbon emissions through its operations (Greenhouse Gas Protocol Scopes 1 and 2) or through its upstream and downstream activities (Greenhouse Gas Protocol Scope 3).[15] Scopes 1 and 2 are emissions from sources that an organization owns or controls directly (for example, from burning fuel in its fleet of vehicles instead of using electrically powered vehicles) or that are caused indirectly when the energy purchased and used by the company concerned is produced. Scope 3, on the other hand, are emissions that are not generated by the company or the result of activities from assets owned or controlled by it, but by activities or assets for which it is indirectly responsible, up and down its value and supply chains. It is estimated that a company's supply chain produces greenhouse gas emissions (Scope 3) 11.4 times more on average than the emissions of its operations (World Business Council for Sustainable Development, 2021). A company's Scope 3 emissions can be significantly improved by choosing suppliers of lower-carbon materials or relocating its energy-intensive industries, such as steel and chemical industries, to

---

[15] According to the Greenhouse Gas Protocol, World Resources Institute and World Business Council for Sustainable Development, the Greenhouse Gas Protocol Corporate Accounting and Reporting Standard outlines requirements and offers guidance for companies and other organizations, for example, non-governmental organizations, government agencies and universities, that commit to cutting to net zero levels their corporate-level, operational and linkages greenhouse gas emissions inventory (Scopes 1, 2 and 3). (See https://ghgprotocol.org/.)

low-cost countries for renewable and green hydrogen power (Albaladejo et al., 2022; Spiller, 2021). Several African economies hold large potential for green hydrogen production and contribution to decarbonization. For instance, solar energy in Africa has the potential to generate 50 million tons of green hydrogen by 2035 (European Investment Bank, 2022). Moreover, green hydrogen is economically viable, produced at less than $2 per kg (equivalent to an energy cost of $60 per barrel) (European Investment Bank, 2022). Its green hydrogen potential makes the continent an attractive destination for supply chain decarbonization in the automotive and pharmaceutical industries.

In focus: Applying inherent and linkage factors to electric vehicle supply chain in Mozambique

Mozambique: A potential supply chain haven

Applying the inherent and linkage factors to the case of Mozambique reveals potential opportunities as a supply chain destination for the electric vehicle industry. The electric vehicle supply chain is discussed in detail in chapter 3. The analysis shows that Mozambique offers many advantages and economic benefits as a potential destination for supply chains of the future – low-carbon transition supply chains. The following section provides an analysis of graphite, a mineral with utility in electric vehicles, and shows that not only can Mozambique supply graphite for global needs for a decade, but also has potential as a haven for the entire supply chain, including the production and distribution of motor vehicles.

Global graphite supplier

As at 2022, Mozambique was one of the world's leading suppliers of graphite, producing 30,000 tons per year. Graphite is used in battery anodes (chapter 3), with demand expected to exceed 2 million tons by 2028. Although graphite is not used in conventional vehicles, about 66.3 kilograms of the mineral are used in electric vehicles (2022 Statista database). It is estimated that Mozambique has 25 million tons in graphite reserves, which at 2028 demand levels, indicates a capability to meet global needs for 12 years as a solo supplier of graphite.

Since 2003, capital has been the main contributing factor to output in Mozambique, peaking in 2013 with the highest contribution to GDP growth, and growing by just under a quarter of the previous year (24.5 annual percentage change). By contrast, the labour growth rate was much lower between 1996 and 2021, averaging 2.5 per cent (figures 17 and 18). The disparity is due to the capital-intensive nature of the extractives sector that makes up most of the industrial sector (aluminium, coal and petroleum products). Nonetheless, about 43 per cent of the country's

Figure 17
Growth of factor inputs in Mozambique

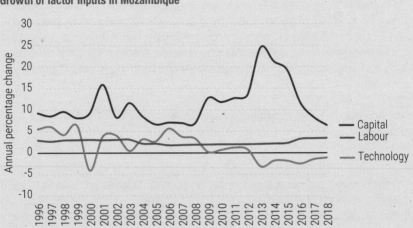

Source: UNCTAD calculations, based on data from the World Development Indicators database (World Bank).

population (just over 32 million in 2021) lies in the 0-to-14 age bracket, an advantage for the future workforce, provided that policies to support labour are implemented properly. Further, policies that promote the development of an electric vehicle or battery manufacturing industry would benefit from labour and capital in the production process, while ensuring value addition in the use of graphite.

Nonetheless, while capital and labour show a promising trend, technology has been declining in the production process. Indeed, between 2011 and 2020, patent applications for Mozambique numbered 196, an indication of scant technological development. However, the country has made strides in the adoption of services technology, such as in the financial technology area.

Distribution and logistics

Between 2011 and 2015, trade tonnage in Mozambique grew overall by 29 per cent, exports by 36 per cent and imports, by 23 per cent. However, the distribution infrastructure in Mozambique has not kept up with the growth in trade. For instance, according to port performance evaluation criteria, such as account infrastructure quality, port operational effectiveness and logistics

Figure 18
Contribution of factor inputs to growth in Mozambique

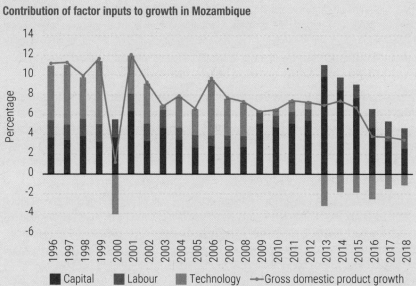

Source: UNCTAD calculations, based on data from the World Development Indicators database (World Bank).

efficiency, Mozambique achieved a score of 58, which is less than half that of the benchmark port, Rotterdam, which scored 129, with performance at 59 per cent efficiency of the top-scoring port in sub-Saharan Africa, Durban, South Africa (PricewaterhouseCoopers (2018).

Since 2013, the Government of Mozambique has ramped up spending on infrastructure aimed at increasing the efficiency of inland infrastructure. For instance, with World Bank support, the Nacala corridor, a highway that links the four provinces of Cabo Delgado, Nampula, Niassa and Tete, as well as the neighbouring countries of Malawi and Zambia (both landlocked countries), is set to improve trade logistics efficiency, saving time and costs with regard to the imports and exports of the three countries. They are part of the Southern African Development Community, where there is free movement of labour, capital and goods.

The extensive and accessible coastline of Mozambique makes it an excellent trade gateway to the rest of Africa, as well as to Asia and Europe, a key advantage for possible future industry and supply chain reshoring.

Macroeconomic and environmental policies: Progress in reforms

In 2013, Mozambique came under scrutiny because of the tuna bond scandal, which had adverse impacts on fiscal sustainability. As a result, Mozambique took steps to carry out institutional and fiscal reforms aimed at strengthening governance and engendering fiscal sustainability. However, the COVID-19 crisis and the war in Ukraine affected the country at a time when fiscal space was limited, before the reforms could be fully implemented.

Nonetheless, the country handled the COVID-19 crisis well, with fiscal policies designed to cushion the economic effects of the crisis and commitments to making reforms aimed at regaining macroeconomic stability (International Monetary Fund, 2022b). Mozambique is committed to climate change mitigation and the low-carbon transition and submitted its first nationally determined contributions in December 2021, with specific emissions-reductions targets in the energy and agricultural sectors.

In short, Mozambique is a frontier for the future economy, with all the strengths of a low-carbon transition economy. The country is a key supply source of minerals of the future that are required for use in the electric vehicle and battery industry (see chapter 3). In addition to supply sources, Mozambique has all the necessary strengths to engage in a production process that could provide value addition in a low-carbon transition, with a logistics system that is not encumbered by legacy high-carbon-emissions infrastructure. Mozambique, therefore, is an example of an African country that provides an opportunity for supply chain participating companies to relocate some of their supply chains so as to diversify their supplier relationships and build resilience to shocks.

2.4 Conclusion

It is evident that the disruption of supply chains is going to become the norm, rather than the exception. Shocks such as the COVID-19 pandemic and the war in Ukraine, which have occurred in quick succession, have had far-reaching implications for supply chains. In addition, the adverse effects of climate change, which have sparked questions on how to change production processes to reduce emissions, will have an impact on supply chains, likely shortening them significantly. Consequently, the discourse, especially among the global North, has shifted toward reshoring or diversifying supply chains. The position of Africa as a low emitter of carbon and its ability to adapt easily to low-carbon transition production, makes it an optimal setting for economies and businesses seeking to decarbonize their industries and diversify into green supply chains.

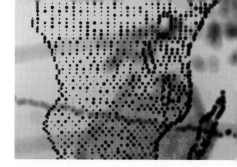

CHAPTER 3

Technology-intensive supply chains and industries: Resetting African markets and businesses for mobility and scale

As stated in chapter 1 of this report, companies are increasingly seeking to diversify their supply chains to reduce their exposure to global shocks and disruptions, such as the COVID-19 pandemic or the war in Ukraine. Such a perspective for supply chain diversification provides opportunities for economies in Africa to position themselves as geographic alternatives. Some industries are more exposed to supply chain shocks than others – this is closely related to their global value chain activity. Figure 19 illustrates that supply chain linkages, measured by imported foreign value added embedded in exports, showing that several areas – computers and electronics, the automotive industry, electrical equipment, machinery and equipment, and chemicals and pharmaceutical products – provide deep supply chain integration.

In countries of the Organisation for Economic Co-operation and Development, refined petroleum products and basic metals depend the most on imported value added. The high trade intensity in these sectors offers scope for regional and global specialization in the production of the various components. The largest growth in supply chain activity is observed for motor vehicles, where foreign value added increased almost fivefold between 2000 and 2018 (on average across non-member countries of the Organisation for Economic Co-operation and Development) (see figure 19).

The strong supply chain activity of these medium- and high-technology manufacturing areas suggests some opportunities for production in manufacturing subsectors that propel growth and development. Recent studies support this assertion by showing that technology-intensive manufacturing can be less emissions intensive than low-technology manufacturing (Altenburg and Assman, 2017; Avenyo and Tregenna, 2022; Zhang, 2012), therefore implying its suitability for sustainable resource-based industrialization. In addition, the evolving scenario of digitizing and greening supply chains, as discussed in chapter 2, provides a window of opportunity for African countries to reposition and integrate into the medium and downstream segments of several supply chains. Specifically, the natural capital of Africa – including opportunity for abundant renewable energy generation and endowments of rare earth metals and critical minerals – can play a pivotal role in attracting investments into productive capacities and promoting the development of domestic and regional linkages.

This chapter discusses the possible paths for the integration of Africa into medium- and high-technology intensive supply chains by using its natural endowments. Global supply chain integration can pave the way for industrialization and sustainable development in the region. Further, the chapter examines the automotive and electronics industries, with special emphasis on mobile telephone supply chains and renewable energy technology (prospects of solar panels). It also explores the medical device and pharmaceutical supply chains. It is vital to understand the relevance and sustainability of the mining industry as a driver of these high-technology supply chains.

Apart from vertical linkages to the supply chain, the chapter will highlight the importance of horizontal integration to leverage increasing demand in Africa and reduce its vulnerability to external shocks. Given its limited manufacturing base and the benefits it stands to gain from greater value addition to its abundant resources, the greater part of the discussion focuses on production and procurement. Nevertheless, aspects of distribution, transport and logistics are considered elements of supply chain integration that can attract investment in production capacities.

Figure 19

Foreign value added embedded in exports by domestic industry and country group

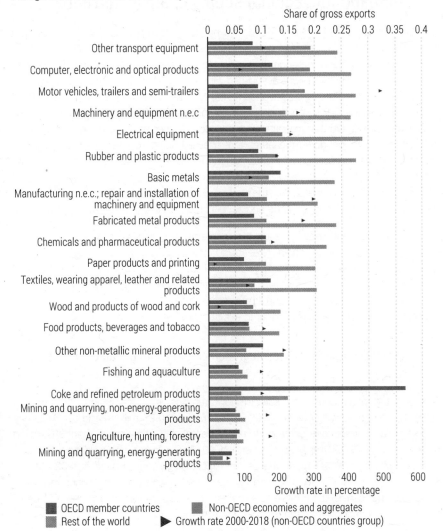

Source: UNCTAD calculations, based on data from the trade in value added database (Organisation for Economic Co-operation and Development and World Trade Organization).

Abbreviations: n.e.c., not elsewhere classified; OECD, Organisation for Economic Co-operation and Development.

3.1 Automotive industry: Leveraging increasing vehicle demand for regional supply chain localization

The automotive industry is one of the most dynamic and complex supply chains and as a result, highly vulnerable to supply chain disruptions. The automotive industry is undergoing far-reaching changes and challenges that can also present opportunities for African countries, owing to supply chain disruptions associated with the COVID-19 pandemic (see chapter 2, box 2), as well as technological advancements, such as connected, autonomous, shared and electric vehicles. For instance, data from the International Organization of Motor Vehicle Manufacturers indicate that the pandemic caused a 16 per cent decline in global vehicle production due to lockdown measures that affected not only assembly but production and shipping of necessary components. Although Africa experienced the sharpest decline (28 per cent) between 2019 and 2020, it also recovered more strongly with an increase of 16 per cent in 2021, compared with the world average of 3 per cent. The robust recovery is also indicative of the recent demand and supply growth of the automotive industry.

In Africa, several factors will provide the momentum to achieve a deeper integration in the automotive supply chain: the abundance of critical metals required for this technology-intensive supply chain, young and fast-growing consumer markets and recent disruptions in the automotive supply chain (see chapter 2). Recent trends in the African automotive industry and the strategic position of African countries in the regional supply chain will be discussed further in this section.

3.1.1 Promising trends for the integration of Africa into the automotive supply chain

Although the registration and sale of new vehicles in Africa is low (1.14 million in 2021), compared with Asia (42.66 million), Europe (16.87 million) and the Americas (22.00 million), projections show that vehicle demand in Africa could reach 10 million vehicles a year by 2030 (Black and McLennan, 2016). Similarly, demand for second-hand vehicles, which dominate many markets in Africa, has also increased. In 2021, Africa accounted for about 40 per cent of the world's used vehicles imports, which represent close to 85 per cent of the total vehicle fleet in Africa (see www.mordorintelligence.com/industry-reports/middle-east-and-africa-used-car-market).

Despite global challenges and concentration in the sector, the production of vehicles is flourishing on the continent. According to International Organization of Motor Vehicle Manufacturers statistics, production increased from 328,749 units in 2000 to

931,056 units in 2021 (see www.oica.net). However, the automotive sector in Africa is still in its early stages, accounting for only 1.2 per cent of global output. Total production units in other regions range from 46.7 million in Asia and the Pacific, to 16.3 million in Europe and 16.2 million in the Americas.

In 2019, the production of vehicles in Africa was dominated by South Africa (631,921 units) and Morocco (403,218 units), followed by Algeria (60,012 units) and Egypt (18,500 units) (figure 20).[16] In Morocco, a sharp increase in vehicle production, from 42,066 in 2010 to 403,007 in 2021, was driven by large investments by original equipment manufacturers from Europe.[17] The geographical location of Morocco, its stable political and macroeconomic environment, investment in infrastructure and a national framework to support the automotive industry were factors that made these investments attractive (see box 6).

Figure 20
Vehicle production trends in Africa, 2000–2021

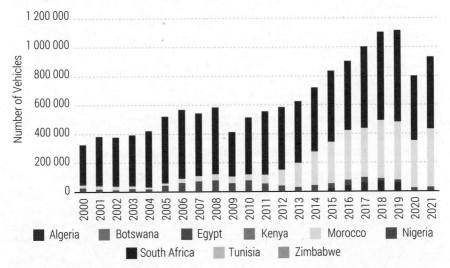

Source: UNCTAD calculations, based on International Organization of Motor Vehicle Manufacturers statistics (www.oica.net/production-statistics/).
Note: Units of vehicles produced in Botswana, Kenya, Tunisia and Zimbabwe were relatively small compared to other reported countries, at less than 3,000 units of vehicles per year during the covered period 2000-2021.

[16] In Algeria, output virtually came to a halt in 2020 due to plant closures resulting from new regulations and a corruption controversy (Agarwal et al., 2022).
[17] In the automotive industry, original equipment manufacturers are the original producers and suppliers of devices or components used in the manufacture of vehicles.

The case of Nigeria, however, differs from that of Morocco. Nigeria used to have a vibrant automotive industry in the 1970s and 1980s, with a production of 149,000 units per annum. Six automobile manufacturers were present on the local market (Leyland, Mercedes-Benz, National Trucks, Peugeot, Steyr and Volkswagen). However, macroeconomic challenges stemming from the 1981 global oil price shock, subsequent recessions and local currency depreciations, led to substantial reductions in the industry's output. To improve on the 2013 National Automotive Industry Development Plan, Nigeria recently announced the adoption of a new plan covering the period 2023–2033. In 2023, Nigeria attracted investment in the automotive industry through a joint venture between Dangote Industries (Nigeria) and Sinotruck (China), raising assembly capacity to 10,000 units (Business Insider Africa, 2023).

Box 6
Morocco: An exemplary domestic automotive industry

Since 1957, the automotive industry in Morocco has evolved from the assembly of vehicles (*Société marocaine de constructions automobiles*) to their production. In 2021, 403,007 units were manufactured, with exports valued at $8.3 billion, $3.4 billion of which were final vehicle exports. Approximately 220,000 jobs were created in the sector, and a burgeoning components network of more than 230 tier 1 and 2 suppliers was set up. This represents a local integration rate of 60 per cent. The country is now positioned as a production platform with the entry of several groups, for example, German Motor Distributors, Renault, Snop (parts and components supplier), Stellantis Sumitomo Electric Wiring Systems (technical array of systems and components) and Yazaki (the world's largest manufacturer of wiring harnesses).

Manufacturing is moving towards more complex components with high value added, such as engine manufacturing, engineering, and research and development. Morocco also produces about 40,000–50,000 electric vehicles per year. However, since the domestic registration of new vehicles is low (175,435 units in 2021; see www.oica.net), the assembly of vehicles is oriented towards the European market. For example, Renault, which has the largest assembly plant with a capacity of 400,000 units, exports most of its production. The Citroën *Ami*, made in Kenitra, Morocco, was the most widely sold vehicle in Spain in 2022. In December 2022, X-Electric Vehicle of China, known commonly as XEV, announced plans to produce electric cars in Morocco for the Italian market.

Various factors have enabled Morocco to attract multinational companies and support local content: investment in infrastructure (domestic and international connectivity); the creation of six special economic zones, in which investors receive tax exemptions and other incentives; and its proximity to Europe. Domestic industrial policies and plans, such as the Industrial Acceleration Plan 2014–2020, have fostered the automotive industry ecosystem and have seen the advent of industrial parks and the automotive cities of Kenitra and Tangier, Morocco. The integration of Morocco into the global economy, facilitated by the signing of various free trade agreements, has also made the country a lucrative investment location. In addition, engineering and research and development capacities have grown with the establishment of a regional technical centre by Stellantis and the first automobile testing centre in Africa, which will allow Morocco to be autonomous in terms of the validation and homologation of parts and vehicles. Systematic investment in education and skill development, digitization and supplier development programmes has also enabled the emergence of Moroccan know-how in the manufacturing of parts and components.

Morocco aims to produce one million cars per year by 2025 and achieve a local integration rate of 80 per cent. In 2020, it already had an installed annual capacity of 700,000 vehicles. The aforementioned government initiatives and plans are designed to enhance local integration, scale up industrial activities, upgrade operations across the value chain, improve levels of technology and knowledge transfer, and diversify export markets. Addressing these challenges could also help increase the participation of small and medium-sized domestic enterprises in the assembly phase, which remains limited. To maintain growth and foster supply chain sustainability, vehicle export destinations should be diversified, and the automotive industry in Morocco should target the African parts market that is dominated by second-hand vehicles. In November 2022, Stellantis announced a $300 million investment in its manufacturing facility to double productive capacity to 400,000 units and serve the Middle East and Africa market.

Source: UNCTAD, based on Auktor 2022; *Automotive News Europe*, 2022; bladi.net, 2023; Economic Commission for Africa, 2018; Hahn and Vidican-Auktor, 2017; Japan International Cooperation Agency and Boston Consulting Group, 2022; Kasraoui, 2022; Khattabi, 2023; Naji, 2020.

Other African countries, such as Angola, Ethiopia, Ghana, Kenya, Lesotho, Mozambique and Namibia, have relatively small-scale assembly operations, mostly semi-knock-down kits with minimal value added. Semi-knock-down kit assembly can be done in low volumes but entails minor assembly with virtually no value addition or employment. The absence of a thriving parts and components industry on the continent is a main challenge to reaping more inclusive benefits in terms of employment creation and the participation of more African countries in the supply chain. However, there is potential to build new capabilities through targeted investment. According to projections for 2025, vehicle bodies will represent the largest global automotive market at $190 billion, followed by electronics ($154 billion), and wheels and tyres ($144 billion) (Deloitte, 2021). Increasing the production of these parts and components provides a major opportunity for African countries to take advantage of and transform available raw materials, such as aluminium, copper and rubber.

Exports of vehicles from Africa to the world have also risen steadily since 2003. Between 2018 and 2020, the two leading African exporters of vehicles were South Africa ($9.2 billion) and Morocco ($3.4 billion).

While Europe is the main destination of vehicle exports from Africa for the transport of persons, mainly driven by exports from Morocco, other types of vehicles, especially vehicles for the transport of goods, such as trucks and tractors, boast a bigger share of intra-Africa exports (30 per cent and 97 per cent, respectively). The majority of intra-African exports of vehicles are trucks (57 per cent), followed by passenger cars (25 per cent). Owing to the potential of the African Continental Free Trade Area to boost trade within the continent, it is likely that there will be a growing demand for regional production and the supply of tractors, buses and vehicles for the transport of goods.

While production facilities of the final vehicle product are generally located in close proximity to the customer, owing to logistical factors such as transport costs, the manufacturing and supply of vehicle parts and components have become more global. Nevertheless, the dependence of the automotive industry on the efficient supply of parts and components often motivates tier 1 (automotive parts and components) suppliers to set up their locations close to large assembling operations, particularly because of high transportation costs. Further up the supply chain, tier 2 (non-automotive parts and components) and tier 3 (raw and semi-raw materials) supplies are also inputs to a range of other industries and hence, less dependent on a particular original equipment manufacturer in the supply chain.

3.1.2 The largest benefits for Africa lie in regional supply chains: A supply chain mapping approach

This section applies a value chain mapping exercise to potentially identify the positions of individual countries in regional supply chains (box 7). The focus on such chains is motivated by the momentum of the African Continental Free Trade Area and the need to achieve greater local and regional value addition. This is important not only to promote industrial growth on the continent but also to meet rules of origin requirements in the various continental trade agreements. The section is also devoted to opportunities in the electric vehicle supply chain.

Box 7
Methodology for identifying regional supply chain opportunities

To position African countries in the global and regional automotive supply chain and to identify feasible opportunities for upgrading, the chapter applies an approach using a mix of sources and existing literature (see sources below).

The methodology uses an input–output table from Canada for the year 2020, as its disaggregation into 234 subsectors allows a detailed identification of potential forward and backward linkages. After matching with the codes of the International Standard Industrial Classification and the Harmonized Commodity Description and Coding System (HS), relevant activities and products are identified along the supply chain.

Identified products are classified under tier 1 (automotive parts and systems), tier 2 (non-automotive parts and system) and tier 3 (semi- and raw materials) suppliers. The mapping of these codes by tier, supporting services and technological equipment is shown in the next figure. Yet, the matching is not perfect, as not all identified inputs are necessarily used in the automotive supply chain, especially in tiers 2 and 3. For instance, all iron and steel subgroups are presented, although not all steel grades can be used by assemblers. Desktop research completes the identification of additional inputs and raw materials used especially in electric vehicle manufacturing. In total, 93 product groups are identified at the HS six-digit level and 28 product groups at the four-digit level, 15 service categories at the International Standard Industrial Classification four-digit level and nine HS product groups as necessary industrial equipment/technology.

It is necessary to identify potential product diversification opportunities by supplementing the input–output approach with the product space method (for an application of the automotive industry in South Africa, see Bam et al., 2021 and for the steel industry, Bam and De Bruyne, 2019). The proposed analysis in this report is the first to apply the input–output product space method to the whole continent. Feasible product diversification opportunities at the HS six-digit level are identified, based on findings from UNCTAD (2022d).

Mapping of automotive parts and components, supporting services and equipment

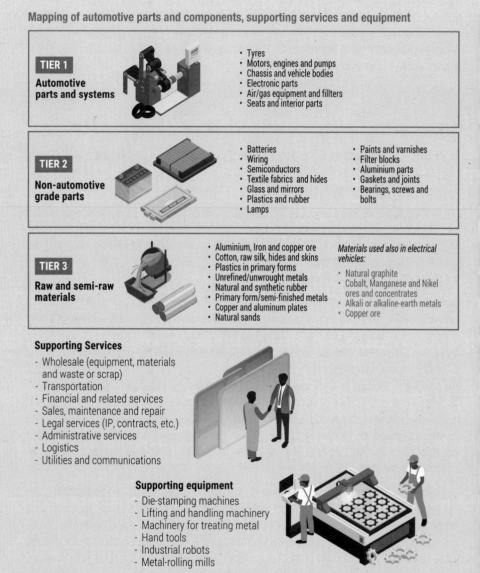

TIER 1
Automotive
parts and systems

- Tyres
- Motors, engines and pumps
- Chassis and vehicle bodies
- Electronic parts
- Air/gas equipment and fillters
- Seats and interior parts

TIER 2
Non-automotive
grade parts

- Batteries
- Wiring
- Semiconductors
- Textile fabrics and hides
- Glass and mirrors
- Plastics and rubber
- Lamps
- Paints and varnishes
- Filter blocks
- Aluminium parts
- Gaskets and joints
- Bearings, screws and bolts

TIER 3
Raw and semi-raw
materials

- Aluminium, Iron and copper ore
- Cotton, raw silk, hides and skins
- Plastics in primary forms
- Unrefined/unwrought metals
- Natural and synthetic rubber
- Primary form/semi-finished metals
- Copper and aluminum plates
- Natural sands

Materials used also in electrical vehicles:

- Natural graphite
- Cobalt, Manganese and Nikel ores and concentrates
- Alkali or alkaline-earth metals
- Copper ore

Supporting Services

- Wholesale (equipment, materials and waste or scrap)
- Transportation
- Financial and related services
- Sales, maintenance and repair
- Legal services (IP, contracts, etc.)
- Administrative services
- Logistics
- Utilities and communications

Supporting equipment

- Die-stamping machines
- Lifting and handling machinery
- Machinery for treating metal
- Hand tools
- Industrial robots
- Metal-rolling mills

Sources: UNCTAD, with input from Bam et al., 2021.

Export data at the HS 1992 six-digit level for 2018–2020 are obtained from the United Nations Comtrade database. Due to data limitations in recent years, only 43 African countries were included (data were not available for 2018–2020 for the following countries: Algeria, Chad, Djibouti, Eritrea, Equatorial Guinea, Gabon, Guinea, Guinea-Bissau, Liberia, Somalia and South Sudan).

Sources: UNCTAD, based on Bam et al., 2021; Bam and De Bruyne, 2019; El Mataoui et al., 2019; International Trade Centre, 2022; UNCTAD, 2022d.

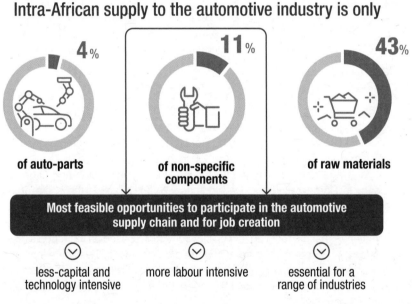

Intra-African supply to the automotive industry is only

4%

of auto-parts

11%

of non-specific components

43%

of raw materials

Most feasible opportunities to participate in the automotive supply chain and for job creation

less-capital and technology intensive

more labour intensive

essential for a range of industries

Although almost all of the 43 African countries for which recent export data were available appear to have some export capacity in either tiers 1, 2 or 3, the share of intra-African inputs to the automotive industry is limited, especially in tiers 1 and 2. As shown in table 4, African imports account for only 4 per cent of total imports of automotive parts and systems owing to the limited productive capacity in Africa; this is largely driven by upper-middle income countries.[18] Most of these products are

---

[18] To align the analysis with that of chapter 2, African countries are classified by income as per the World Bank classification.

Table 4

Import supply to Africa, by region and tier category, 2018–2020 average exports

	Tier 1		Tier 2		Traditional tier 3		Tier 3 (including electric vehicle materials)	
	Value in million dollars	Share (percentage)	Value in million dollars	Share (percentage)	Value in million dollars	Share (percentage)	Value in million dollars	Share (percentage)
Africa	887.37	4	817.13	11	5,684.09	38	7,171.99	43
Low-income countries	49.68	0	34.02	0	4,127.55	28	4,890.86	29
Lower-middle-income countries	144.56	1	316.25	4	429.84	3	956.08	6
Upper-middle-income countries	693.11	3	466.84	6	1,126.70	8	1,325.047	8
Americas	1,401.15	6	222.64	3	1,395.75	9	1,622.11	10
Asia	10,911.06	47	3,973.35	53	4,244.77	29	4,248.99	25
Europe	9,266.04	40	2,500.51	33	3,450.76	23	3,592.95	22
Oceania	46.79	0	18.73	0	28.98	0	28.98	0

Source: UNCTAD calculations, based on data from the United Nations Comtrade database.

exported by South Africa, especially to member countries of the Southern African Development Community, where the bulk of components exports are destined for the aftersales market (that is, repair and maintenance of cars), including for instance, tyres, engine parts and transmission shafts (African Union Commission and Organisation for Economic Co-operation and Development, 2022). In tier 2, the share of import supply of African countries to other African countries is 11 per cent, and low-middle-income African countries also have a larger share. Finally, Africa is the largest supplier of raw materials that are required for vehicle production. Based on the report's research findings (box 7), 38 per cent of tier-3 imports are from Africa. This share increases to 43 per cent when considering new materials (electric vehicle materials) used to make electric vehicles. Africa holds about 19 per cent of the global metal reserves required for building electric vehicles.

Figure 21 maps the number of products, with a minimum value of $100,000, that African countries exported to the continent between 2018 and 2020. It illustrates the dominant role of South Africa, especially in tier 1. About 75 per cent of the countries covered (31 out of 43) exported at least one product in tier 1 (figure 21(a)).[19] Thirty

[19] In reality, the number of countries exporting a certain product based on actual production is probably much lower. However, re-exports as part of export are poorly reported, which poses a key limitation on the chapter's export data-based analysis.

Figure 21

Number of countries currently supplying inputs, including new electric vehicle materials, to African markets: (a) tier 1, (b) tier 2 and (c) tier 3, 2018–2020 average

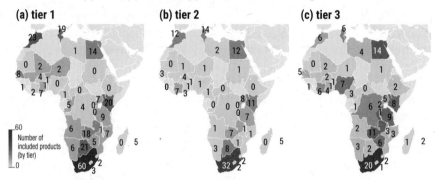

Source: UNCTAD, based on data from the United Nations Comtrade database.

Note: Tier 1 includes 63 product groups; tier 2, 34 product groups; and tier 3, 26 product groups.

The boundaries and names shown and the designations used on these maps do not imply official endorsement or acceptance by the United Nations.

African countries exported at least one product in tier 2 (figure 21(b)), and 36 African countries exported at least one product in tier 3 (figure 21(c)). The identification of feasible export diversification opportunities suggests that through targeted investment in capabilities, African countries can fill recent gaps in the regional supply chain. For instance, the report's analysis (box 7) shows that Uganda, which currently exports eight products in tier 2, could diversify into 25 other products in tier 2, given that tier 2 products require similar capabilities and could be realized through relatively small jumps in the product space.

Parts and components are not only relevant for final vehicle assembly but increasingly for the aftersales market. In Ghana, for example, the aftersales market has an estimated revenue of $500–$575 million per year, which is approximately twice as much as revenue stemming from new vehicles sales. The supply of parts, in particular, tyres, but also batteries, brake pads and filters, accounts for about 60–65 per cent of the aftersales market in Ghana, while the costs of repair services contribute about 25–30 per cent. About 70–80 per cent of the aftersales market in that country is run by informal small and medium-sized enterprises. Given the constraints faced by the informal sector, such as limited access to finance and higher costs of importing parts and components, tackling such barriers could trigger greater expansion in the automotive industry in Ghana.

Similarly, in Nigeria, the aftersales market is estimated at $1.5 billion (2020) of which tyres contribute the largest part (Japan International Cooperation Agency and Boston Consulting Group, 2022).

Despite the abundance of rubber in Africa, more than 85 per cent of tyres are still being imported from China, thus suggesting little existing local capacity for rubber processing and tyre export. For instance, in Côte d'Ivoire, the largest supplier of natural rubber in Africa, rubber output was estimated at 1.1 million tons in 2021, a 16 per cent increase from 2020, while the country's processing capacity was estimated at only 664,000 tons. Despite planned investment in rubber-processing plants (for example, by Saph), local processing and capacity remains low, compared with the output of natural rubber (Reuters, 2021). Considering the example of car seats, intra-African export mapping prepared for this report shows that Africa can provide almost all the inputs necessary to produce car seats. Leather, for example, could be made by Kenya, Namibia and the Niger; textiles fabrics, by Botswana, Côte d'Ivoire and Eswatini; bolts and screws, by Côte d'Ivoire, Egypt, Kenya, Mauritius, Morocco, Senegal, the United Republic of Tanzania and Zambia; and propylene polymers, by Burkina Faso, Côte d'Ivoire, Egypt, Eswatini, Kenya, Morocco, the Niger, Nigeria and Senegal. On the whole, however, inputs continue to be largely imported from other countries (International Trade Centre, 2022).

Given the increasing adoption of automation and technology, such as artificial intelligence, machine learning and additive manufacturing, in the automotive production and supply chain processes, the potential impact of the automotive industry on employment creation in Africa is worth exploring in more detail. According to statistics from the data portal of the United Nations Industrial Development Organization (see https://stat.unido.org), Morocco experienced an increase of 147 per cent in the number of people employed in the manufacture of motor vehicles between 2000 and 2016, as well as a growing share of industrial employment, from 2 per cent to 4 per cent during the same period. Similarly, between 2000 and 2019, the number of employees in South Africa rose by 14 per cent, and the share of total industrial employment increased from 8 per cent in 2010 to 9.7 per cent in 2019. Input–output table analysis suggests that assembly manufacturing contributes only 1 per cent to total value added of the sector's output. The majority is contributed by automotive parts and components (for example, metal stamping contributes 11 per cent value addition; engine manufacturing, 9 per cent; and seat manufacturing, 7 per cent). In addition, non-automotive sectors that contribute high value addition are plastic manufacturing, financial services and transport services. While it is difficult to estimate the multiplier effects for African countries, this analysis gives an idea of the additional employment created in more labour-intensive sectors, such as seat manufacturing, including the leather and textile industry. In South Africa, for example, final assembly employment grew slightly from 28,100 people in 2010 to 30,000 people in 2017 and 33,000 people in 2022, owing principally to technological progress and the increased use of robots. Employment figures in the automotive component manufacturing sector increased form 65,000 people in 2010 and 80,000 in 2017 to 83,000 in 2022 (Mashilo, 2019; National Association of Automobile Manufacturers of South Africa, 2023). In addition, employment along the entire auto supply chain in South Africa is estimated at more than one million people, implying a multiplier effect of 14 jobs upstream and downstream in the supply chain (National Association of Automobile Manufacturers of South Africa, 2023).

In focus: How the electric vehicle trend leads to new opportunities for African countries

To achieve the climate goals, the share of electric vehicles, alongside the electrification of buses, freight trucks and commercial vehicles, must reach 40 per cent by 2030 (International Energy Agency, 2022). In 2020, electric car sales worldwide climbed by 40 per cent to about 3 million, attaining a market share of over 4 per cent. According to the International Energy Agency (2022a), an electric car requires about six times the mineral inputs of a conventional car: One electric car requires 53 kg of copper, 13.3 kg of cobalt, 8.9 kg of lithium, 39.9 kg of nickel, 24.5 kg of manganese, 66.3 kg of graphite and 0.5 kg of rare earth metals. By contrast, a conventional car requires 22.3 kg of copper and 11.2 kg of manganese. In a sustainable development scenario, demand for these minerals will rise (International Energy Agency, 2022a).[20] At the time of writing, nine African countries hold a significant share of world exports in these critical materials.[21] Africa accounts for 97 per cent of world cobalt exports, and 84 per cent of world manganese exports (see figure 22).

---

[20] The International Energy Agency (2022a) estimates that the demand for minerals will increase sharply between 2020 and 2040. The demand for nickel will multiply 41 times to 3,300 kilotons; for cobalt, 21 times; for lithium, 43 times; for copper, 28 times, reaching about 3,000 kilotons for new electric vehicle sales; and for graphite, 25 times (from 140 kilotons in 2020 to over 3,500 kilotons in 2040).

[21] These countries are Botswana (copper), the Democratic Republic of the Congo (manganese, copper, cobalt), Egypt (natural graphite), Morocco (manganese), Mozambique (natural graphite), South Africa (manganese, copper), the United Republic of Tanzania (natural graphite), Zambia (manganese, copper, cobalt) and Zimbabwe (nickel).

Figure 22
Share of critical electric vehicle materials in world exports, by region, 2018–2022 average

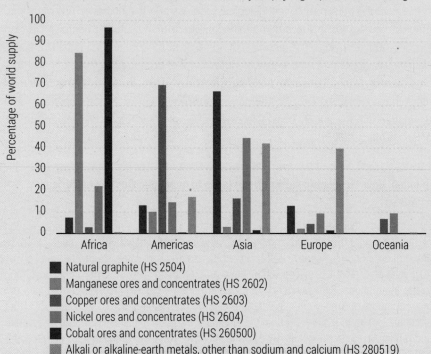

- ■ Natural graphite (HS 2504)
- ■ Manganese ores and concentrates (HS 2602)
- ■ Copper ores and concentrates (HS 2603)
- ■ Nickel ores and concentrates (HS 2604)
- ■ Cobalt ores and concentrates (HS 260500)
- ■ Alkali or alkaline-earth metals, other than sodium and calcium (HS 280519)

Source: UNCTAD calculations, based on data from the United Nations Comtrade database.
Note: HS code 280519 (alkali or alkaline-earth metals) includes lithium.

African countries abounding in electric vehicle minerals are exploring opportunities on how best to exploit their resources to attract downstream investment in battery production. South Africa launched a programme to develop a lithium battery value chain in 2011, focusing on cell and battery manufacturing, testing and validation and recycling. South Africa holds vast resources of some of the minerals that go into that supply chain, including manganese, cobalt, iron ore, nickel and titanium, and it has lithium reserves (Mordor Intelligence, 2022; Trade and Industrial Policy Strategies, 2021).[22] To date, however, there is little value addition and transformation of minerals to battery grade in the country. Only manganese and aluminium are refined to battery grade, while nickel and lithium are in the pipeline. Downstream of the supply chain, some battery manufacturing activities depend on imported battery cells (Trade and Industrial Policy Strategies, 2021).

Paradoxically, proximity to the mineral source is only a minor factor in the location of downstream industries, since processed metals are relatively easy and inexpensive to transport (Trade and Industrial Policy Strategies, 2021). However, transport cost is still relevant for products closer to the raw extraction stage, especially in its raw form. For instance, to reduce the weight of exports, Zambia has succeeded in developing copper smelting and refining copper from concentrates to cathodes. Conversely, there is only a small manufacturing sector that uses this copper, despite the emerging demand for the mineral in battery production.

With regard to the demand side in battery production, all vehicle assemblers in Africa are multinational companies with their own core technology and research and development at headquarters or other plants outside the continent. Despite the encouraging trend in electric vehicle demand, the demand in Africa for electric vehicles is simply not sufficient to make new battery cell production plans competitive without securing demand from the major companies. It is estimated that by 2040, at current production capacity and demand, only 20 per cent of vehicles in Africa will be electric vehicles (Conzade et al., 2022). Necessary investment in battery or electric vehicle production plants is also costly and requires private–private and public–private partnerships. Electric vehicle producers could serve more aptly as alternative capital providers to accelerate projects, while gaining supply security.

Given the fast-developing battery supply chain in terms of technology advancements and research and development spending, African countries need to actively make deals with car companies and producers of car batteries to acquire technology and knowledge and engage local processing and go beyond the supplying of raw materials. Moreover, national incentives and regional cooperation should allow local African car companies to source first and provide local companies with the competitive advantage of localization or local content.[23] As they access such market advantages domestically and gain skills and technologies

---

[22] Minerals used in the cell and battery supply chain include lithium, cobalt, manganese, nickel, graphite, bauxite, copper, iron, phosphate rock and titanium.

[23] Local companies can have a competitive advantage if they are granted preferential access to local resources. Such measures can take the form of a specific percentage of mining products that must be used or transformed locally. However, investment in infrastructure is needed to reduce local transportation costs and promote the provision of services that facilitate local market linkages (Korinek and Ramdoo, 2017).

from their relationships with leading multinational companies, local African companies will also be in a better position to encourage battery assembly. This entails the improvement of battery management systems, which include a range of parts and components, such as chargers, battery packaging and harnessing. Enlarging development capacity in recycling or supplying the circular economy is also necessary. Recycling will be a key feature of automakers and electric vehicle battery manufacturing operations by transforming current supply chains into a circular economy. This will enable firms to reuse the critical raw materials in electric vehicle batteries at low cost, which will be important for automakers as electric vehicle adoption grows exponentially throughout the world over the next decade or so (see section 3.5.2).

3.1.3 Realizing industry potential by achieving scale and mobility

Despite the growing exports of parts and components in some African countries, the intra-African supply of tier 1 and tier 2 components remains small. The minimum production capacity of an automotive assembly plant is estimated at 80,000 vehicles per year, requiring an investment of $200 million (Natsuda and Thoburn, 2021). Hence, to reach greater scale and mobility in the automotive industry, it is necessary to institute favourable policies and incentives to localize supply chains, including parts and components, distribution and aftersales goods and services.

Promoting national demand for locally produced vehicles and parts and components
First, new vehicle-financing mechanisms should be developed. Current financing options come with high interest rates and strict repayment terms. In Ghana, for example, interest rates can be as high as 30 per cent, resulting in only 5 per cent of new car sales being financed by banks (*Automotive News Europe, 2020*). The Government announced a vehicle-financing scheme in 2023, an initiative that would allow more Africans to purchase new, locally manufactured cars (Ghana News Agency, 2023).

Second, the regulation of used-car imports and minimum standard requirements on imported parts and components aimed at promoting the aftersales market should be harmonized further. The lack of harmonization of standards makes it difficult for parts and components suppliers to produce at sufficiently large scale. There are about 1,432 international automotive standards worldwide. The African Organization for Standardization expects that some 250 standards relating to basic components and replacement parts will need to be harmonized in Africa to keep vehicles safe and operational (African Export–Import Bank, 2021).

Third, regional integration efforts should favour locally produced vehicles and components. As shown in figure 23, tariffs on imports from Africa are currently more advantageous than imports from outside the continent. However, to benefit from tariff advantages under the African Continental Free Trade Area (see International Trade Centre and UNCTAD, 2021 and UNCTAD, 2021b), rules of origin must be certified. Rules of origin are an important instrument to promote regional value addition. The African Continental Free Trade Area rules of origin are being negotiated on a sector-by-sector basis, resulting in product-specific origin rules (Agarwal et al., 2022; Trade Law Centre, 2021). As of January 2023, negotiations relating to the automotive sector had not yet been concluded.

Fourth, the regional supply chain can be leveraged to reduce overall costs. For that, intraregional supply chain efficiency can be enhanced through better regional logistical coordination facilitated by custom harmonization, single-window arrangements and simplified regional sourcing of parts and components.

Figure 23
Tariff advantage for sourcing inputs from Africa

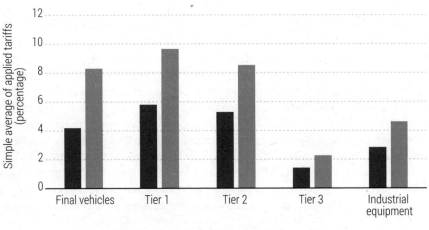

■ Average applied tariffs on imports from Africa
■ Average applied tariffs on imports from the world

Source: UNCTAD calculations, based on the World Integrated Trade Solution database.
Note: Final vehicles include HS 8701–8705; tiers 1, 2 and 3 and industrial equipment discussed in box 7.

Realizing scale through the identification of niche areas and clustering production
Clearly, not all African countries have the same opportunities, depending on their initial capabilities and their location. For instance, countries and close neighbours can use existing assembly hubs to target the production of heavier and model-specific parts, such as engines, transmissions, seats and other car interior parts. Countries farther away, which is true for most African countries, can still benefit from the automotive industry through the production of lighter, less complex and more labour-intensive components to take advantage of economies of scale and low labour costs (for example, tyres and wire harnesses). The niche areas in countries and regions should be identified through detailed research in the future, fostered through bilateral and multilateral cooperation.

Due to high operating costs, lack of electricity and infrastructure, African countries find it difficult to compete with imports from China and India. To overcome this challenge, clustering production through special economic zones and industrial parks can be a viable option. For instance, under an agreement between the Democratic Republic of the Congo and Zambia to build a battery supply chain, the creation of a special economic zone for batteries was officially confirmed in March 2023 (United Nations, Economic Commission for Africa, 2023).

Attracting investment and facilitating financing options
Foreign investments are necessary for companies to acquire the technological capabilities required to manufacture more sophisticated automotive components (Wuttke, 2022). The experiences of Morocco (box 6) and Thailand (see box 8) highlight the importance of original equipment manufacturers and parts and component manufacturers in the growth of local industry. Strong domestic demand (Thailand), favourable locations (Morocco), infrastructure investments (Morocco and Thailand) and supportive trade and industrial policies, such as local content requirements and tax incentives, are key incentives to investment in the automotive supply chain. Other performance requirements to increase local benefits for the economy include requirements relating to local training, joint ventures, technology transfer and exports. Such requirements, for instance to transfer technology or research and development findings, should, however, be coupled with national efforts to build national innovation systems that include the promotion of education and training to be effective. For instance, export-related performance requirements have been widely used in various countries, for example, Chile (diversification of resource-based exports), in Costa Rica (example of a leading manufacturer of microprocessors and chipsets attracting exports of medical devices), Malaysia (electronic components industry), South Africa (automotive industry) and Mexico and Thailand (export-focused investment in the automotive industry) (UNCTAD, 2003; UNCTAD, 2022d; World Economic Forum, 2016).

Other localization policies include requirements relating to the transfer of knowledge and technology to local firms and employment and skills creation. Yet, according to UNCTAD research, the driving force behind export performance is supply capacity; and those requirements alone would suffice to build domestic production capabilities and localize more parts of the supply chain (UNCTAD, 2003; UNCTAD, 2005).

To avoid national strategies that would impede economies of scale and necessary investments, a regionally harmonized policy aimed at attracting large-scale investment in both assembly and parts and components and facilitating public procurement would be advantageous.

Access to financing remains one of the key challenges of African companies as they strive to integrate supply chains. Therefore, to support financing of industrial players in the automotive supply chain, African Export–Import Bank and the African Association of Automotive Manufacturers have entered into a memorandum of understanding in which the African Export–Import Bank has committed to providing $1 billion (African Continental Free Trade Area, 2023). Possible areas of intervention include direct financing, project financing, guarantees and equity financing. Additional financing instruments, such as supply chain financing, is discussed further in chapter 4.

Box 8
Automotive industrial policies: Lessons from Thailand in the context of the Association of Southeast Asian Nations

In 2019, 4.2 million vehicles were manufactured in countries of the Association of Southeast Asian Nations. Thailand produced about 2 million units; Indonesia, 1.2 million units; and Malaysia, 700,000 units. Most of the vehicles are sold in the countries of origin, except for Thailand, which exports 52 per cent of production, 14 per cent of which is exported to countries in the region. The Philippines and Viet Nam have some small-scale production and contribute substantially to component supply, for which there is strong demand within the countries of the Association of Southeast Asian Nations. Thailand has emerged as the main automotive hub of the region, ranking as the third-largest exporter of automotive products in Asia after Japan and the Republic of Korea. Countries in the region have supported that growth. For example, in 2014, 82 per cent of households owned a car. Under the Industrial Promotion Act (1960), Thailand established the first vehicle assembly firm in 1961. High tariffs and restrictions on imports of completely built units, as well as fiscal incentives, promoted import substitution. Once local assembly was set up, localization policies, such as local content requirements, targeted an increase in local content ratios. Since then, there has been a gradual shift to greater localization of auto parts production. In 1991, the first research and development centre in the country was founded.

The success of the automotive industry in Thailand can be attributed to firm-level costs and market advantages. The local auto industry benefited from large-scale export-oriented investments, which were facilitated by a favourable physical environment, substantial infrastructure investments and supportive trade and industrial policies. Further, Thailand had used local content requirements widely as an industrial policy to promote local sourcing before joining the World Trade Organization. As local content requirements are not allowed under article 2.1 of the Agreement on Trade-related Investment Measures of the World Trade Organization, they were abolished after Thailand joined the Organization. The liberalization of inputs through the abolition of local content requirements has even increased local content, combined with the relaxation of restrictions on the foreign entry of input suppliers. Even if Thailand does not have its own brand, the country added value to the production process by localizing research and development activities through multinational original equipment manufacturers. Thailand is indeed an important example of a country that uses existing supply chain facilities to achieve further value addition for domestic industries.

While Thailand has benefited from investments from Japan, the creation of a full regional supply chain still remains difficult, as other members of the Association of Southeast Asian Nations (Indonesia and Malaysia) are also developing their local car brands. Yet, regional integration under the Association has supported the industry's growth. The Industrial Cooperation Scheme (1996) of the Association grants preferential tariff rates if two companies set up an industrial cooperation arrangement. The products included under that arrangement must have at least 40 per cent content from countries of the Association. It is considered by some authors that this policy (although only used by Toyota and its major supplier Denso in Thailand), coupled with regional integration and increased regional demand, leveraged additional foreign investments and helped create a regional market that was large enough to achieve economies of scale. In Thailand, the automotive industry is supplied at small but increasing scale through imports of wiring harnesses and seat covers from Cambodia, the Lao People's Democratic Republic and Myanmar. Although the experience of building a regional supply chain of components is encouraging, it took decades of efforts and growth before culminating in a regional production of 3 million units per year.

Source: UNCTAD, based on Barnes et al., 2017; Ing and Losari, 2022; Japan International Cooperation Agency and Boston Consulting Group, 2022; Markowitz and Black, 2019; Natsuda and Thoburn, 2021.

3.2 Electronics: Favourable prospects for mobile telephones supply chains

The electronics industry is an interesting case, owing to the pivotal role of information and communications technology and digital technologies in industrialization (United Nations Industrial Development Organization, 2019). Between 2019 and 2021, the consumer electronics industry attracted 20 greenfield investment projects to the continent. According to the fDi Markets database, the largest investment was announced by Bosch ($70 million), concerning plans to build a home appliance factory in Egypt. Recent decisions by industry leaders to diversify their supply chains in response to major disruptions can be promising for the growing mobile telephone market in Africa. For example, Apple and its key tier 1 supplier, Foxconn, decided to make a major investment in India in 2023 (*Financial Times, 2023*).

3.2.1 Promising demand and supply trends in the mobile telephone sector

Africa has a diverse mobile telephone market. Mobile cellular subscriptions are far in excess of 100 per 100 inhabitants in 13 out of 44 countries considered, namely Botswana, Cabo Verde, Côte d'Ivoire, Gabon, the Gambia, Ghana, Kenya, Mali, Mauritius, Namibia, Senegal, Seychelles and South Africa. Twenty countries have subscription rates per 100 inhabitants below the African average of 82.3, while 12 others have less than 50 subscriptions per 100 inhabitants (International Telecommunication Union, 2021).

Africa has seen tremendous growth in the mobile telephone industry in recent years, with a rising demand for affordable and reliable smartphones. Stiff competition on the continent is taking place in the middle-range smartphone and budget-telephone brackets (on average below $200). The leading competitor is Transsion, a Chinese-led group that started in Africa in 2006 and focuses on emerging markets outside China. Its brand Tecno is the single biggest smartphone seller in Africa. For instance, since 2011, every telephone Transsion sells in Ethiopia has been assembled at its facilities in the suburbs of Addis Ababa (Dahir, 2018).

Several African companies have emerged, offering a range of products that cater to the needs of consumers in different countries. For example, in South Africa, Onyx was launched in 2017 as a start-up. Onyx imports its components from overseas and builds its smartphones from the circuit board on up in South Africa (Scott, 2017). In the

Republic of the Congo, a local startup, VMK, opened a plant in Brazzaville in 2015 to produce smartphones, including its Elikia brand (van Zyl, 2013). In 2018, Mara Group, a pan-African multisectoral business services company opened a smartphone factory in Rwanda. These encouraging trends provide a strong case for relocating parts of the electronics supply chain to Africa and producing locally components of mobile telephones that are largely imported from outside the continent (World Economic Forum, 2019). In 2021, the mobile technology company Africell and Industry Five, a global smart manufacturing vendor, collaborated to develop assembling facilities for mobile telephones in the Democratic Republic of the Congo. The factory in Kinshasa is equipped with modular and mobile workstations, and workers are trained to reach quality standards and handle proprietary handsets. In addition, workers are assisted by state-of-the art robots. Performance testing and quality checks are also to be carried out at the facility (Barton, 2021; Boyadzhieva, 2021).

3.2.2 Leveraging horizontal and vertical linkages to localize supply chains

The mobile telephone global supply chain – from product conception to after-use – includes the following segments: input materials, hardware manufacturing, software development, sales and marketing, mobile service and use, and after-use (Lee et al., 2013). Indeed, the supply chain combines hardware and software, and it has spread worldwide as the integration of developing countries has deepened.

With regard to the first step in the supply chain, sourcing raw material, the composition of telephones varies, depending on the brand. Figure 24 provides a breakdown of the raw materials used to make mobile telephones in African countries.

Overall cobalt demand from the lithium-ion industry is expected to grow 1.5 times between 2021 and 2030. Nickel, used in cathodes, should see demand rise to about 1.4 million metric tons by 2030, five times that of 2021. Annual copper demand from the industry is estimated to reach 3.9 million tons by 2030, and aluminium, 3.1 million tons. In addition, the market size for both metals is projected to grow sixfold during that period (Bloomberg Finance, 2021; Daly, 2021).

In the next steps in the supply chain, manufacturers transform the raw material into a usable material or component. Component suppliers are numerous and will often specialize in particular parts that may be used by many different brands. A smartphone, for example, can contain components from more than 200 suppliers. Components include circuit boards, antennae, liquid crystal displays, microphones, speakers,

Figure 24
Raw materials used in the manufacture of mobile telephones

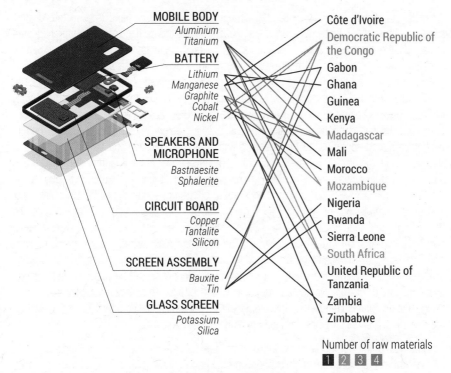

MOBILE BODY
Aluminium
Titanium

BATTERY
Lithium
Manganese
Graphite
Cobalt
Nickel

SPEAKERS AND MICROPHONE
Bastnaesite
Sphalerite

CIRCUIT BOARD
Copper
Tantalite
Silicon

SCREEN ASSEMBLY
Bauxite
Tin

GLASS SCREEN
Potassium
Silica

Côte d'Ivoire
Democratic Republic of the Congo
Gabon
Ghana
Guinea
Kenya
Madagascar
Mali
Morocco
Mozambique
Nigeria
Rwanda
Sierra Leone
South Africa
United Republic of Tanzania
Zambia
Zimbabwe

Number of raw materials
1 2 3 4

Sources: UNCTAD, based on data from United States Geological Survey.

batteries and cameras (Webb, 2022). Once the components have been sourced from manufacturers, they are taken to a factory for assembly. To make lithium-ion batteries for mobile telephones, sulphates for cobalt, nickel and manganese are combined to form precursor cathode-active materials (precursors). These are then combined with graphite, an anode material, to form battery cells. Owing to the abundance of cobalt, nickel and manganese, the production of precursors provides a good manufacturing opportunity for the Democratic Republic of the Congo and for building a regional supply chain (Bloomberg Finance, 2021; UNCTAD, 2022c).

In focus: Opportunities for regional supply chains in precursor development

According to Bloomberg Finance (2021), annual lithium-battery demand is expected to grow rapidly, topping 4.5 terawatt hours annually by 2035. Meeting this demand requires unprecedented but achievable increases in metals, precursor and cell production. In April 2021, a leading battery manufacturer, Contemporary Amperex Technology, announced it would acquire a 25 per cent stake in China Molybdenum in the Kisanfu mine in the Democratic Republic of the Congo. The Democratic Republic of the Congo, which produced about 70 per cent of global cobalt supply in 2020, unveiled plans to produce battery precursors (Daly, 2021). The production of cathode precursors (nickel-manganese-cobalt oxide), a main ingredient in the manufacture of battery components, can contribute to the country's higher value capture in the battery industry and integration into the electric vehicle supply chain. The investment in the country's infrastructure to support industrialization totals $58 billion (roads, ports and electrical infrastructure) (Argus Media, 2022; Eyewitness News, 2021). According to a feasibility study requested by the United Nations, Economic Commission for Africa, building a 10,000-ton precursor facility in the Democratic Republic of the Congo could cost $39 million, which is three times cheaper than what it would cost for a similar plant in the United States. The precursor plant would need to procure nickel from the Ambatovy mine in Madagascar and then ship it through the United Republic of Tanzania or Mozambique into the country. It is assumed that manganese will be procured from Gabon and transported into the Democratic Republic of the Congo. The Democratic Republic of the Congo has manganese deposits that could benefit from the potential demand stemming from the precursor plant, should it be established (Bloomberg Finance, 2021).

The potential of the Democratic Republic of the Congo for cathode precursor development could also contribute to increased mobile phone production capacities in the country by enabling companies to develop further stages upstream in the electronics supply chain. There are already some positive signs. For example, in 2021, Africell undertook a record-breaking network expansion in the country, extending infrastructure and launching telecommunications services in several new provinces. At the same time, Industry Five began diversifying facilities in the Democratic Republic of the Congo to focus on tablets, laptops, high-performance servers and data storage solutions. The company expects to generate up to 5,000 skilled technical jobs in the country by 2026 (Barton, 2021; Boyadzhieva, 2021).

The Agreement Establishing the African Continental Free Trade Area and other existing subregional free trade agreements offer opportunities for regional value and supply chains development for battery minerals and electric vehicles. For instance, the Regional Mining Vision of the Southern African Development Community proposes a mechanism to redistribute benefits across countries, for example, a common fund that pays the additional cost of transporting inputs from countries with weak transport infrastructure to where the activity is taking place (Natural Resource Governance Institute, 2022). By locating domestic strategies as part of regional industrial development plans, African countries could exert more bargaining power and realize greater cluster and scale economies.

3.3 Renewable energy technology: Prospects for solar panels supply chains

3.3.1 Importance of solar photovoltaic supply chains

The International Renewable Energy Agency and African Development Bank (2022) estimate the solar photovoltaic potential of Africa at 7,900 gigawatts, underscoring the continent's unique untapped potential for solar generation. Yet, despite the continent's enormous potential to generate energy from renewable sources and its urgent need to bring modern energy services to the millions of people still lacking access to electricity – about 43 per cent of the total population – only 2 per cent ($60 billion) of the $2.8 trillion invested in renewable energy worldwide between 2000 and 2020 went to Africa (International Renewable Energy Agency and African Development Bank, 2022). According to the African Union (2022), there remains an annual financing gap of $90 billion for the region to meet energy-access and transition goals. However, during this period, renewables investment in Africa grew at an average growth rate of 96 per cent per year, compared with 15 per cent in Asia–Oceania (excluding China and India) and 7 per cent globally (International Renewable Energy Agency and African Development Bank (2022). Between 2019 and 2021, 134 greenfield investment projects in Africa were announced, 86 of which were made in solar energy, representing a total value of $10.8 billion. Of these investments, 98 per cent were made in solar energy for the supply of electricity, the rest, in maintenance and services, and sales and marketing. According to the fDi Markets database, most of these investments were announced by France and Norway as the source countries. The bulk of investments in renewables was driven by structured procurement programmes, such as the Renewable Energy Independent Power Producer Procurement Programme in South Africa (South Africa, 2023). In 2020, 57 per cent of total installed solar generation capacity in Africa (10,431 megawatts) was generated by South Africa, followed by Egypt (16 per cent) and Morocco (7 per cent) (International Renewable Energy Agency and African Development Bank, 2022).

Traditionally reliant on hydropower, Africa is increasingly turning to solar photovoltaics to bolster energy security and support rapid economic growth in a sustainable manner. Economies of scale and continuous innovation throughout the supply chain have enabled steep reductions in manufacturing costs at every step of the production process. As a result, module prices declined by more than 80 per cent over the last decade, making solar photovoltaics the most affordable electricity-generation technology in many parts of the world. With regard to solar energy production, most African countries have a competitive advantage, given their high horizontal irradiance levels (International Renewable Energy Agency, 2016). Solar thermal investments, mainly in concentrated solar power, were made in Morocco and South Africa, primarily between 2012 and 2018. For instance, the Noor-Ouarzazate concentrated solar power complex in Morocco is the world's largest (World Bank, 2016).

Nevertheless, Morocco heavily depends on foreign sources for over 97 per cent of its energy. Harnessing energy from the sun will free Morocco from the volatility of import costs and create the potential for green energy exports to neighbouring countries. An ambitious national energy strategy, issued by the Government of Morocco in 2009, drove a strong expansion of wind and solar energies over the following decade. By 2020, solar photovoltaic capacity in Morocco had increased sixteenfold, albeit from a low base, and wind, sixfold (Alami, 2021).

In addition, the Government of Morocco encouraged private sector investments by implementing a number of measures: increasing the installed capacity threshold of hydro projects, enabling renewable electricity producers to access electricity networks (low, medium, high and very high voltage) and allowing the sale of excess electricity from renewable sources to the national electricity and water utilities office of Morocco for facilities connected to high and very high voltage networks (World Bank, 2018). Morocco plans to increase renewables capacity to reach 52 per cent by 2030. This ambitious goal requires massive investment in solar power (solar panels and batteries) (International Energy Agency, 2019). Although several sources of critical minerals are available in the country for the manufacture of solar power components, these minerals continue to be largely imported.

3.3.2 Diversification opportunities through the solar panel supply chain

Figure 25 illustrates the main stages in the manufacturing process for solar photovoltaic systems, including crystalline silicon and cadmium telluride systems, although they require different materials. In recent years, a major geographical shift has occurred in solar photovoltaic manufacturing capacity and production. Top solar panel manufacturers include Canadian Solar (Canada), First Solar (United States), Hanwha Q Cells (Republic of Korea), Jinko Solar (China), Sun Power (United States) and Trina Solar (China) (UNCTAD, 2023). China further strengthened its leading position as a manufacturer of wafers, cells and modules between 2010 and 2021, while its share of global polysilicon production capacity almost tripled. Today, the country's share in all manufacturing stages exceeds 80 per cent, more than double its 36 per cent share in global photovoltaic deployment.

The manufacture of the physical components of solar panels and solar storage relies on the combination of a variety of metals, metalloids, non-metallic minerals and polymers, with material needs differing across technologies and segments. Critical minerals and rare earth metals needed to make these components are aluminium, cadmium, copper, gallium, indium, lead, molybdenum, nickel, silicon, silver, selenium, tellurium, tin and zinc. These minerals are deployed at different stages of the solar photovoltaic value chain. International Energy Agency (2022b) estimates suggest that raw materials make up 35–50 per cent of the total cost of a solar photovoltaic module at 2021 prices.

Figure 25
Key stages of solar photovoltaic manufacturing

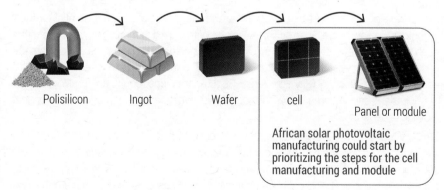

Polisilicon   Ingot   Wafer   cell
                                                    Panel or module

African solar photovoltaic manufacturing could start by prioritizing the steps for the cell manufacturing and module

Source: UNCTAD.
Note: Production of solar photovoltaics is limited in Africa, with some initial opportunities materializing in Egypt, Morocco and South Africa, which are also countries with the strongest demand pull.

Capital requirements are a key consideration when companies consider investing in solar photovoltaic manufacturing and when policymakers design incentives to support businesses. High investment requirements for certain segments of the supply chain, in particular polysilicon, ingots and wafers, may increase risk and reduce project bankability (International Energy Agency, 2022b). According to recently commissioned plant and equipment price data, polysilicon plants and ingot and wafer factories require significantly more capital expenditure than cell- and module-manufacturing facilities (International Energy Agency, 2022b). For instance, owing to the considerable infrastructure investment requirements, estimated at $200–$400 million, greenfield polysilicon plants are not usually bankable for capacities of less than 10,000 megatons (about 3 gigawatts) (International Energy Agency, 2022b). Again, economies of scale are necessary to attract investment. According to the International Renewable Energy Agency (2016), the rapid growth in demand for solar home systems in the African market is being driven by lower system costs and innovative new business models. Yet, systems in Africa, typically under 100 watts, are tiny compared with their counterparts in the developed countries and require batteries and charge controllers to ensure stable output.

The concentrated solar power supply chain is even more complex, requiring a range of manufacturing steps. Here, the solar field represents the biggest value share of a concentrated solar power plant, largely due to labour costs rather than equipment costs, offering great local content potential. With regard to components, for example, ball joints, bearings and cables, most inputs are not specialized and are also used by other industries. This lends opportunities to already established companies for the lateral diversification of customers, and the joint demand for these components by several industries can make investments in productive capacities more lucrative. Assembly of the solar field, which must be performed at the site, especially offers potential for local manufacturing and installation services (box 9). With regard to more critical components, such as mirrors or heat exchangers, joint ventures with international market players are necessary to successfully adapt already existing production lines to meet needs and to achieve the necessary quality standards. Such adaptations require an initial investment in equipment and skilled workers. To justify this investment, a long and stable project pipeline is necessary.

Similarly to the early development of the automotive industry in Africa, which began with the assembly stage, African solar photovoltaic manufacturing could start by prioritizing the steps for the cell manufacturing and module assembly. This is feasible, owing to the less technological and chemical complexity of these processes, input–import and product-export opportunities, labour availability and existing solar panel assembly. Polysilicon and wafer production could be considered when other manufacturing steps scale up, as production of these components is complex and requires high energy availability. In addition, for latecomers to the industry, opportunities further down the supply chain, such as project development, procurement and construction, should be considered (UNCTAD, 2023; box 9).

Box 9
Kenya: Participation of domestic companies in solar panel supply chains

Kenya has made great strides in securing access to electricity. According to World Bank world development indicators, the share of population with access to electricity increased from 19.2 per cent in 2010 to 71.4 per cent in 2020. Yet, this still lags behind the Government's goal, outlined in a national electrification strategy, to achieve universal access to electricity by 2022. Apart from the dominant energy sources (geothermal, representing 36 per cent of total energy sources, and hydropower, 36 per cent), solar power contributes 6 per cent to renewable energy capacity in Kenya. It therefore has promising potential to accelerate access to electricity, owing to its high horizontal irradiation levels.

Growth in the solar panel market provides a vast opportunity for the economy through private sector development and job creation. However, much of the market is held by internationally owned companies. A study by the United Nations Environment Programme assesses how the solar market can be better leveraged by domestic companies through supply chain linkages. Most domestic companies operate in services, offering project-development services, consultancy and after-sales services. A few companies also focus on product sale and distribution, often using informal sales and distribution channels, such as churches, local retail stores or supermarket chains. The participation of domestic companies is particularly high in the installation of commercial and industrial rooftop systems and mini-grids, as this market requires an in-depth engagement with customers and local skills, such as language and cultural knowledge.

Future expansion in industrial parks promises to grow business opportunities for domestic companies and employment in the solar panel supply chain. According to the United Nations, Economic Commission for Africa, for every megawatt of mini-grid capacity developed, approximately 800 full-time-equivalent job-years are created in Kenya. To maximize the benefits from increased investment for domestic employment and supply chain participation, the Government, as part of the Kenya Vision 2030 development plan, aims to promote local manufacturing through the Energy (Local Content) Regulations, 2014. However, skills development must be promoted. On one hand, this can be done through mentoring programmes between large experienced and new domestic companies, and on the other, through organized training. For instance, Renewable Energy Solutions for Africa has established a microgrid academy with local partners to develop skills needed for the sector. Further, vocational training and university curricula in energy offer courses in business, finance and technology.

Source: UNCTAD, based on United Nations, Economic Commission for Africa, 2020a; International Renewable Energy Agency and African Development Bank, 2022; United Nations Development Programme, 2017; United Nations Environment Programme, 2021; World Bank, 2019c.

3.4 Building resilience and improving public health by strengthening supply chains in pharmaceuticals and medical devices

3.4.1 Promising trends in relocating health-care supply chains

As mentioned in chapter 1, medical devices and pharmaceuticals are among the top five supply chains most exposed to shocks and disruptions. Such exposure poses a considerable risk to African countries, which are heavily dependent on the import of pharmaceuticals goods and medical devices. However, the rising middle class and increasing consumer demand, as discussed in chapter 2, are assets the continent can exploit to attract horizontal investment, for example, by lead companies, and to diversify global supply chains in the pharmaceutical and medical device sectors.

In 2021, greenfield investments of $19 billion dollars were recorded in the global pharmaceutical industry, with an increase of 26 per cent over 2020 (UNCTAD, 2022d). In Africa, 28 greenfield investment projects were recorded between 2019 and 2021, mostly in the manufacturing of pharmaceutical products and related processes. The largest project recipients were Kenya ($108 million), Ethiopia ($98 million), Lesotho ($79 million), Morocco ($65 million), and Uganda ($64 million). For instance, a $47 million investment in Ethiopia by a firm based in India, Africure Pharmaceuticals, aimed to build manufacturing plants to better serve regional demand, while circumventing lengthy and costly shipping (Gupta, 2022). Similarly, an Egyptian-based company announced plans to invest $30 million to build a factory in the United Republic of Tanzania. In comparison, fewer investment projects (nine) were announced for the medical device sector between 2019 and 2021, including a $130 million investment in the United Republic of

Tanzania by a producer of medical devices from the Republic of Korea, providing access to a lucrative pharmaceutical market (fDi Markets database).

Despite these investments and the abundance of key materials that go into the manufacturing of medical products and devices, the pharmaceutical industry in Africa remains highly dependent on the import of pharmaceutical products. Between 2018 and 2020, the number of imported pharmaceuticals, accounting for 4 per cent of total imports, has risen steadily since 2006, to $13.6 billion. Most of these imports originated in India (20 per cent) and France (16 per cent); 4.5 per cent of these products were imported from Africa due to limited productive capacity. Imports are expected to increase further by 79 per cent by 2026 (International Trade Centre, 2022). Although total exports grew from $695 million in 2008–2010 to about $1.06 billion in 2018–2020, the billowing trade deficit in the pharmaceutical sector, which increased from minus $2.3 billion in 2000 to minus $12.5 billion in 2020, points to the need to set up more production facilities of pharmaceuticals in Africa to facilitate access to medicine.

ONLY 20 AFRICAN COUNTRIES HAVE PHARMACEUTICAL PRODUCTION CAPACITY

Access to affordable medical devices is still a challenge due to:
→ High costs
→ Poor logistics and distribution
→ Limited financing instruments

However, Africa's rising middle class and increasing consumer market are demand factors the continent can exploit
→ To attract investment in the production of active pharmaceutical ingredients
→ Integrate the pharmaceutical and medical devices supply chains

According to 2021 figures, only 20 African countries have pharmaceutical production capacity; less than half (eight) produce about 80 per cent of total local output. The top eight producers and exporters are South Africa, Egypt, Kenya, Morocco, Tunisia, Mauritius, Ghana, and Uganda. Production focuses mostly on generic products, which represent about 70 per cent of total local production value (African Development Bank, 2022a). However, a large part of today's health challenges come from non-communicable diseases, such as cardiovascular diseases, cancer and diabetes, cancer and diabetes, which may not respond effectively to generic products. For instance, unlike generic medicines, insulin, which is used to treat diabetes, is a biological product, for which creating an exact copy requires a complex, high-knowledge-intensive manufacturing process, generating unique challenges to supply chain development and resilience (Perrin et al., 2017). In addition, non-communicable diseases necessitate regular health examinations and medical devices for diagnosis and monitoring. However, while global trade in medical devices[24] more than tripled between 2000 and 2020, limited access to diagnostic equipment, especially in rural areas, is still a major constraint to public health. According to data from the United Nations Comtrade database, the trade deficit in the medical device sector amounted to minus $2.6 billion in 2018–2020, compared with minus $1.3 billion in 2008–2010, despite a slight increase in exports from $237 million in 2008–2010 to $404 million in 2018–2020. Based on growing GDP and population figures and increasing demand for medical devices, the negative trade balance is expected to rise further.

3.4.2 The non-communicable disease supply chain: A special case

Deaths from non-communicable diseases are on the rise in Africa, owing to weaknesses in prevention, diagnosis and care. For instance, data from the International Diabetes Federation show that the prevalence of diabetes in Africa has been increasing rapidly (see https://diabetesatlas.org/data/en/). In 2021, 44 million adults (20–70 years old) in 53 African countries were living with diabetes; this figure is expected to increase by 34 per cent to 59 million in 2030 and by 109 per cent to 91 million in 2045. Access to affordable insulin is limited, due to high prices and poor infrastructure (logistics and distribution). In addition, syringes and needles are needed, and patients require medical devices to monitor glucose levels regularly. According to the World Health Organization, only 46 per cent of people living with diabetes in Africa know their status. The end consumer, be it an institution or a patient, requires the technology, medicine and equipment to treat diabetes (World Health Organization, 2022). Therefore, two distinct supply chains are of relevance: First, the insulin supply chain in Egypt, and second, the supply chain of medical devices. The following section discusses the position of Egypt in the supply chain to deliver insulin to hospitals and patients, as well the procurement of necessary materials and production relating to medical devices.

---

[24] This section focuses on medium- and high-technology medical devices and provides an analysis of trends and supply chains of HS group 9018, instruments and appliances used in medical, surgical, dental or veterinary sciences.

In focus: Case study of the insulin supply chain in Egypt

Egypt has significantly boosted its export capacity in pharmaceuticals by 300 per cent since 2006, according to data from the United Nations Comtrade database. It is one of the biggest pharmaceutical importers and exporters on the continent, contributing to 17 per cent of total pharmaceutical imports and 24 per cent of total pharmaceutical exports. Based on estimates by the International Diabetes Federation (2021), Egypt has one of the highest estimated projections for the prevalence of diabetes, with 22 per cent of its adult population (20–79 years) at risk of being affected by diabetes in 2030. Access to quality diabetes care is thus an urgent consideration.

Insulin production is complex and highly concentrated globally. The three leading multinational insulin manufacturers, Novo Nordisk, Sanofi and Eli Lilly, controlled over 90 per cent of the insulin market in 2016. Until 2002, over 90 per cent of total insulin needs in Egypt were imported from Novo Nordisk (Abdelgafar et al., 2004). When the country suddenly faced an acute insulin shortage crisis in 2002, it cooperated with international partners from China and Europe. Vacsera rapidly started to produce recombinant human insulin locally, resulting in a two-year supply of insulin, substantial cost savings for the Government of Egypt and independence from foreign monopoly. Nevertheless, Egypt still imports about $103 million of insulin per year. Reported exports amount to $1.1 million, mainly to Iraq, the Sudan and Yemen.

With regard to the supply chain of insulin in Egypt (figure 26), pharmaceutical localization has occurred mainly at the manufacturing stage, with Amoun, Sedico and Vacsera as lead manufacturers. Logistics and distribution are also localized, largely through Ibnsina Pharma, the fastest growing pharmaceutical distributor in the country. Limited backward linkages to the manufacture of active pharmaceutical ingredients pose a challenge to the development of a competitive pharmaceutical industry. Egypt still imports 90 per cent of its pharmaceutical raw materials (Agiba, 2022; UNCTAD, 1999), mainly from China, India and the United States, which implies long transport routes. Overall, considering the growing importance of sophisticated biotechnology in pharmaceutical manufacturing, lowering cost through economies of scale, improved technology and stronger industrial production infrastructure are key to attracting the multinational companies to establish local production sites (Agiba, 2022; UNCTAD, 1999).

Certain upstream inputs, such as the active pharmaceutical ingredients of insulin that are biotechnologically processed, require deep sophistication and technological intensity in their production. Yet the trade deficit of Egypt in the production of active pharmaceutical ingredients is large (based on data from the United Nations Comtrade database). This suggests that even active pharmaceutical ingredients used in the manufacture of more common generic drugs,

Figure 26
Insulin supply chain in Egypt

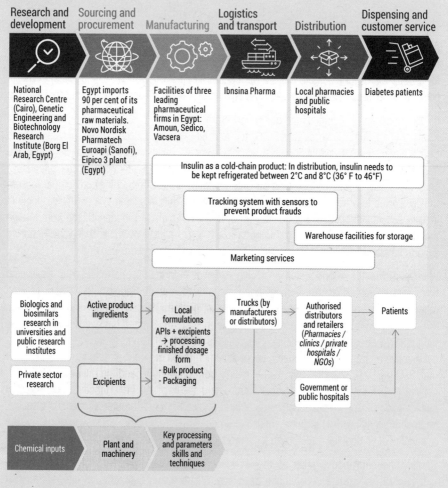

Source: UNCTAD.
APIs: Active product ingredients
NGOs: Non-governmental organizations

and which require lower technology, are not manufactured locally. To overcome the constraint of limited production of active pharmaceutical ingredients, Egypt has encouraged local companies to establish new facilities for sourcing raw materials (Business Today Egypt, 2021; Egypt, 2021a). Examples include Pharco B International for Chemicals, a subsidiary of Pharco, a domestic firm, which has been producing active pharmaceutical ingredients and raw materials since 2016 (Agiba, 2022; World Economic Forum, 2022).

More recently, Egyptian International Pharmaceuticals Industries, the largest pharmaceutical company in Egypt by units and fifth largest by value, in collaboration with the Egyptian pharma group Acdima, invested $103 million to build a biological and biosimilar production plant. It would be the first such facility in Egypt and is expected to commence production at the end of 2023 (Agiba, 2022; Garcia, 2022). According to data from the United Nations Comtrade database, imports of active pharmaceutical ingredients declined by 21 per cent between 2019 and 2021, partly due to increased capacity to manufacture such ingredients as part of the long-term national strategic plan for pharmaceutical localization.

With regard to research and development in the supply chain (figure 26), Egypt has been less successful in building local capacity. According to the World Bank Enterprise Surveys (various years), Egypt has introduced fewer new products, services, or improved processes in pharmaceutical manufacturing and spent less on research and development, compared with China and India, for instance. As the pharmaceutical industry is a high-knowledge-intensive sector, particularly for the manufacturing of biologics and biosimilars, which requires more advanced biotechnological processing, it is necessary for Egypt to increase research spending and innovation to further develop its long-term competitiveness in the pharmaceutical sector and reinforce its supply chain flexibility and resilience.

3.4.3 Strengthening the position of Africa in the medical device supply chain

Between 2018 and 2020, imports of medical devices were valued at $6 billion (data from the United Nations Comtrade database). With a high prevalence of diabetes, the continent imported $1.8 billion of electro-diagnostic apparatus and $295 million worth of syringes, where imports from African countries accounted for only 0.45 per cent and 3.5 per cent, respectively. Yet, access to medical devices is still a challenge, largely due to high costs and limited financing instruments. Further, the COVID-19-related shortages in medical equipment, including medical devices, have made Africa vulnerable to these external shocks.

Access to medical devices is a challenge largely due to high costs and limited financing instruments

viable solutions

| innovative and digital solutions | pooled public procurement | localized production by leveraging available raw materials |

As the largest exporters of medical devices in Africa, Tunisia ($193 million in 2018–2020), South Africa ($119 million), Egypt ($35.8 million) and Mauritius ($32.2 million) can readily serve as potential hubs (data from the United Nations Comtrade database). Such potential can be leveraged through the implementation of technologies and innovative solutions, especially in rural areas (see box 10). On the other hand, to be competitive in a technology- and digitization-driven industry such as this, the digital capability of firms must be high (United Nations Industrial Development Organization, 2019). Despite digital transformation on the continent, the region's capabilities to absorb new technologies are small, due to the lack of skilled labour, efficient logistics and infrastructure. Yet, African countries can integrate the medical supply chain through a combination of vertical or horizontal linkages and thus leverage the regional supply chain.

Box 10
Innovation in medical device solutions

An encouraging example of how innovation and technology in medical supplies can enhance health care in rural areas in Africa is the cardiopad device, designed by a Cameroonian engineer. Since its launch in 2016, sales of the device have been rising steadily. It enables cardiac screening, and the results are sent remotely to specialists for analysis without patients needing to travel to urban centres. Public procurement by the Ministry of Public Health of Cameroon played an important role in boosting interest and demand.

Another example is the first solar-powered hearing-aid unit, manufactured by Deaftronics, based in Botswana. There are only a few audiology centres in the country where patients can test levels of hearing impairment or obtain a suitable hearing aid. Unlike conventional hearing aids, the device developed by Deaftronics eliminates the need for expensive batteries that are often not available. In addition, the solar rechargeable solar device is accessible to rural and poorer parts of the population.

Women's entrepreneurship also plays an essential role in innovative solutions. For instance, Medsaf, a company led by women, offers a medication supply chain management solution for hospitals and pharmacies based on blockchain technology.

Sources: UNCTAD, based on Hendricks, 2015; Mbodiam, 2021; Roland Berger, 2018.

Figure 27 illustrates the different stages of the supply chain: sourcing and processing mining and plastics materials; procuring additional parts and components, such as semi-conductors; assembly of the final products; and distribution.[25] Similarly to the automotive industry, medical devices are part of producer-driven supply chains, and global trade is led by vertically integrated lead firms with worldwide production facilities. Owing to the high safety standards and quality requirements of medical devices, many principal firms maintain some production of critical components in house, which explains the remaining dominance of traditional exporters. Africa accounts for 12 per cent of global exports of key mining materials, emphasizing their importance for future growth of the industry and for increasing the resilience of lead firms. The most important minerals and metals include titanium as the pillar of many medical applications, especially in devices to control heart function, where nine African countries have a substantial export supply (Arima, 2022).

South Africa is the world's largest titanium exporter, representing 35 per cent of global reserves of the mineral, followed by Mozambique (12 per cent) and Kenya (10 per cent). Yet, imports to Africa in 2018–2020 came primarily from Ukraine (55 per cent), followed by Mozambique (29 per cent) and Senegal (16 per cent) (based on data from the United Nations Comtrade database). South Africa accounts for only 5 per cent of imports

---

[25] The analysis presented here is one the first that attempts to identify supply chains in the medical device sector. This section follows a similar methodology to that described in section 3.1 (box 7). First, based on Canadian input–output tables, key economic activities in the manufacturing of medical supplies are identified; second, additional supply chain direction and linkages, especially with regard to the sourcing of raw materials, are identified through desktop research, for example, Hendriwardani and Ramdoo, 2022 (see www.pekoprecision.com/blog/medical-device-manufacturing-critical-processes/); third, inputs and activities are matched with trade in products (at the HS six- or four-digit level).

Figure 27

Medical devices supply chain and number of African countries with export supply to the world, by supply chain category

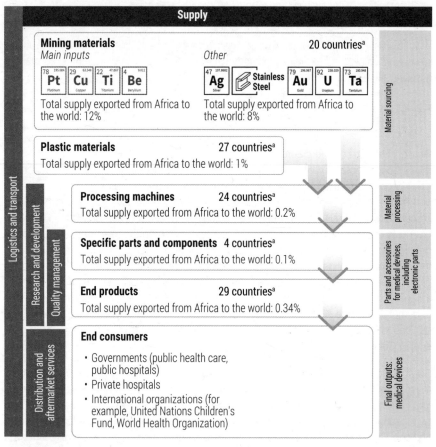

Source: UNCTAD.

Notes: Product codes with number of countries in parentheses are included in each supply chain category as follows: Mining materials: 2603 (12), 7110 (4), 261400 (9), 811211 (0); other: 7218 (6), 7402 (6), 7403 (21), 7901 (8), 261210 (2), 261590 (10), 710691 (8), 710692 (7), 710812 (26), 710813 (18); plastic materials: 3901 (16), 3902 (20), 3903 (7), 3904 (10), 3907 (16); processing machines: 8302 (12), 8466 (12), 847710 (10), 847759 (5), 847780 (10), 848079 (7); specific parts and components: 903300 (3), 854150 (2), 854390 (4); end products: 901811 (3), 901812 (4), 901813 (3), 901814 (1), 901819 (6), 901820 (2), 901831 (6), 901832 (3), 901839 (7), 9018416(1), 901849 (3), 901850 (4), 901890 (24).

[a] Number of African countries that export at least one product or product group at the HS four- or six-digit level to the world, at a value of $100,000.

to Africa, despite its leading role in the world market. A similar case is observed for platinum metals, where South Africa is the top exporting country, representing 21 per cent of world exports but it exports these metals mainly outside Africa, principally to the United States, the United Kingdom and Germany. The leading importers of platinum from Africa are the United States (32 per cent), Zimbabwe (31 per cent) and Germany (29 per cent).

Increasing intra-African trade can be a good starting point to leverage the comparative advantage of Africa in metal supply for use in the medical device supply chain. The African Continental Free Trade Area can play an important part in facilitating this. For instance, the tariff applied to unwrought platinum imports from South Africa to Tunisia amounts to 15 per cent of the value of the metal shipped; to Kenya, 25 per cent but 0 per cent to Germany and the United States. This poses a clear competitive disadvantage for African countries aiming to produce medical devices. However, African Continental Free Trade Area tariff liberalization targets can be a solution. Many African countries have a competitive advantage in supplying key inputs to the production of medical devices. To strengthen these supply chain linkages, tariff and non-tariff barriers must be tackled and stronger collaboration encouraged to access the inputs.

Based on data from the United Nations Comtrade database, African countries play a limited role further along in the global supply chain (figure 27). However, some African countries show some export capacity in plastic materials, an important input for the manufacture of medical devices.[26] Hence, African countries could serve regional inputs but plastic processing capabilities must be improved. Manufacturers are increasingly turning to technologies, such as artificial intelligence, robotics and three-dimensional printing, to improve the affordability of medical devices. For instance, injection-mould manufacturing is key to producing plastic parts for use in such devices.[27] This stage of the supply chain is concentrated in China, which supplies 46 per cent of global exports in mining and metal processing machines (data from the United Nations Comtrade database).

---

[26] According to data from the United Nations Comtrade database, 27 African countries already export one type of plastic material to the world for a value of at least $100,000. These countries are Angola, Botswana, Burkina Faso, Cameroon, Côte d'Ivoire, Egypt, Eswatini, Ethiopia, Ghana, Kenya, Lesotho, Madagascar, Malawi, Mali, Mauritius, Morocco, Mozambique, Namibia, the Niger, Nigeria, Senegal, South Africa, Tunisia, Uganda, the United Republic of Tanzania, Zambia and Zimbabwe.

[27] For low volumes, three dimensional-printing is an alternative to work around injection-moulding parts but this technology is also limited on the continent.

However, regulatory and digital solutions can help boost processing capabilities and facilitate access to medical device supply chains. Regulation of medical devices varies widely across countries in Africa and can be lengthy and lack transparency, often delaying access to medical products and devices. Harmonization towards internationally recognized registration or certification programmes (Saidi and Douglas, 2019) and the possibility to apply digital solutions for procurement, production, quality control, distribution, logistics and traceability should be explored. Innovative and technology-based solutions already play an important role in facilitating public health-care supply chains in Africa. Some examples include Mdaas Global, which provides a network of physical and virtual diagnostic and primary care facilities; Infiuss Health, the first remote clinical research platform in Africa; Koniku, a technology company working in visual processing, data processing and pattern recognition; and Instantrad, an as-a-service teleradiology platform (see https://healthcap.co/portfolio/). Box 11 illustrates the importance of partnerships in facilitating research and development and technology, as well as public procurement.

Box 11

Building research and development capacity and enhanced technology transfer through partnerships

More than in other high-technology industries, patents and trademarks play a crucial role in the competitiveness of the pharmaceutical industry. The low levels of patenting activity by countries in Africa is indicative of the need to develop and strengthen health innovation systems in the region. This can be done through policies that support health research systems and a local incentive structure that focuses research on local health challenges.

There are various global health innovation and entrepreneurship initiatives under way. These include an initiative launched by UNCTAD, aimed at sparking the post-COVID-19 resurgence of the micro, small and medium-sized enterprise sector (2020–2022). Other such initiatives are a global digital health strategy (2020–2025) and a special toolkit, the Mobile Health Assessment and Planning-for-Scale Toolkit, developed by the World Health Organization. Other means of strengthening health innovation systems would include the development of local scientific and biomedical research capacities and local manufacturing capabilities. For example, in South Africa, funding is being provided for research and development through a technology and human resources for industry programme. Targeted special economic zones with a focus on the health sector can also enhance knowledge and technology transfer. Medical cities have, for instance, been promoted by investment promotion agencies in Rwanda.

Emulation has become more difficult, owing to increasing protection of intellectual property rights through the 1994 Agreement on Trade-related Aspects of Intellectual Property Rights. The African Pharmaceutical Technology Foundation, established in 2022, is expected to support the practical implementation of trade-related intellectual property rights in Africa. It is supposed to act as an intermediator to advance the sharing of intellectual property-protected technologies, know-how and patented processes. In 2020, India and South Africa submitted a proposal for a waiver of four forms of intellectual property of the Agreement (patents, copyrights, industrial design and undisclosed information) for COVID-19-related vaccines, treatments and diagnostics. By May 2021, the waiver proposal had gained 65 official co-sponsors. However, only patents have been included in the waiver for vaccines. Hence, the final adoption fell short of what was in the original proposal.

Although national enforcement of intellectual property rights is important to promote innovation, the provisions concerning special and differentiated treatment are not linked to objective measures for technological or productive capacities. An UNCTAD study recommends that manufacturers in technologically weak and less-diversified countries should be allowed to imitate the production of more technologically advanced economies.

Some patent holders also grant voluntary licences to local manufacturers through contractual arrangements or mechanisms such as the Medicines Patent Pool. It is common practice, however, to restrict the location where the product can be sold. For instance, in Egypt, partnerships between multinational companies and local companies have allowed exchanges for technology transfer and intellectual property, while producing locally for the Egyptian market. For example, Sun Pharma of India opened its first manufacturing site in Egypt in 2017; Gypto Pharma, a domestic company, worked with Otsuka of Japan; and Eli Lilly collaborated with the Egytian firm, Eva Pharma. The Government of Egypt encourages local pharmaceutical production and aims to become self-sufficient in pharmaceuticals by 2030, as part of its national sustainable development strategy, Egypt Vision 2030, launched in 2016.

Sources: UNCTAD, based on African Development Bank, 2022b; Agiba, 2022; Egypt, 2016; Egypt, 2021b; Iqvia, 2022; Lilly, 2022; Motari et al., 2021; UNCTAD, 2021c; UNCTAD, 2022f; UNCTAD, 2023; World Trade Organization, 2020b; World Trade Organization, 2021; Youssef, 2021.

3.5 Making resource-based supply chain integration work for sustainable development

3.5.1 Local content requirements in the mining supply chain

Despite the vast mineral wealth of Africa and the significant foreign investment that the sector has attracted throughout the years, many resource-rich African countries have not been able to translate their resource wealth into sustainable economic, social and environmental development. In an effort to reverse this trend and ensure that capital-intensive large-scale mining becomes an engine of inclusive and sustained development, many resource-rich Governments have established policies and measures that can catalyse lateral linkages between large-scale mining and local productive industrial development. Developing an African supplier base in the mining industry has perhaps the most potential among all the benefits countries can derive from mining. Suppliers provide goods and services to mining companies. This can range from products such as pick-up trucks, tyres, drills, conveyor belts and specific replacement parts, to services, such as catering, surveying and human resource management. Efficient local suppliers lead to lower costs for mining companies. Mining companies need to import fewer goods, and local expertise solves local problems. By procuring more from the local market and establishing a wide network of local suppliers, the mining industry also has stronger ties to their host countries, reducing disputes and discontent (Kemp et al., 2011; Ross et al., 2012). Governments that are aware of the industrial value represented by critical minerals and the opportunities to develop domestic production capabilities to yield cluster and scale economies, instituted measures to incentivize local procurement and local content production (see the example of South Africa, box 12).

However, in most African countries, much procurement value is spent on imported goods and resold by domestic suppliers, without creating additional employment, transferring business knowledge to other economic sectors (Korinek and Ramdoo, 2017). The case of the mining value chain in Zambia (Lombe, 2020) is illustrative in that regard, with foreign suppliers accounting for 96 per cent of goods and services[28] supplied to the mines. Domestic suppliers in Zambia contribute about 1 per cent to total supplies for mines,

---

[28] About 98 per cent of core services (drilling services, underground development, instrumentation services) and 95 per cent of core goods (explosives, mill balls and rods, chemicals); 95 per cent of non-core services (security, customs handling, cleaning, transportation) and 87 per cent of non-core goods (safety and office equipment, nuts and bolts, light fittings).

mainly in catering, security services and office maintenance. Despite industry supplier development programmes at the firm level, these have not successfully included many domestic companies. The reasons can be mainly attributed to limitations, such as a lack of access to long-term capital, restricted access to production technologies, high costs of production inputs and a lack of full quality control of production, as well as a lack of legislative provisions favouring domestic production and sourcing (Lombe, 2020). Current incentives reward mining firms for importing goods rather than encouraging domestic manufactures. In the past, more focus was placed on capturing tax benefits but local participation in the mining value chain through infrastructure about mines would provide larger gains. Structured support requires incentives for imports of raw materials and equipment, access to technology and structured finance, and technical mentorship.

Box 12
South Africa: The mining equipment sector

South Africa plays a central role in the trade of processed platinum and primary aluminium and uranium across the continent. This suggests the central role of South Africa in leading these regional value chains. Mining equipment production and services are today's most relevant and technologically advanced segments of the broader special-purpose machinery industry in South Africa. Specifically, the mining machinery and equipment sector represents the largest contributor to employment, turnover and exports of the special purpose-machinery industry, and it also stands out with respect to total plant, property, equipment and intangible assets, expenditures in research and development, royalties and patent rights, and staff training.

Proximity to the mining sites and demand for customized and niche technology solutions well suited for the peculiar geological conditions of South Africa have been important drivers of learning and, thus, of global competitiveness for local companies that, over the years, have developed production and service operations across major extractive industries and countries, actively engaging in the technological race in the global mining value chain. However, although a number of these companies are large by local standards, they are still significantly smaller than the leading multinational corporations operating in South Africa, and their expertise and competencies are particularly advanced and at the global frontier only in specific product segments, such as deep-level mining and related areas.

With the amendment of the Mining Charter in 2010, the Government of South Africa introduced a black economic empowerment programme, requiring that black ownership of mining companies reach 30 per cent and that the companies purchase 80 per cent of their services, 50 per cent of their consumable goods and 40 per cent of their capital goods from entities participating in the programme.

Since 2013, however, the global competitiveness of South Africa in the mining equipment sector has been on the decline, owing to a combination of factors. These factors include domestic bottlenecks, such as the shrinking domestic mining industry, and global threats, such as the increasing foreign competition faced by local players. The country has experienced a drop in its export shares of mining machinery and equipment to traditional markets in the aftermath of the global financial and economic crisis and it is losing its appeal for leading multinational corporations as a preferred and strategic location in which to undertake research, product development, engineering and production activities.

Local content requirements policies have played an important role in the mining policy of South Africa to increase the participation of local actors; however, in some cases, they have also introduced unnecessary rigidities, such as a more limited choice of inputs or potentially higher costs of inputs, which have prevented alternative pathways to increasing domestic value addition. The local procurement and content policy framework could be reformed along two main directions: first, by introducing specific categories of procurement reserved for local suppliers, based on a thorough assessment of goods and services to target; second, by linking local procurement and content requirements with export promotion where companies would be allowed to import more of the products they need, to the extent that they also increase the local content value of the exported products.

Source: UNCTAD, based on Andreoni and Torreggiani, 2020; Andreoni et al., 2021.

To unlock the potential of capital-intensive large-scale mining for inclusive and sustained development, Governments in Africa have started adopting local content policies to harness business opportunities for domestic enterprises by developing local supply chains and facilitating the creation of backward linkages in the mining sector, for example, generating value addition in domestic supply sectors, creating local employment opportunities or transferring technology. In many resource-rich countries, Governments adopt local procurement policies to foster greater participation of domestic industries in the mining supply chain. International Institute for Sustainable Development and Intergovernmental Forum on Mining, Minerals, Metals and Sustainable Development (2019) define local procurement as the purchase of goods and services from domestic suppliers. A supplier is considered local when it originates from, is registered or incorporated in, and conducts business in the country where the mining project or site is physically located.

The definition and practice of "local" can vary across countries. However, in the absence of a clear definition and applicable regulations, this can result in a situation where mining companies end up sourcing imported goods from companies in the local area and therefore report on having met their local procurement targets. Although in such a situation a proportion of value addition is performed within the country, it does not create meaningful economic benefits for the host country. Local employment is not necessarily created, domestic manufacturing industry is not promoted, and the growth of local suppliers is not adequately supported. It is therefore vital for mineral-rich countries in Africa to put in place sound local procurement policies based on clear local sourcing and local ownership criteria.

To date, 17 African countries have local content regulations in place, namely Angola, Botswana, Burkina Faso, Cameroon, Côte d'Ivoire, the Democratic Republic of the Congo, Ghana, Guinea, Mali, Mozambique, Namibia, the Niger, Sierra Leone, South Africa, the United Republic of Tanzania, Zambia and Zimbabwe. Of these, only nine – Cameroon, the Democratic Republic of the Congo, Guinea, Mozambique, Namibia, the Niger, Sierra Leone, the United Republic of Tanzania and Zambia – have introduced negotiated local content requirements in their mining regulations (Fofaria, 2020). While the implementation of local content measures will require regulatory and monitoring capabilities to ensure compliance by investors and foreign firms, their success will also depend on domestic capabilities – adequate infrastructure, strong institutions, a supportive local business environment and a skilled labour force.

Although local content requirements are established through domestic policies, their scope can extend beyond national borders and contribute to the development of regional supply chains (International Institute for Sustainable Development and Intergovernmental Forum on Mining, Minerals, Metals and Sustainable Development, 2019). Promoting local content from a regional perspective will also contribute to expanding local suppliers' access to wider regional markets and thus create larger business and economic gains for domestic firms. In Africa, opportunities for regional markets and more efficient rules of origin under the African Continental Free Trade Area, combined with the commitment of the Africa Mining Vision to promote economic linkages in the mining sector, can help optimize regional content in local procurement rules and foster regional supply chains on the continent. The Africa Mining

Vision (box 13) was formulated in 2009 by African Heads of State as a pathway for catalysing more sustainable backward (upstream industries) and forward (downstream industries) linkages in the mining sector that will help establish more competitive local suppliers and manufacturing industries (Ackah-Baidoo, 2020). The continued commitment of resource-rich countries to such a vision will serve as a springboard for the materialization of local content to support the growth of African industries and their integration in regional and global supply chains.

Box 13
Africa Mining Vision

In 2009, the African Union put forward the Africa Mining Vision to ensure that Africa utilizes its mineral resources strategically for broad-based, inclusive industrial development. This vision identifies several areas of intervention where improvements can be made:

- Quality of geological data.

- Contract negotiation capacity.

- Capacity for mineral sector governance.

- Capacity to manage mineral wealth.

- Infrastructure constraints.

- Artisanal and small-scale mining.

However, implementation has been slow, and there is a low level of awareness of the framework among key stakeholders in the mineral sector. As recommended in an UNCTAD study, countries should use existing guidelines to enact policies and regulations aimed at its implementation. The expectations of mineral-rich countries in Africa with regard to development benefits from the extractive sector are justified by its status as a key generator of export revenues and foreign exchange in mineral-exporting economies. Mindful of the magnitude of the extractive sector as a source of illicit financial flows, African countries should build on lessons learned from past engagement in international commodity governance to meet these expectations.

Sources: UNCTAD, based on Africa Centre for Energy Policy, 2020; United Nations, Economic Commission for Africa, 2014; Oxfam, 2017; UNCTAD, 2020c.

3.5.2 Enforcing sustainable development standards in materials supply chains

The increasing demand and supply of minerals and metals gives rise to environmental and social concerns, owing to the possible negative externalities of extractive industries on local communities (Marin and Goya, 2021; UNCTAD, 2020c). For instance, copper and lithium are particularly vulnerable to water stress, given high water-consumption requirements (International Energy Agency, 2022a). Although African countries, intergovernmental organizations and companies have intensified efforts to clean up mineral supply chains, raw materials often come from mines that provide poor environmental and labour protection; further, their profits are sometimes linked to armed conflicts. Referred to as conflict minerals, the supply chains of gold, tantalum, tin and tungsten are now subject to regulations issued by China, the United States and the European Union that aim to prevent the profits being used to fund armed groups in unstable or fragile resource-rich countries. The mining of other critical minerals used in the manufacture of batteries for electrical vehicles (cobalt, for example) but not currently listed as conflict minerals under the Dodd–Frank Act,[29] is, however, subject to risks. These include poor working conditions, child labour, the sexual exploitation of women and other human rights concerns (Honke and Skender, 2022; International Labour Organization, 2019). Women workers are particularly affected by issues of social and environmental practices in the mining sector, despite their potential to contribute to the development of large-scale mining and related capital- and technology-intensive industries (see box 14). The spillover of economic and social benefits of gender equality and decent work are increasingly recognized, calling for the need to reinforce efforts aimed at securing equal rights and opportunities for women workers and entrepreneurs in the mining sector (International Labour Organization, 2021). In Africa, the Africa Mining Vision proposes actions favouring gender equity and the empowerment of women (International Labour Organization, 2021).

---

[29] The Dodd–Frank Wall Street Reform and Consumer Protection Act was passed in 2010 by the United States Congress to curb risky financial industry activities that had led to the global financial and economic crisis of 2008-2009. It established a wide range of reforms throughout the entire financial system, aimed at providing greater financial market regulation, which includes improving transparency in the over-the-counter derivatives markets. In 2018, the United States Congress passed a new law that rolled back some of the restrictions of the Act, relaxing some of the regulations for smaller and medium-sized banks. The main purpose of the Dodd–Frank Act remains to protect consumers and taxpayers from egregious practices, such as predatory lending.

Box 14
Women in high-technology industries

To realize a more equal distribution of the benefits of high-technology supply chains, the integration of women is important. This section of the report is a first attempt to assess women's participation in high-technology industries. World Bank Enterprise Surveys are used to provide information on top women managers and the share of women production and non-production workers. On average across all industries, the survey reveals that only 13 per cent of the surveyed businesses in Africa are managed by women, compared with 27 per cent in East Asia and the Pacific, 16 per cent in Latin America and 8 per cent in South-East Asia. In addition, 17 per cent of all productive workers and 21 per cent of non-productive workers in the surveyed African countries are women, compared with 33 per cent and 34 per cent, respectively, in East Asia; 27 per cent and 40 per cent, respectively, in Latin America; and 5 per cent and 0.5 per cent, respectively, in South Asia. That comparison indicates that opportunities for women are currently greater in the areas of sales, advertising, servicing of products, routine office tasks and financing and legal functions, rather than in production. Across high-technology industries, the largest share of female workers is in communications equipment: they account for 26 per cent of employers in production and 44 per cent of non-production workers (see table).

Share of female workers in high-technology industries, various years

Industry and International Standard Industrial Classification of All Economic Activities code	Share of production workers	Share of non-production workers	Share of enterprises with women as top managers
		percentage	
Motor vehicles (ISIC 34)	11	25	6
Communications equipment (ISIC 32)	26	44	0
Electrical machinery (ISIC 31)	18	30	10
Pharmaceuticals (ISIC 2423)	12	30	7
Medical instruments (ISIC 33)	18	28	8
Machinery and equipment (ISIC 29)	13	27	7
All industries (average)	17	21	13

Source: UNCTAD calculations, based on World Bank Enterprise Surveys.
Note: Classifications used in this table are based on ISIC Revision 3.1.
Abbreviation: ISIC, International Standard Industrial Classification of All Economic Activities.

Source: UNCTAD, based on World Bank Enterprise Surveys.

There is a need for a new global governance architecture that addresses the needs for structural transformation in resource-dependent countries and improves the social benefits of mining (United Nations Environment Programme, 2020). An example is the Sustainable Development Licence to Operate, which is a holistic multilevel and multi-stakeholder governance framework aimed at enhancing the contribution of the mining sector to sustainable development (Pedro, 2021). For many years, the extractive industry focused on securing a social licence to operate as a measure to relieve social tensions and mitigate environmental damage at the operational level, mostly from local communities and other stakeholders. The approach is based on joint responsibility and recognizes how these conditionalities must be more stringent and go far beyond minimum standards of corporate social responsibility and compensations. Corporate social responsibility perspectives still range from being focused on economic benefits and compliance with ethical expectations, to being merely philanthropic (Singh et al., 2015) but they are nevertheless useful to improve social and environmental outcomes of economic activity.

Technological advancements, such as blockchain technology, can enhance corporate responsibility and environment sustainability by providing information to buyers on the origin of products and guarantees as to the authenticity of the information (Lema and Rabellotti, 2023). By leveraging blockchain technologies to collect and track reliable and trusted environmental, social and governance-related data and supply chain information more accurately and in a consistent manner (Capgemini, 2021), companies and suppliers will be able to monitor their carbon footprint and ensure accountability and sustainability throughout their supply chains.

A number of companies are also involved in marketing second-life batteries, highlighting the potential role of the circular economy, not only in increasing sustainability but also adding local value to the supply chain. To date, there is no facility that can fully recycle lithium-ion batteries – a potential investment opportunity. The International Energy Agency (2022a) estimates that by 2040, recycled quantities of copper, lithium, nickel and cobalt from spent batteries could reduce combined primary supply requirements for these minerals by about 10 per cent. The global capacity for battery recycling is currently only about 180 kilotons per year, of which China accounts for 50 per cent. To state a recent example, a joint venture between a United States company, Ace Green Recycling, and a leading investment company based in South Africa, Tabono, is investing in two battery-recycling facilities (*Mining Review Africa*, 2023). Progress towards the circular economy has also been made in Morocco. Given the country's large potential in high-technology supply chains, the development of a circular economy model in Morocco – end-to-end electric vehicle production – would potentially attract a string of complementary investments into the upstream, midstream and downstream sectors of the electric vehicle supply chain. Such investments would open the way to the development of domestic vertical integration for electric vehicles, involving the production of electric vehicle battery metals, batteries, electric vehicles and battery recycling. It could further position the country as an attractive destination for the European electric vehicle market. By closing the loop in the supply chains, firms will be able to reuse the critical raw materials in electric vehicle batteries at low cost and render their electric vehicle supply chain more resilient, especially during periods of global commodity price volatility (Tanchum, 2022b).

3.6 Conclusion

The high-technology supply chains discussed in this chapter –the automotive industry, mobile telephones, solar panels, pharmaceutical products and medical devices – all involve a variety of economic activities and require many different inputs and raw materials. Although countries in Africa are marginally integrated in the supply chains of high-technology intensive industries, except for the export of raw materials, there is potential for deeper substantive integration in local and regional supply chains. Final assembly and export activity is largely concentrated in South Africa and some countries in North Africa, such as Egypt, Morocco and Tunisia; yet, even in these middle-income countries, most inputs are still imported from outside Africa. This is a hindrance for these supply chains to engage in employment creation and diversification. Acknowledging the potential of these high-technology supply chains for sustainable development, middle-income countries in Africa have already attracted investments in upstream activities and encourage local sourcing, for instance, through partnerships and local content requirements.

Although the limited productive capacities of low-income countries in Africa currently restrain their participation in high value added activities in these supply chains, this chapter demonstrated that the employment benefits stemming from the provision of services, such as those relating to consulting, project development and aftermarket-sales of goods and services, should not be neglected. Stronger partnerships with multinational companies can provide skills and knowledge spillovers.

Effective implementation of the African Continental Free Trade Area will be essential to leverage these opportunities, not only with regard to tariff liberalization but most importantly, in harnessing joint investments in infrastructure and facilitating the building of clusters, which benefit from quicker, more flexible delivery to customers.

Given the abundance of critical minerals in Africa to meet demand in high-technology supply chains, the chapter argued that countries in Africa must significantly scale up investment in infrastructure, especially electricity and transport infrastructure, to increase the competitiveness of local suppliers and revise mining legislation to ensure greater benefits for the local economy. Local content regulations and conditionalities can set requirements for technology transfer and investments in community infrastructure. Moreover, a significant amount of production has already been committed to overseas buyers through offtake agreements; therefore, it is urgent for Governments to seek options for securing supply for value chains in Africa. These options could include public procurement engagement and measures to strengthen procurement options by local companies through digital transformation, technology-enabled services and improved supplier and customer management (see chapter 4).

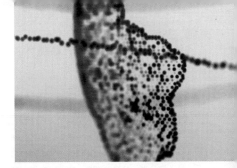

CHAPTER 4

Optimizing supply chain opportunities in Africa through enablers and incentives

It is evident from the analysis in chapters 2 and 3 of this report that African countries offer untapped potential for global supply chain diversification. For instance, the geographic proximity to source inputs, such as mines, and the associated reduced cost of transport and shipping, can be a major motivation for manufacturers of mineral-intensive products to relocate some of their supply chains to Africa and invest in refineries or other entry- to mid-level tier 2 or 3 suppliers (see chapter 2). However, to unlock such potential and become an attractive destination for the diversification of global supply chains, African countries should create enablers and leverage incentives that could be a catalyst for the relocation of some of the supply chains to the continent and increase investment in efficient and cost-effective continental supply chains.

For instance, investment in improved local manufacturing capacity; enhanced labour force skills; adequate infrastructure, including for distribution and logistics; and reduced trade barriers[30] could trigger competitive advantages and make Africa attractive to global manufacturers and suppliers. UNCTAD (2021b) found that through tariff liberalization and the removal of non-tariff barriers, the African Continental Free Trade Area is expected to increase trade and attract investment to build productive capacities, therefore expanding supply in Africa to serve rising regional demand. Such regional opportunities could foster the competitive position of Africa in global supply chains.

Diversifying and making supply chains more resilient is also associated with digitization and the adoption of digital technologies through the supply chain. In complex, high-value products and shorter lead-time supply chains, such as medical devices and electrical equipment, digitization is a necessity for production, processes and supply. Digital technologies, such as advanced automation, additive manufacturing (three-dimensional printing), machine learning, artificial intelligence, robotics, the Internet of things and blockchain technologies are a step change in productivity, distribution, logistics and procurement efficiency. At the firm level, the increased adoption of such technologies facilitates efficiency, cost reduction, valuation and competitive advantage. Goering et al. (2018) estimate that companies "that aim well and execute effectively" can expect technology-enabled manufacturing and delivery in advanced industries to bring productivity gains and cost savings, with a near-term impact of 200–600 basis points of margin expansion, of about $200 billion to $500 billion. As the use of new technologies and digital platforms has become essential for the operational effectiveness and cost-efficiency of firms and for heightened supply chain resilience, the affordability and increased access to such digital technologies will be required for African economies to be become attractive partners or destinations in the quest for supply chain diversification and resilience. Accelerating technological transformation in Africa will not only foster its supply chain and operational capabilities but will allow African firms to better position themselves to take advantage of supply chain opportunities.

Companies that have an interest in expanding their supply chains and building partnerships with suppliers located in new markets, such as Africa, could access potential African markets through joint ventures with domestic firms or mergers or acquisitions with foreign manufacturers and supply chain service providers that have a presence on the continent. Creating such partnership opportunities between well-established firms

---

[30] Lowered tariffs and other preferential access to materials and inputs under free trade agreements and regional trade agreements.

in the global supply chain and emerging domestic firms in Africa will have spillover effects relating to specialization, innovation, digitization, knowledge and skills, resulting in higher-value activities, productivity gains, job creation opportunities and enhanced competitiveness in global supply chains (Research Network Sustainable Global Supply Chains, 2022).

This chapter explores the role of technology-enabled services and financing mechanisms that global companies and economies are increasingly leveraging to diversify and facilitate the resilience of their supply chains. In addition, the chapter analyses the challenges African countries and firms are facing to digitize their supply chains and build stronger supplier capabilities, which can offer African suppliers and buyers a range of opportunities for value creation and value capture in global supply chains. To become an attractive destination for technology-intensive industries and digitally interconnected production and supply chain networks, Governments in Africa and the private sector will need to ensure the necessary incentives and policies to boost local capacity, infrastructure, production, supply chains and demand.

4.1 The value of technology-based enablers and firm innovation

There is strong evidence that technology plays a vital role in the diversification and resilience of supply chains. It contributes to production efficiency, faster delivery, cost-effective product customization, enhanced information flows across supplier networks and increased supply chain integration. For instance, digital platforms and technology-enabled services allow better integration and smooth coordination between different sectors and processes and across miles-away markets, thus facilitating supply chain diversification. In addition, various technology services, including supply chain connectivity and logistics, supply chain digitization, electronic data interchange, supply chain traceability software and smart services, enable supply chain resilience and sustainability.

To address the effects of supply chain disruptions from global crises and other external shocks, companies participating in global supply chains are adopting strategies to overcome obstacles by leveraging digital technologies across multiple aspects of their supply chains. Smart manufacturing, flexible automation, optimized connectivity, digital intelligence and other advanced technology-based analytics and applications are some of the technologies and digital tools paving the way for better firm performance, productivity and supply chain resilience. This section analyses the contribution of digitization and technology-enabled services to supply chain diversification and resilience, highlighting the potential role of African firms and incentives in boosting investment for the adoption of digital technologies.

4.1.1 How supply chain digitization could promote integration and efficiency in African firms

As diversifying and building resilient supply chains can be challenging for firms, capabilities to do so can be unlocked by the increased use of digital technologies. The complexity of supply chains, spanning multiple interconnected countries with varying taxes and regulations, servicing numerous e-commerce platforms and customers with high demand or changing behaviour, and involving broad ranges of relationships and collaborative efforts, can be a race to the bottom for many small and medium-sized enterprises. Supply chain technology thus offers an immense opportunity for small-scale firms to build and strengthen their technological capabilities and optimize their production, operations, logistics and distribution services. As data and analytics, artificial intelligence, machine learning, additive manufacturing and other technology-enabled processes and services can be utilized at all levels (from micro to large at firm level or within a supply chain), leveraging those technologies can improve the much-needed efficiency within a firm and its participation in a supply chain (Pitchbook, 2022).

According to UNCTAD (2023), blockchain technology can be used to enhance supply chain management and sustainability. Adopting digital technologies could facilitate the participation of small and medium-sized enterprises in supply chains or linkages with firms that are already part of global supply chains. Indeed, digital technologies, through online marketplaces and digital supply chain platforms, autonomous supply chains and technological devices, could improve business-to-business and business-to-consumer services between small and medium-sized enterprises and large companies that are already integrated in supply chains, thus contributing to supply chain regionalization. This also applies to those firms, regardless of size, that are not located in the same geographical areas. For instance, Internet-of-things technologies allow a digital interconnection between several machines and industries or companies in different places. Baldock (2022) demonstrates that through technology-enabled services, the integration of digitized machinery, combined with cyberdata streams and the Internet of things, facilitates supply chain efficiency.

Furthermore, supply chain digitization through supply chain automation enables greater sustainability and resilience in supply chains. An autonomous supply chain is a digital supply chain that leverages the robust combination of digital business ecosystems, the Internet of things, artificial Intelligence and blockchain technology on a digital foundation to enable connected, highly intelligent, self-aware and trusted supply chains in firms (Morley, 2022; Supply Chain Brain, 2018). For instance, a digital business ecosystem consists of the digitization of all activities, business, production, trading and finance within firms and with suppliers and customers, operating throughout the supply chain of the firms and companies concerned.

While the Internet of things ensures interconnection with all the partners within a supply chain network, blockchain technology protects the digital system again external attacks and data falsification. According to Supply Chain Brain (2018), a blockchain organizes data into a digital ledger of transactions, shared among a network's participants through a distributed computer network. In addition, blockchain can contribute to efficiency in production, supply chains and improved access to markets by facilitating different stages of the supply chain, including the following factors: procurement; information on the origin, quality and costs of goods; and closer access of small and medium-sized enterprises to corporate clients (UNCTAD, 2022d). Moreover, blockchain technology facilitates supply chain traceability, which in turn facilitates secured access to and sharing of information on data, customers, suppliers and operation time of goods and services throughout the supply chain network, from production to transformation and final consumption. Supply chain traceability also allows firms to have complete visibility, meet market demands and maximize profits.

In addition to traceability software, electronic data interchange, global business-to-business electronic trading networks, and smart services and manufactures, technology devices of autonomous supply chains offer attractive benefits. UNCTAD (2022d) shows how technology and smart services can provide conducive platforms for efficiently linking output and markets, enabling intermediate inputs of key technology-intensive services in production that facilitate complexity and diversity of manufacturing outputs. These technology devices reinforce supply chain capabilities to overcome supply chain disruption. The adoption of these digital technologies greatly depends on capabilities within a sector or country.

Most domestic firms in Africa are predominantly small and medium in size and operate outside the global supply chain network (United Nations, Economic Commission for Africa, 2020b). However, these enterprises can play an important role in supply chain diversification by integrating vertically or horizontally into the supply chain. For instance, by engaging in business-to-business or business-to-consumer collaboration, they can set up complementary businesses (vertical integration) or similar businesses in other localities (horizontal integration). Also, larger firms could seek vertical or horizontal integration in start-ups and small and medium-sized enterprises to diversify and regionalize their supply chains. Vertical integration enables a company to expand into upstream or downstream activities, thus allowing the integrated companies to streamline their operations and supply chains by acquiring or establishing their own suppliers, manufacturers, distributors or retail locations instead of outsourcing or relying on external suppliers (Hayes, 2022). Horizontal integration, on the other hand, enables a company to broaden its operations at the same value or supply chain level and within the same industry, thus allowing the integrated companies to reach into new markets, diversify their product offerings and reduce competition (Kenton, 2022). These two types of integration are better facilitated with the use of technology services at all stages, whether transactional or operational.

Collaboration and horizontal integration could be particularly beneficial for informal small and medium-sized enterprises, providing them with added opportunities to formalize, access markets and information, and create profits margins or turnover. For instance, the digitization of their operations, production and distribution or the business or operational integration of technological services, for example, through the creation of company webpages, online marketplaces and e-commerce platforms, provide more visibility for firms throughout regional and global supply chains. Furthermore, integration with small and medium-sized enterprises in different localities (horizontal integration) and as part of post-sale services in localized economies (vertical integration) will allow large companies to obtain channels closer to customers in various localities and enable the regionalization of their supply chains.

However, most of the technology-enabled services and digital platforms required for supply chain diversification and resilience are non-existent in many African countries, owing to infrastructure challenges, limited investment in innovation, lack of institutional framework and regulation, as well as information asymmetry and lack of visibility (Kuteyi and Winkler, 2022). Except for some pockets of achievement in countries that have developed logistics and smart services for business-to-business platforms – Egypt, Kenya, Mauritius, Nigeria and South Africa – countries in Africa have generally failed to integrate global supply chains. Autonomous supply chains, considered the supply chains of the future, do not exist in Africa, except in South Africa. Box 15 illustrates the case of South Africa and how its technological advancement has been a driving force for its competitiveness and integration into global supply chains.

Moreover, Organisation for Economic Co-operation and Development (2022a) showed that digital transformation in Africa could strengthen producer competitiveness, reduce cross-border trade costs, make trade-related institutions more efficient and facilitate the implementation of the African Continental Free Trade Area. Digital transformation also allows firms, including small and medium-sized enterprises, to work around formal contract enforcement constraints and integrate informal actors. It will enable them to realize productivity gains, streamline cross-border trade and ensure the safe and seamless flow of data across borders for competitive regional and global supply chains (Organisation for Economic Co-operation and Development, 2022a).

Box 15
South Africa: An example of successful diversification through supply chain networks

As an upper-middle-income country and the most industrialized economy on the continent, South Africa is the regional leader in supply chain diversification. It is also one of the world's leading mining and mineral-processing countries, with a diversified portfolio of minerals and large shares of world production. The county has developed robust backward linkages in mining equipment technologies and forward linkages in metal fabrication and automotive technologies. The mining upgrading and mineral beneficiation of South Africa were achieved on the back of technological innovation. The country benefited significantly from Government and private sector commitment to and investment in diversification, which bolstered its capabilities in the domestic and global supply of mining equipment for extraction, processing and beneficiation for mining houses.

The integration of companies in South Africa into global supply chains was also facilitated by the country's technological advancement, road and maritime transport networks, partnerships and regional integration. Indeed, the Government is developing an industrial strategy based on economically competitive technology platforms that address its economic and social imperatives to improve competitiveness and prepare for the fourth industrial revolution.[31] Moreover, the country is developing technological leadership in mobile software, security software, electronic banking services, and digital landscape and transformation, including the

---

[31] The fourth industrial revolution refers to the growing application of digital technologies at any stage of industrial production, from conceptualization to product design, manufacturing, distribution and recycling.

move to increasingly software-centric networks and cloud-based infrastructure to improve operational agility.

South Africa has one of the largest information and communications technology markets on the continent, and its electronics sector, similarly to the information and communications technology sector, is sophisticated and growing. In addition, the Government is embarking on an extensive skills-development programme aimed at training one million young people by 2030 in robotics, artificial intelligence, coding, cloud computing and networking. This technology boom has allowed the private sector and micro, small and medium-sized enterprises, as well as banking and other financial institutions, to embed some of the new technologies, such as machine-to-machine communication, the Internet of things, cloud computing, big data analytics, the monetization of growth in data tracking, cybersecurity, advanced robotics, artificial intelligence, smart sensors, augmented and virtual reality, and three-dimensional printing. As a result, these technologies are transforming manufacturing in South Africa and placing it among the world's 30 most highly diversified and integrated supply chains.

Moreover, the technological integration of South Africa is illustrated by its score in the frontier technology readiness index and the logistics performance index, putting the country in the first position in Africa for both indices. Its frontier technology readiness index was 0.61, compared with a global average of 0.50 in 2022[32]. The other African countries with a frontier technology readiness index above the average global index are Tunisia, 0.56; Morocco, 0.55; and Mauritius, 0.54. In the overall logistics performance index, South Africa also performed relatively well on a global scale and ranked the highest in Africa (3.38), followed by Côte d'Ivoire (3.08) and Botswana (3.05). South Africa performed better on average in logistics than other regions, except North America (3.81); the global index was 2.87 in 2018. See figures I and II. The logistics performance of South Africa explains the development of its supply chain connectivity and logistics.

---

[32] The frontier technology readiness index assesses a country's readiness for using, adopting and adapting frontier technologies. It is comprised of indices of information and communications technology deployment, skills, research and development activity, industrial activity and access to finance. It ranges between 0 (lowest score) and 1 (highest score). Principal component analysis was conducted to generate the index (UNCTAD, 2021d; UNCTAD, 2023).

Figure I

Overall logistics performance indices for countries in Africa, 2018

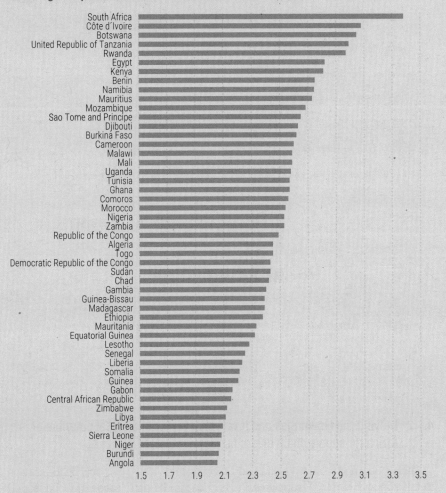

Source: UNCTAD calculations, based on World Development Indicators (World Bank).
Notes: Index scores range from 1 (low) to 5 (high). Data were unavailable for Cabo Verde, Eswatini, Seychelles and South Sudan. For Botswana, Ethiopia, Namibia, Mozambique and the United Republic of Tanzania, data were reported in 2016.

Figure II

Overall logistics performance indices for South Africa and selected world regions, 2018

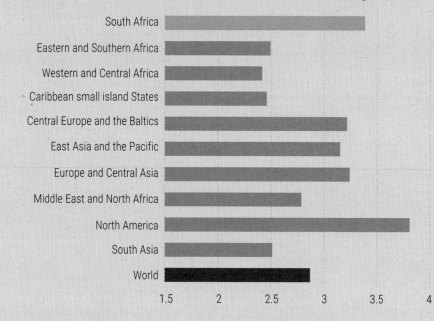

Source: UNCTAD calculations, based on World Development Indicators (World Bank).
Note: Index scores range from 1 (low) to 5 (high).

Source: UNCTAD.

4.1.2 Defying the challenges and leveraging the technological potential of Africa for supply chain diversification

Creating robust and resilient regional supply chain corridors in Africa could be the solution to its integration in global supply chains and lead to its participation in global supply chain diversification. Africa, with its growing economies, consumer markets and regional opportunities to achieve regional market access and economies of scale under the African Continental Free Trade Area, for example, is a strategic option for moving towards resilient supply chains. However, analysing foreseeable challenges and opportunities to ensure the establishment of resilient networks on the continent (for example, facilitating good visibility and resilient sourcing, manufacturing and distribution activities) will be foundational knowledge and provide the basis for assessing the benefits and anticipating the risks of diversifying into Africa as a road map for global supply chain diversification and resilience.

Many of the foreseeable challenges are not new and include inadequate infrastructure capacity, low level of skills and technology capacity, and lack of access to affordable working capital and other financing means. Such operational and structural challenges affect the ability of African companies to supply goods and services efficiently and reliably, and therefore are perceived as uncompetitive in a dynamic and ever-evolving globalized world. For instance, the high cost and low quality of infrastructure in Africa, including information and communications technology, railways and road transportation, can easily have an impact on supply chains, causing delays in ports and on the roads and increasing the cost of transaction and exchange of information at every stage of the supply chain. As a result, this reduces the effectiveness of supply chain logistics and management. The continent operates less than 70 ports, many of which are poorly equipped and uneconomically operated, with delays two or three times greater than the global average (UNCTAD, 2022a). Efforts at increasing the levels of digitization and technology, in tandem with adequate transport infrastructure and Internet connectivity, will be necessary to address the operational and structural challenges affecting supply chain diversification in Africa.

Despite the importance of technology in the supply chain, most African countries are not entirely up to date in trading technology-enabled goods and services. The level of transformation of raw materials for high-skill technology-intensive manufactures is low, limiting opportunities for value capture and participation in global supply chains. While on average, high-skill technology-intensive manufactures[33] represented almost 30 per cent of total exports of goods worldwide in 2017, in Africa, these goods made up only 7.7 per cent of high-skill technology-intensive manufactures in 2017–2021 (figure 28). This is the smallest proportion in all regions, except Oceania (6 per cent), behind the Americas (23 per cent), Europe (28 per cent) and Asia (36 per cent). In Africa, the share of medium-skill technology-intensive manufactures is also low.[34]

---

[33] High-skill technology-intensive manufactures include office and automatic data-processing machines, telecommunication equipment, chemical products, medicinal and pharmaceutical products, fertilizers, and cinematographic and photographic supplies.

[34] Medium-skill technology-intensive manufactures include household-type equipment, apparatuses for electrical circuits, boards, panels, articles and materials of rubber, engines and motors, agricultural machinery, civil engineering and contractors' plants and equipment. Low-skill technology-intensive manufactures include food products, beverages, tobacco, textiles and apparel, leather and footwear, and wood and paper and related products.

Figure 28
Share of low-, medium- and high-skill technology-intensive manufactures in exports and imports, 2017–2021

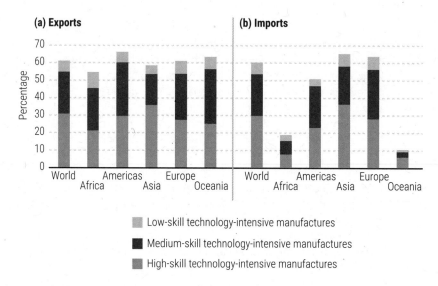

(a) Exports

(b) Imports

Low-skill technology-intensive manufactures

Medium-skill technology-intensive manufactures

High-skill technology-intensive manufactures

Source: UNCTAD calculations, based on data from UNCTADstat database.
Note: The classification is derived from the UNCTADstat database (2023) on manufactured goods by degree of manufacturing groups (Standard International Trade Classification Revision 3).

The low level of technology in African exports is not compensated by its imports, as Africa remained in the last position for imports in high- and medium skill technology-intensive manufactures (figure 28) in 2017–2021. In addition, the imports of high and medium skill technology-intensive manufactures have experienced a slow increase over the last ten years in Africa. The share of high-skill technology-intensive manufactures in total imports in goods has increased from 18.6 per cent in 2011 to 22.3 per cent in 2021, while the share of medium-skill technology-intensive manufactures in total imports in goods has decreased from 24.1 per cent in 2011 to 23.8 per cent in 2021 in Africa. The low levels of technology-intensive manufactures imply very limited or lack of research and development and innovation in African manufacturing industries. It is clear that African countries need to invest more in innovation and technology and provide conducive environments for technological transformation to unfold in order to develop its manufactures and integrate more effectively global supply chains.

The levers of the emerging digital ecosystem in Africa

As global companies are embracing technology and innovations to optimize supply chain practices, their appetite to expand their sourcing locations will generally materialize in markets with readily available advanced technologies and capabilities. While such technological capabilities are lacking in many African markets, the digital momentum on the continent, compounded by its demographic dynamics (a young and growing population, a promising large consumption market and technology-oriented small and medium-sized enterprises) can favour the adoption of new digital technologies and create greater opportunities that can deepen the region's footprint in global supply chains. See chapter 2 for additional analysis on demographic dynamics in Africa. It is broadly acknowledged that the use of digital technologies[35] can improve end-to-end supply chains with increased traceability, transparency and information flow and enable firms to generate maximum benefits from the production and supply of higher-margin products (Gandhi, 2022).

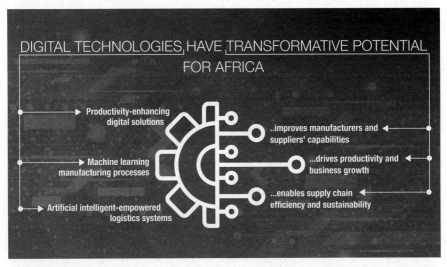

DIGITAL TECHNOLOGIES HAVE TRANSFORMATIVE POTENTIAL FOR AFRICA

- Productivity-enhancing digital solutions
- Machine learning manufacturing processes
- Artificial intelligent-empowered logistics systems

- ..improves manufacturers and suppliers' capabilities
- ...drives productivity and business growth
- ...enables supply chain efficiency and sustainability

In Africa, the adoption and use of these new digital technologies can also contribute to increased entrepreneurship, job creation and better incomes. This, in turn, can increase consumer welfare and purchasing power, an important decision-making factor for industries looking into supplying the growing consumer markets in Africa. For

---

[35] Digital and data infrastructure, productivity-enhancing digital solutions, machine-learning manufacturing processes, artificial intelligent-empowered logistics systems and other technology-enabled procurement, marketing and financing solutions.

instance, in Nigeria, improved digital and data infrastructure and a wider use of digital communication technology, measured by three or more years of exposure to Internet availability, resulted in greater labour force participation (by 3 percentage points), wage employment (by 1 percentage point) and total consumption (by 9 percentage points). Further, the proportion of Nigerians living below the extreme poverty line of $1.90 per person per day declined by 7 per cent (World Bank, 2023b). Similar welfare outcomes and firm productivity through innovation and the use of more sophisticated digital technologies are also observed in other African countries – Ghana, Kenya, Malawi, Senegal and the Republic of Tanzania, to name a few.

In Senegal, for example, Cirera et al. (2021) find a position correlation between a firm's use of more sophisticated digital technologies and better productivity performance, measured by value added per worker. Under the UNCTAD frontier technology index (UNCTAD, 2023), Senegal in 2022 obtained a low score (128), which can be partly explained by obstacles to adopting technologies that are associated with higher productivity. In a survey of about 1,800 small, medium and large firms in Senegal for the use of digital technologies, about 70 per cent of respondents considered the lack of capabilities to be major barriers to the adoption of technologies in their operations, while 60 per cent cited the lack of finance (Cirera et al., 2021). This suggests that appropriate policy measures to overcome these obstacles could improve the effective diffusion and adoption of frontier technologies by firms in Senegal. The policy implications are presented in greater detail in chapter 5.

Another market that has rising potential for innovation and digital technologies is Kenya. It has one of the highest digital skill adoption rates in Africa, meaning that about one third of its population is able to use digital devices and applications. By 2030, about 55 per cent of jobs in Kenya will require some level of digital skills, with the industry and services sectors requiring the highest rates of digital adoption (International Finance Corporation, 2021a). The country's high digital literacy and its thriving information and communications technology sector are key drivers of the adoption of digital technologies, giving impetus to the rise of cutting-edge start-ups and technology-empowered companies. According to International Telecommunication Union (2021), Kenya has one of the largest and growing international bandwidths per Internet user on the continent, with 566.41 kilobits per second and a compounded annual growth rate of 52 per cent during the period 2015–2019. Some of the emerging technologies that are increasingly being deployed in Kenya and which can be leveraged to boost specific industries and supply chains (for example, innovation, product design, manufacturing, logistics and supply chain management), include artificial intelligence, the Internet of things and cloud-computing technologies, such as blockchain. This growing technology-aware ecosystem in Kenya, also known as the Silicon Savannah, has benefited from sound policies, a business-friendly regulatory environment and other government-led skills, upgrading and digital technology adoption programmes, including the establishment of technology hubs and incubators (International Telecommunication Union, 2021).

One technology that is becoming the norm in optimizing supply chain operations and is gaining momentum and widespread use in Africa is blockchain. The use of this technology in supply chains enables fast and efficient sourcing and delivery of products, enhances coordination between suppliers and buyers and can improve supply chain participating firms' access to finance (Gaur and Gaiha, 2020). A blockchain, which is a digitally distributed ledger or data-recording technology that can record supply chain transactions, such as information flows, inventory flows and financial flows among multiple suppliers, buyers and service providers in a transparent, verifiable and tamperproof way, does not only improve traceability of end-to-end supply chains, but it can also reduce operational, administrative and logistics costs and mitigate potential risks from supply chain malpractice (Deloitte, 2017a). Mining companies, such as DeBeers of South Africa, are increasingly using blockchains to ensure the traceability of authentic, registered and conflict-free movement of minerals within their supply chains, from mining to delivery, thus minimizing the risk of corruption, cutting transaction costs and increasing profit margins (Oke et al., 2022).

Blockchain and other advanced technologies provide valuable tools and platforms that can meet the financing needs of African firms and potential suppliers or service providers in supply chains. For instance, banks and other credit providers can also use blockchains to improve supply chain financing, as they will enable them to make better lending decisions in a fast and cost-efficient manner by having access to real-time and verifiable transactions between suppliers and buyers without having to conduct physical audits or pay for financial reviews (Gaur and Gaiha, 2020). And for firms, whether suppliers or buyers, the increased visibility between the different supply chain partners and the traceability of supply chain operations and transactions through the use of blockchain-enabled solutions or other secured digital platforms can also help tackle some of the operational and financial challenges they encounter when participating in supply chains, and thus improve their operational reliability and creditworthiness (Loannou and Demirel, 2022). The next section will analyse in greater detail the financing solutions that are necessary for a firm's operational efficiency in supply chains. Opportunities for firms in Africa seeking to integrate supply chains and optimize their potential for supply chain diversification will also be explored.

4.2 Financing solutions for market-creating innovations

Enabling technologies such as artificial intelligence, the Internet of things, three-dimensional printing, robotics, machine learning, digital manufacturing solutions, logistic technology and blockchain, can provide competitive advantage and cost-efficient business models to companies and suppliers that may decide to diversify in Africa and build relationships between suppliers and customers. Targeting or investing in market-creating innovations can also have a spillover effect on local entrepreneurs in terms of improved innovation, skills and management, with the potential to drive growth and the funding of future innovations and supply chains in African countries. Christensen et al. (2019) define market-creating innovations as new markets that serve people for whom no goods or services exist or are made accessible and affordable. Therefore, innovations will be required to make new goods or transform complex and expensive goods and services into simple and affordable ones that "unconsumers",[36] a group of consumers or population not previously targeted, can easily access. Facilitating such market-creating innovations will not only create new goods, services and markets, but they will also develop the necessary distribution and logistics infrastructure and generate employment – new job opportunities to manufacture, distribute, sell and service goods (Christensen et al., 2019).

In Africa, the burgeoning private sector, especially start-ups and small and medium-sized enterprises, will be key in leveraging potential market-creating innovations. The growth of small and medium-sized enterprises has long been a strong driver of economic development and employment, while financial constraints have been shown to be barriers to innovation, which is necessary to improve long-run productivity levels (Elshaarawy and Ezzat, 2022). Small and medium-sized enterprises have been characterized as the missing middle in financing: they are underserved by financial institutions because they tend to be too small and high-risk to make it profitable for the formal banking sector, yet too large to be served by microfinance institutions.

This presents a significant challenge to their potential role in market-creating innovations and high-knowledge-intensive supply chains, therefore limiting prospects to become suppliers of inputs and contribute to making supply chains more resilient to external shocks. A possible solution for creating new market innovations and facilitating the participation of small and medium-sized enterprises in supply chains in Africa is to increase the use of supply chain-related investments and finance. The section reviews

---

[36] See www.shareable.net/the-unconsumption-un-manifesto/ (accessed 2 July 2023).

the concept of supply chain finance and the financing solutions it offers firms (suppliers and buyers) that face liquidity constraints, which could be opportunities for the integration of small and medium-sized enterprises in supply chains. It also explores the current development of supply chain finance in Africa, paying particular attention to addressing the barriers to supply chain finance development and highlighting the potential role of sustainable supply chain finance initiatives, especially with a view to fostering industrial development and structural transformation in Africa.

Supply chain finance has gained increasing attention in recent years through greater consideration for the value-enhancing effect of operations-finance integration that emphasizes how the material, financial and information flows in the supply chains complement each other to optimize profit and better match supply with demand (Zhao and Huchzermeier, 2018). In 2022, the global supply chain finance market value, was $2.187 trillion (BCR, 2023), a 21 per cent increase from 2021, and is expected to grow at a compound annual growth rate of 8.8–17.1 per cent (Allied Market Research, 2022; BFSI Network, 2021; Maximize Market Research, 2022). Africa recorded the strongest growth in supply chain finance by volume at about 40 per cent between 2021 and 2022 (from $29 billion to $41 billion), compared with a growth of 28 per cent for Asia, 21 per cent for the Americas and 18 per cent for Europe (BCR, 2023). Given the $5.2 trillion global finance gap of micro, small and medium-sized enterprises in developing countries, 6.5 per cent of which came from Africa (International Finance Corporation, 2017), the growth of supply chain finance markets and products offers an opportunity to bridge this gap by providing liquidity, enhancing working capital efficiency and improving cash conversion cycles.

4.2.1 The role of supply chain finance in developing market capabilities

Access to finance for firms participating in supply chains generally involves two areas of finance: real investment and working capital financing. Real investment includes, for example, investment in physical and technological infrastructure; fixed assets, such as offices, warehouses, plants and equipment; human resources; research and development; procurement; marketing; and sales and services.

Working capital financing bridges the payment time gap between buyers and sellers or the time gap of a business between incurring costs and generating sales, so that it can manage its cash levels and needs from daily operations in an efficient manner and reduce stress to the balance sheet (BCR, 2022; Zhao and Huchzermeier, 2018). While both areas of finance are important to economic development and supply chains integration in Africa,, the next section will focus on working capital financing from the perspective of supply chain finance.

Defining supply chain finance

The world of supply chain finance is varied, complex and constantly evolving, and as such, presents definitional challenges. As there are no internationally agreed standards for supply chain finance – unlike the International Chamber of Commerce rules for letters of credit[37] or the Incoterms rules[38] – terminology relating to supply chain finance is not standardized, and it is often up to each finance provider to decide how to designate supply chain finance product offerings – whether supplier finance, payables finance, supplier payments, approved payables finance or reverse factoring. However, the term supply chain finance is also treated as the parent category that encompass all of the aforementioned variations (BCR, 2022; Trade Finance Global, 2023). In common references to supply chain finance in finance, business and international development, it is often considered as part of, or together with, trade finance (see box 16).

The standard definition of supply chain finance established by the International Chamber of Commerce divides diverse, yet related, financial instruments available across supply chain activities into two categories:

- Receivables purchase-based supply chain finance products, where suppliers obtain financing by using their receivables as collateral or selling them at a discount to a finance provider (receivables discounting, forfaiting, factoring), or a better-rated buyer initiates financing for the supplier from the finance provider (payables finance).

- Loan- or advance-based supply chain finance products, under three scenarios: suppliers or buyers receive loans and advances against an underlying asset (for example, receivables and inventory), a distributor of a large manufacturer obtains financing to hold goods for sale (distributor finance) or a supplier receives a loan for sourcing, manufacturing or conversion of semi-finished into finished goods (International Chamber of Commerce et al., 2016; International Finance Corporation, 2014).

An effective supply chain finance solution is conceived in the context of trade finance products, external guarantees, risk-sharing mechanisms and other innovations to

---

[37] Uniform Customs and Practice for Documentary Credits is a set of detailed international rules developed by the International Chamber of Commerce in 1933 to govern commercial letters of credit.

[38] The Incoterms rules were formulated by the International Chamber of Commerce and are the world's essential terms of trade for the sale of goods (see https://iccwbo.org/business-solutions/incoterms-rules/incoterms-2020/).

address the risk aversion of finance providers, particularly when financing for non-investment-grade-rated small and medium-sized enterprises in Africa, where the financial product landscape is generally less developed.

Box 16
Supply chain finance and trade finance

Trade finance refers to the global trade-enabling instruments used by financial intermediaries to overcome the payment time gap between exporters and importers. Examples include letters of credit, guarantees, documentary collection and open accounts. The boundaries between trade finance and supply chain finance are generally unclear. This can be illustrated by how international financial institutions deal with the issue. For example, the Asian Development Bank offers a trade and supply chain finance programme, the African Export–Import Bank presents some of its supply chain finance products under its trade finance programmes and the African Development Bank continues to offer mainly trade finance products. In the private sector, supply chain finance solutions have long been offered by big banks to large corporations, such as fast-moving consumer goods and manufacturing companies to support trade.

While it has long been suggested that more than one third of international trade is supported and enabled by trade finance, since the 2000s, open account trade, to which supply chain finance is typically applied, has grown exponentially, while traditional trade finance saw relatively slow growth. Open-account trade focuses on transactions, rather than collateral, and occurs when goods are shipped and delivered before payment is due. The buyer is directly responsible for meeting the payment obligation of the underlying transaction, as it is not supported by banking or documentary trade instruments issued on behalf of the buyer or seller. Open-account trade is no longer reserved solely for established trading relationships or trade with low-risk markets.

In addition, regulatory changes since the 2008–2009 global financial and economic crisis have favoured supply chain finance over traditional trade finance, as the Basel II Capital Accord treats trade finance more harshly, requiring a minimum duration of one year for loans and emphasizing counterparty risk. With COVID-19 commanding global attention on rethinking supply chain disruption and resilience, supply chain finance has been met with greater interest in recent years, and its potential in developing supply chains in Africa could be transformative.

Sources: UNCTAD, based on African Development Bank, 2023; African Export–Import Bank, 2017; African Export–Import Bank, n.d.; Asian Development Bank, 2023; Garnizova and Khorana, 2021; Herath, 2015; International Chamber of Commerce et al., 2016; Shrivastava et al., 2019.

In recent years, supply chain finance has benefited from the emergence of technology-enabled service platforms, which connect counterparties more efficiently and enable innovative solutions in the face of growing trade complexities. Figure 29 provides a stylized illustration of how supply chain finance products work. For example, the availability of procure-to-pay automation, in which purchasing and accounts payable systems are integrated in the buyer's procurement management process relating to independent third-party platforms, has allowed buyers and suppliers to gain better access to financial services and facilitated access to multiple liquidity providers, and thus more efficient matching of demand for and supply of funds. Buyers and suppliers could electronically submit approved invoices to a supply chain finance platform, and the financial provider partnered with this platform would receive and review the payment requests and provide funding to the supplier after risk assessment (Herath, 2015). As more supply chain finance actors participate in these integrated platforms, data analytics can be conducted more effectively to predict supply chain finance demand and supply.

At the most granular level, supply chain finance can be defined as approved payables finance or reverse factoring. This is commonly accepted as equivalent to supply chain finance by business and financial practitioners, although it is one of various supply chain finance products available (BCR, 2023; International Chamber of Commerce et al., 2016; International Finance Corporation, 2014). Payables finance is a buyer- or consumer-driven supply chain finance programme in which a large buyer approves a supplier's invoice and requests one or more finance providers to set up a receivable discounting line in favour of its suppliers. This allows the supplier, typically a non-investment-grade-rated small and medium-sized enterprise that often suffers from liquidity squeeze and difficulty in accessing sufficient working capital, to access credit based on the buyer's credit worthiness. The finance provider grants the financing without recourse to the supplier, which is related to the risk of non-payment by the buyer of the invoice or account payable. *World Supply Chain Finance Reports* issued by BCR usually adopt this definition of supply chain finance.

The global supply chain finance ecosystem has been changing. Global universal banks have traditionally dominated the supply chain finance space, holding over 95 per cent of programmes as of 2005, the remainder being split between platform providers, such as Orbian and Prime Revenue (Herath, 2015). However, the growing importance of supply chain finance has attracted rapid innovative development in the space with financial technology firms entering the market that offer greater digitization in supply chain finance product offering and implementation, such as innovative business models, improved digital interfaces and simplified onboarding (Herath, 2015). The innovation of financial technology firms has the potential to significantly improve the reach of supply chain finance products and facilitate economic activities along the supply chains.

Figure 29
How supply chain finance works

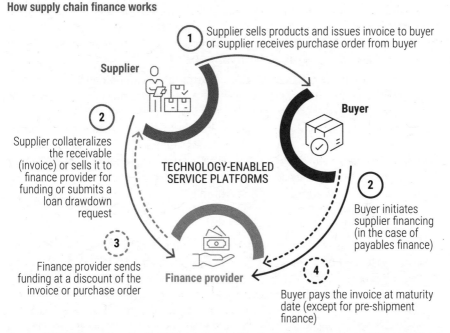

Supplier sells products and issues invoice to buyer or supplier receives purchase order from buyer

Supplier

Buyer

2 Supplier collateralizes the receivable (invoice) or sells it to finance provider for funding or submits a loan drawdown request

TECHNOLOGY-ENABLED SERVICE PLATFORMS

2 Buyer initiates supplier financing (in the case of payables finance)

3 Finance provider sends funding at a discount of the invoice or purchase order

Finance provider

4 Buyer pays the invoice at maturity date (except for pre-shipment finance)

Source: UNCTAD, based on Herath, 2015; International Chamber of Commerce et al., 2016; International Finance Corporation, 2014.

4.2.2 How supply chain finance can drive the participation of small and medium-sized enterprises in supply chains in Africa

Scaling innovative supply chain finance solutions has the potential to significantly improve small and medium-sized enterprises' access to financing and competitiveness in a well-integrated supply chain that could further increase employment, income, quality of life and economic growth in Africa (International Finance Corporation, 2021b).

Indeed, supply chain finance enables small and medium-sized enterprises previously considered unbankable for traditional trade-finance products to access credit. According to Auboin et al. (2016), factoring, which is mainly employed by firms involved in global supply chains, has a positive effect in allowing small and medium-sized enterprises to access capital and international trade, given its availability. For example, Kenya faces a financing gap of $19.3 billion with a lack of financial products for the missing middle (firms valued at K Sh100,000–K Sh1,000,000) as microenterprises benefit from the microfinance market. Scaling supply chain finance could bridge 54 per cent of small and medium-sized enterprises' financing gap and reduce liquidity gaps between suppliers and buyers (International Finance Corporation, 2022a).

More importantly, beyond financing, supply chain finance can be particularly effective in forming forward and backward business linkages and facilitating clusters of small and medium-sized enterprises by providing the well-needed financing at each different trigger event along the physical supply chains, which improves the competitiveness of firms along the supply chains (Garnizova and Khorana, 2021). For example, a China-based pharmaceutical wholesaler (Real Can or Ruikang) built a blockchain solution for supply chain finance with China Zheshang Bank that would give it faster, more reliable data, financing needs assessment and payment with nearly 1,000 pharmaceutical manufacturers that it works with, thus strengthening its backward linkages (Wood, 2019).

As many small and medium-sized enterprises struggle to manage cash flow and working capital and are unable to buy inventory due to the liquidity gap created by delayed payments, supply chain finance can allow them to better manage liquidity and cash, giving room to both buyers and sellers to undertake other physical or financial transactions without harming their cash flow, reducing transaction costs and decreasing risk associated with serving smaller and riskier firms (International Finance Corporation, 2014; Trade Finance Global, 2023). For example, factoring may allow a high-risk supplier to transfer its credit risk to a highly rated buyer (Klapper, 2006). Payables finance also takes the underlying receivable off the supplier's balance sheet, thus improving its credit metrics. More importantly, supply chain finance could potentially help not only tier 1 and 2 suppliers, but also last-mile merchants in delivery of goods up to the last stage (consumer), helping them to expand and increase revenues (BCR, 2023).

In Africa, the use of supply chain financing mechanisms can enable small and medium-sized enterprises to obtain improved access to working capital and provide them with a cushion to further invest and develop the technological and knowledge intensity of their production of goods and services along the supply chains. And for foreign firms looking into diversifying their supply chains, supply chain finance can provide them with a powerful way to enter the African market and relocate some of their production and distribution to the continent, with improved assurance that local suppliers and buyers will not be financially constrained, thus lowering financial risk. Supply chain finance products, such as factoring, facilitate access to new territories without taking on country risk, as underwriters mainly place the risk on the receivables, payables, inventory, or purchase orders and unapproved invoices (which display varying degrees of risk themselves), rather than the firm itself.

Supply chain finance also provides valuable benefits for finance providers. It helps broaden a financial institution's customer base by providing access to new, small and medium-sized-enterprise clients, which increases opportunities for cross-selling (International Finance Corporation, 2014). With improved relationships and understanding, finance providers can further expand their range of products, focusing on core customers to maximize synergies and gains. In addition, automation in a typical supply chain finance transaction could ease reconciliation and forecasting processes of trade transactions. Compared with traditional trade finance, this can lower costs for banks that lend money to firms. At present, however, too few African banks are providing supply chain finance solutions or promoting a continent-wide supply chain finance market, which hinders data collection related to supply chain finance potential in Africa and thus makes it difficult to predict trends accurately in supply chain finance.

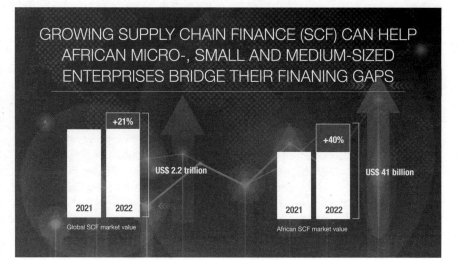

GROWING SUPPLY CHAIN FINANCE (SCF) CAN HELP AFRICAN MICRO-, SMALL AND MEDIUM-SIZED ENTERPRISES BRIDGE THEIR FINANING GAPS

+21%

US$ 2.2 trillion

2021   2022

Global SCF market value

+40%

US$ 41 billion

2021   2022

African SCF market value

Although supply chain finance is seen as a productive way to grow businesses and finance trade and liquidity for an economy's long-term structural transformation since its use in the 1990s, it has remained a financial product mostly used in advanced economies and emerging markets in Asia and Latin America, reflecting the levels of financial market development across regions. Looking at supply chain finance defined solely as payables finance, Africa contributed to only 1.9 per cent of the global supply chain finance volume of $2.2 trillion in 2022 and remains the most underdeveloped supply chain finance market across regions (figure 30(a)). However, supply chain finance growth in Africa is accelerating, led by financial technology companies offering digital platforms for collection, payment and lending (BCR, 2023), especially after experiencing supply chain disruptions during the outbreak of COVID-19. Furthermore, while the year-on-year growth of global total supply chain finance volume has stayed in a consistent range of 25–38 per cent, Africa has experienced a much more volatile growth path, compared with other regions, suggesting relatively unpredictable supply chain finance market supply and demand (figure 30(b)). However, the bright spot is that while other regions witnessed a slowdown in supply chain finance market growth in 2022 due to the lingering effects of the COVID-19, Africa was the only region that saw an accelerated growth at 41 per cent year-on-year, owing to its sustained growth momentum from a low base and potential financial technology and financial technology-enabled investments, which have increased by more than 200 per cent to $2 billion in 2021 over 2020 (UNCTAD, 2022d).

Another fast-growing and evolving financing solution that can provide opportunities for African firms to access finance and build supply chain relationships with foreign companies are mergers and acquisitions. Box 17 highlights recent merger and acquisition investment trends in Africa and describes how these investment opportunities can make Africa an attractive destination for multiple investors and companies participating in global supply chains.

Overall, the supply of supply chain finance continues to be far below demand, with diverse situations across the continent. For instance, in Kenya, supply chain finance supply has only reached 7–10 per cent of the $24.8 billion (K Sh2.8 trillion) estimated market, or 25.1 per cent of GDP, of which small and medium-sized enterprises generate about 42 per cent, in terms of annualized value of financial payables, receivables and inventory (International Finance Corporation, 2022a). In Nigeria, the estimated market for supply chain finance is $6.6 billion (₦2.7 trillion) of which small and medium-sized enterprises generate more than half (International Finance Corporation, 2022b). In both Kenya and Nigeria, the manufacturing sector generates the greatest demand of the supply chain finance market – almost 40 per cent in Kenya and 35 per cent in Nigeria – owing to

Figure 30

Global supply chain finance volume and growth, 2015–2022

(a) Volume

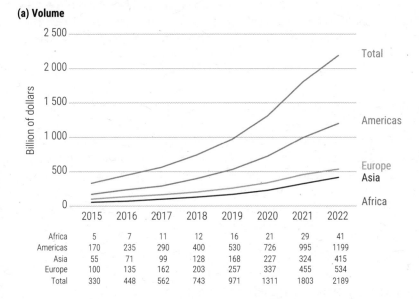

	2015	2016	2017	2018	2019	2020	2021	2022
Africa	5	7	11	12	16	21	29	41
Americas	170	235	290	400	530	726	995	1199
Asia	55	71	99	128	168	227	324	415
Europe	100	135	162	203	257	337	455	534
Total	330	448	562	743	971	1311	1803	2189

(b) Year-on-year growth

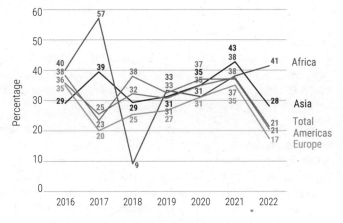

Source: UNCTAD, based on data from BCR, 2023.
Note: Global supply chain finance refers to payables finance only.

the high volume of transactions in the sector's supply chains. International Finance Corporation surveys (2022a, 2022b) further show that in Kenya, commercial banks are the largest providers of supply chain finance at about $1.7 billion–$2.6 billion, while microfinance banks, microfinance institutions, and factoring and financial technology companies have also started to launch supply chain finance products to close financing gaps. In Nigeria, commercial banks do not lend much to micro, small and medium-sized enterprises, while 80–90 per cent of lending is working capital financing; non-bank financial institutions, such as merchant banks, financing companies and microfinance banks, offer limited supply chain finance products. In countries such as South Africa and Zambia, supply chain finance programmes were set up to unlock working capital and support local businesses. For example, South African Breweries Miller adopted an advanced supply chain finance solution facilitating the production and supply of empty bottles in soft-drink plants and breweries. (African Export–Import Bank, 2017). In Zambia, a supply chain finance programme to manage pharmaceutical supply chains, involving technical assistance and lending, was implemented through a government contract with International Business Machines.

Box 17
Opportunities in the area of mergers and acquisitions

Mergers and acquisitions hold significant potential for small and medium-sized enterprises in terms of efficiency, capability and innovation. By definition, these transactions provide integrated firms and their suppliers with a powerful platform to merge and transform two distinct supply chains into an integrated model that creates competitive advantage in terms of cost and operations. While the objectives of entering into such a transaction can vary, most firms that do so consider assessed risks or vulnerability in the supply chain. These firms share similar objectives: improving supply chain visibility, securing supply sourcing, expanding scale capacity, broadening capabilities and increasing value chain adaptability.

A look at the performance of merger and acquisition and private equity markets in Africa, especially in 2019–2020 when the world was in turmoil and supply chains were disrupted, can reveal key trends in investment opportunities. Figure I shows a spike in investment in mergers and acquisitions and private equity in Africa during the first half of 2021, despite the impact of the COVID-19 pandemic and other global pressures on markets. Merger and acquisition and private equity investment flows into the continent peaked at a total value of $50.82 billion during the second quarter of 2021.

Figure I

Africa: Investment in mergers and acquisitions and private equity, third quarter 2019–fourth quarter 2022

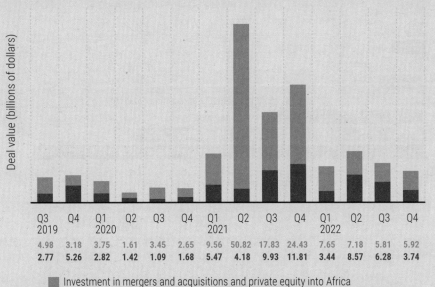

	Q3 2019	Q4	Q1 2020	Q2	Q3	Q4	Q1 2021	Q2	Q3	Q4	Q1 2022	Q2	Q3	Q4
	4.98	3.18	3.75	1.61	3.45	2.65	9.56	50.82	17.83	24.43	7.65	7.18	5.81	5.92
	2.77	5.26	2.82	1.42	1.09	1.68	5.47	4.18	9.93	11.81	3.44	8.57	6.28	3.74

Investment in mergers and acquisitions and private equity into Africa
Investment in mergers and acquisitions and private equity from Africa to the world

Source: UNCTAD calculations, based on Mergermarket database (see https://info.mergermarket.com/).
Abbreviation: Q, quarter.

Figure II demonstrates the significance of the energy, mining and utilities sector, as well as the pharmaceutical, medical and biotechnology sectors for African acquirers and local entrepreneurs, whose share of transaction value has been growing by about 5 per cent per year. When combined with financial services, the energy, mining and pharmaceutical sectors account for about 74 per cent of total merger and acquisition investment by African firms on the continent. The growing African-led mergers and acquisitions on the continent and the emergence of African private equity investors can be explained by two major trends: the rise and attraction of technology-based start-ups and the growth potential of regional markets (African Continental Free Trade Area), which are opening up more and more opportunities for domestic acquirers and foreign players.

Figure II

Investment in mergers and acquisitions by companies based in Africa, 2022

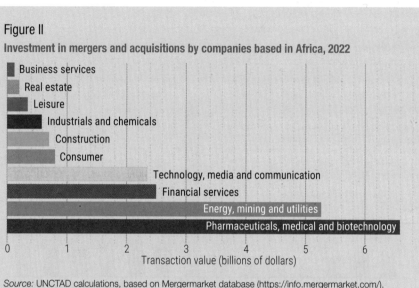

Source: UNCTAD calculations, based on Mergermarket database (https://info.mergermarket.com/).

Sources: UNCTAD, based on Deloitte, 2017a; El Fihri et al., 2021; Kearney, 2022.

4.2.3 Financing solutions as enablers of liquidity and innovations in supply chains

Supply chain finance growth is needed to raise the industrial output and stimulate structural transformation in Africa as regional supply chains become more sophisticated in the context of the African Continental Free Trade Area. For firms (designers, manufacturers, distributors, sellers and buyers) to enter and operate in supply chains, barriers to the greater use of supply chain finance pose major limitations to their competitiveness. In the case of factoring, for example, its development could be impeded by anti-money laundering or know-your-customer regulations, and buyer performance, which is related to supply chain finance default risk and profitability, according to members of Factors Chain International, widely known as FCI (Factors Chain International, 2022).

In general, African countries often face a disproportionately higher risk perception by major global financial players, which hinders the expected and necessary financial flows into the continent and feed into their currency risk. Some countries in Africa are constrained by low or nonexistent country risk ratings, weak banking systems, lack of credit information and regulatory requirements. A survey of small and medium-sized enterprises across 49 countries in Africa conducted by the African Development Bank concluded that such enterprises exhibited a default rate of 10–11 per cent during 2015–2019, which is materially higher than the default rate observed in global trade finance portfolios of below 1 per cent (African Development Bank, 2020). This prevents some financial institutions from extending credits to certain countries altogether, as their credit selection process might include minimum rating and information requirements. The high rate of informality among micro, small and medium-sized enterprises in Africa further prevents their eligibility for formal-sector financing, including supply chain finance. A lack of infrastructure, in particular reliable electric power, transport and telecommunications, compounds the difficulties of establishing well-integrated supply chains across the continent.

Challenges to supply chain finance growth:

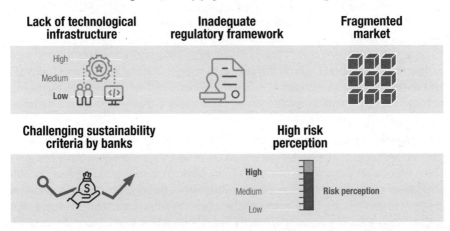

| Lack of technological infrastructure | Inadequate regulatory framework | Fragmented market |

| Challenging sustainability criteria by banks | High risk perception |

There are five main types of barriers to supply chain finance service provision in Africa: technological infrastructure; legal and regulatory framework; knowledge, education and risk perception of local firms; a fragmented market; and sustainability (African Export–Import Bank, 2017; International Finance Corporation, 2021b). Addressing these challenges will not only increase innovative opportunities for African firms, specifically in the realm of liquidity and working capital management, but it will also help overcome some of the obstacles multinational companies could face when they relocate part of their upstream production of supply to Africa. This section provides detailed information on some of the main barriers that constrain the deployment of supply chain finance in

Africa. Chapter 5 provides key recommendations for leveraging supply chain finance to unleash the profit potential of African firms along the supply chains.

Technological infrastructure uptake and upgrade

Currently, there is a low level of technological capacity within banks to provide for themselves and manage supply chain finance, and they are sometimes unable to cover the costs of technology development to reach the necessary scale required of efficient operations and product offerings of supply chain finance (International Finance Corporation, 2021b). As a result, across the continent, there is insufficient digitization and adoption of technology in the financing process. Processing financing applications remains a highly labour-intensive process, with excess paperwork, such as for letters of credit that incur high operational and transaction costs. Based on the experience of other developing and emerging countries, such as Peru, overcoming this type of barrier could reduce trade finance operating costs by 50 per cent on average (International Finance Corporation, 2020). Although digitization and automation are in place, such innovations are not yet widespread in Africa. Integrating digital invoicing or payments systems and customer relationship management systems with those of suppliers, buyers, financial institutions and other service providers continues to be a challenge (International Finance Corporation, 2022b). Since supply chain finance requires real-time supply chain performance data flows, which can indicate fraud potential and whether lenders can conduct sufficient know-your-customer due diligence on buyers, access to reliable statistical data continues to be a major challenge to the expansion of supply chain finance in Africa.

It is therefore essential to develop technological infrastructure and the digitization of payment and invoicing processes, which is a key potential transformative factor of supply chain finance on economies. Digitization can serve as a new enabler to reconceive and develop supply chain finance ecosystems – electronic invoicing, application programming interfaces, blockchain and cloud-based solutions, for example – to improve supply chain efficiency and transparency (International Finance Corporation, 2021b). Many actors in the supply chain finance market contend that mobile technology will be key in developing supply chain finance; therefore, carrying out cross-border trading transactions with mobile platforms will be a game changer (BCR, 2019), especially since Africa is a leader in mobile banking.

Conducive legal and regulatory frameworks

Across the continent, there is a lack of a necessary homogeneous and favourable regulatory and legal framework and infrastructure to ensure the enforcement of creditors' rights in cases of conflicting claims, and to support financial technology, know-your-customer compliance challenges, public registers, electronic invoicing and electronic signatures, for example (BCR, 2022). The legal framework is usually unable to facilitate the use of assets as collateral. This makes the expansion of supply chain finance, or generally credit financing, difficult. To build the foundation of an enabling environment for a well-functioning supply chain finance market, it is necessary to improve and enforce legal and regulatory frameworks, with more homogeneous legal frameworks to facilitate financial investment, aligned with supply chain finance pre-requisites, such as ensuring the application of laws related to dematerialization for digital invoicing, signatures and accounting (International Finance Corporation, 2020). For instance, contractual enforcement is important, as under a supply chain finance programme, the ownership of the receivables could be reassigned to a finance provider, which needs to enforce the contract and apply to court in case of non-repayment. However, this varies across the continent: Ethiopia and Morocco achieved a contract enforcement score of about 63, compared with 40 for Egypt and 28 for Angola (World Bank, 2020). Furthermore, Governments are encouraged to rigorously enforce the law, limiting payment periods to 60–90 days and setting penalties for late payers.

Regulations should be favourable but should adapt to the changing realities of global supply chains, while being vigilant of fraudsters. For example, the rise of supply chain financier Greensill Capital[39] was partly the result of the increasingly stringent regulations and capital restrictions on traditional banks engaging in supply chain finance. However, Greensill and other similar firms did not face levels of regulatory scrutiny that could affect their profit, which facilitated its fraudulent behaviour and eventually its bankruptcy in March 2021. This is a reminder of the need for suitable enabling government regulatory frameworks in Africa and the careful scrutiny of non-bank financial institutions and platforms.

Moreover, some observers argue that some supply chain finance products, such as payables finance, allow firms to obscure debts as they go off-balance sheet after debts to suppliers are settled quickly by a financial intermediary[40] and encourage late payments through a buyer–supplier relationship that draws from strong bargaining power. Recently, however, the Financial Accounting Standards Board in the United States required companies to disclose the terms and size of supply chain finance programmes in financial statement footnotes (Neu Group, 2022). While the level of hidden debt should be concerning for highly indebted firms, especially in countries with more advanced financial development,

---

[39] The bankruptcy of Greensill Capital, a financial services company founded in 2011 and based in Australia and the United Kingdom, was the result of risky large, multi-party supply chain financing transactions and related services (Pickard et al., 2021).

[40] This is the case of Carillion, a British multinational construction and facilities management services company that was liquidated in January 2018. It was a supply chain finance user influenced by Greensill. According to a rating agency, Carillion may have misclassified up to £498 million of debt (Pickard et al., 2021).

this should not be a major concern for firms in certain African countries that are still at the stage of increasing financial inclusion and have barely utilized their credit capacity.

Knowledge and risk perception of local firms

As supply chain finance is a relatively new trend in Africa, promoting it is a lengthy process, as most buyers and sellers still do not fully understand or accept the use of supply chain finance. Indeed, supply chain finance solutions are broadly unknown to both the banking sector and its clients on the continent. As a result, bankers lack adequate skills to effectively implement supply chain finance programmes. In a typical capital market, credit ratings are used by banks and investors to help assess credit and counterparty risks, and thus the risk premium required: A good credit rating allows the company to borrow at a lower interest rate. As such, credit ratings are essential to a company's funding access. Supply chain finance products, such as payables finance, particularly rely on the differential ratings between suppliers and buyers. However, small and medium-sized enterprises are the missing middle in financing. The traditional methods of conducting due diligence required for assigning ratings of borrowings by large companies – meeting with their management, collecting and analysing their financial statements and legal documents, conducting industry research, speaking with their suppliers and customers and making cash-flow projections – are too expensive to be applied to small and medium-sized enterprise loan applicants, who often lack financial records, credit histories and collateral (Alpert and Turlakova, 2014). Research has acknowledged the importance of credit ratings to small and medium-sized enterprise financing, proposing the use of alternative credit-rating methodologies, such as statistical analysis techniques that group small and medium-sized-enterprise customers according to financial health and adjust the interest rates for each group (Yoshino and Taghizadeh-Hesary, 2015; Yoshino et al., 2015), and integrating both the financial and vendor ratings in supply chain finance assessment (Moretto et al., 2019).

Some countries in Africa have also recognized the importance of credit ratings. In Egypt, for example, the financial regulatory authority agreed to allow small and medium-sized credit-rating companies to receive licences to operate in the country in 2019, and in 2022, the regulatory authority began facilitating the expansion of a credit-rating system based on consumer behaviour and non-financial data (Moneim, 2019; Salah, 2022). Credit-rating agencies aimed at enhancing access to affordable formal financial services have been established in a number of African countries, such as Kenya, Mauritius, Nigeria, Rwanda and Zimbabwe. Box 18 illustrates how applying private sector credit-scoring systems within supply chain finance can facilitate access to finance when supplying or buying parts, goods and services in a supply chain.

Box 18
The potential of micro-, small and medium-sized enterprise ratings to improve access to affordable supply chain financing

Ratings of micro, small and medium-sized-enterprises are a little-known concept. They have the ability to trigger financing opportunities and address the ubiquitous funding issues that plague such enterprises in developed and developing countries alike. These ratings broadly represent a large category of underlying ratings (credit, due diligence and environmental, social and governance ratings) that have been designed to facilitate access to finance from traditional and non-traditional sources, and market access as well. The non-traditional application is particularly useful, as the ratings can complement these alternative funding channels well. A pertinent example of this is within the supply chain finance channel, which is often hampered by information asymmetry among key stakeholders.

The primary objectives of small and medium-sized-enterprise-credit ratings are to decrease information asymmetry and properly articulate a business's financial, strategic, operational and economic positioning. Of relevance to the supply chain finance channel is the focus of these ratings on the rated entity's financial health, main suppliers and customers, and strategic advantages. These metrics are of particular importance within a supply chain finance transaction and could be further tailored to include a specific ranking scale that could compute the probability of default for such transactions. The structured finance market linked to supply chain finance providers and related stakeholders is a viable concept in principle; however, events such as the global financial and economic crisis or the collapse of financial services companies highlighted the importance of obtaining comprehensive information on underlying individual credit exposure.

The aforementioned rating concept can provide such information, thereby improving transparency, credit quality and investor confidence. This could have positive effects on the credit quality of overall structured finance issuances, as well as the underlying costs associated with such transactions. The rating concept can be used to rate individual exposures or an entire portfolio of supply chain finance exposures and can thus be an optimal solution to increase the availability and viability of these structured transactions. Furthermore, micro, small and medium-sized enterprises are in some instances excluded from supply chain finance transactions due to the tenuous availability of information on these entities. As such enterprises make up the largest number of businesses within emerging markets, these ratings could then be a viable tool to increase the feasibility of supply chain finance on a wide scale and address the perennial issue of access to finance. Although these ratings have been effective at delivering on their intended mandate, the concept is not widely available.

Sources: UNCTAD, based on Credit Rating Analytics, 2023 (see www.creditratinganalytics.co.za).

Lowering barriers to financing through regional integration of supply chains and innovative foreign exchange hedging

As distribution and logistics channels and infrastructures across Africa remain weak, economies of scale are difficult to achieve, when compared with China, India and countries in South-East Asia. There are still challenges to integration and coordination between supply chains in different markets. Fragmented markets often see extremely competitive markets with price-sensitive buyers, which reduces potential profit and makes supply chain finance products appear too expensive (International Finance Corporation, 2022c). With the implementation of the African Continental Free Trade Area, regional trade is expected to pick up, and networks of raw material inputs, production and distribution will become better integrated, reducing the relative cost of supply chain finance products. Supply chains across Africa will experience much less friction and will benefit from both the flow of physical goods and of finance.

The small and fragmented markets and political risks across the continent have also made it easy for domestic and foreign firms to manage their currency risk. Great currency volatility has contributed to high foreign exchange hedging costs that makes it difficult for companies and financial institutions to conduct businesses or lending operations. For example, the onshore and offshore forward markets of the Moroccan dirham and the non-deliverable forwards of the Egyptian pound, the currencies of two of the largest economies in Africa, were overly expensive (Castell, 2021). In view of such levels of currency fluctuation, some foreign banks might choose not to extend trade finance or finance at critical stages across the supply chains related to businesses in these countries, threatening urgently needed financing for supply chain development in Africa. While it is difficult to address the issue of currency stability within a short period of time, innovative and agile foreign exchange hedging strategies could be useful in overcoming certain currency risk management concerns (Buck, 2019). Given that currencies across the continent have vastly diverse characteristics and are managed differently by central banks with heterogeneous political and economic objectives, it is essential for companies and financial institutions, both in Africa and abroad, to fully understand these dynamics when devising foreign exchange management strategies.

4.4 Conclusion

Supply chain diversification improves supply chain resilience, avoids supply chain disruption, increases demand flows and unlocks supply chain potential. Other benefits include supply chain sustainability and the ability to maximize profitability and assess customer and supplier communities. However, Africa has little involvement in supply chains, and its supply chains are poorly diversified. The main factors constraining its participation in technology-intensive industries and supply chains are inadequate infrastructure capacity, lack of technology and skills, and poor access to liquidity and working capital.

This chapter described how viable technology-enabled services and financing solutions, such as supply chain finance, can provide innovative solutions to increase the competitive position of Africa in upgrading its industries and businesses and developing supply chain linkages to become an attractive destination for multinational companies and ultimately, to achieve supply chain diversification and resilience. In terms of technology-enabled services, most small and medium-sized enterprises in Africa are not digitized and rarely use technology-enabled services for supply chains, preventing them from forming linkages with firms already part of global supply chains. The main technology-enabled services –supply chain connectivity and logistics, supply chain digitization, autonomous supply chains, intellectual property rights and technological devices[41] – are nonexistent in most of Africa.

A wide variety of innovative supply chain finance products has been developed, and it has been shown that supply chain finance plays an important role in economic development for firm competitiveness, finance providers and the economy as a whole. Yet, Africa remains the most underdeveloped supply chain finance market across global regions, including emerging markets such as Asia and Latin America. Apart from the general financial barriers faced by African firms, small and medium-sized enterprises are confronted with a fragmented market, inadequate technological infrastructure, insufficient legal and regulatory frameworks, and inadequate knowledge when engaging in supply chain finance transactions. To overcome barriers and constraints in global supply chains, small and medium-sized enterprises in Africa should reinforce their collaboration with larger domestic companies or foreign companies to create complementary businesses (vertical integration) or similar businesses in other localities (horizontal integration). Building supply chain partnerships will not only give such enterprises the opportunity to integrate domestic or global supply chains, but it will also give them a competitive edge in regional and global markets.

Furthermore, it is essential for African economies to create an enabling environment for the supply chain finance market. Such an environment will feature enhanced legal

---

[41] Examples of technological devices are electronic data interchange, traceability software, and smart services and manufacturing.

and regulatory frameworks that can facilitate financial investment and law enforcement, improved access to business lending markets, as well as increased investment in technological infrastructure, services and digitization. Policymakers may therefore consider technology-enabled services and supply chain finance, along with supporting infrastructures and institutions, including human capital and regulations, to holistically implement policies aimed at diversifying African economies and facilitating their integration in regional and global supply chains.

CHAPTER 5

Conclusions and policy recommendations

5.1 An opportune global situation

The global supply chain disruptions caused by recent crises, such as the 2008–2009 global financial and economic crisis, the COVID-19 pandemic, the war in Ukraine and the resulting global market slowdown, have intensified the need to promote resilience by diversifying supply chain operations across various countries and regions. The risks of concentrating manufacturing and supply chains in a few markets and of sourcing and supplying sector-specific intermediate goods from a few locations can increase exposure to shocks and disruptions in production networks and supply chains. By diversifying or relocating to Africa, supply chain participating companies can source some of the inputs (raw materials and intermediate goods) from the continent, while reducing the costs of transportation and logistics and minimizing risks of supplier delivery delays and other challenges. These disruptions and opportunities for supply chain diversification or relocation come at a time when African economies are growing more sustainably.

African consumer markets are increasingly transitioning towards middle- and low- middle-income status with an appetite for more sophisticated goods and services. Moreover, the need for supply chain diversification emerges at a time when Governments in Africa and regional institutions have reinforced their commitments to push forward their regional integration, diversification and industrialization agendas, which are viable strategies for developing industrial capabilities and creating prosperity on the continent.

The aforementioned global trends and pressures have given many economies and businesses pause for thought; they are now rethinking strategies for recovery, renewal, and resilience. Many multinational companies are looking into how they can reduce their dependence on a single supplier and diversify their supply chains to build resilience to current and future global turbulence. Others have explored a more regionalized approach with greater security, allowing firms to source and produce within their home countries and regions. While some of these evolving scenarios may have far-reaching implications for investment and fixed cost – and some companies may not be able to pay the cost – their potential benefits and impacts far outweigh the cost. This is particularly so for supply chains and industries that are highly exposed to geo-physical events, trade disputes and other global stresses. *The Economic Development in Africa Report 2023: The Potential of Africa to Capture Technology-intensive Global Supply Chains*, focuses on the high-knowledge and technology-intensive industries – automotives, electronics, green energy technology and medical devices – that are vulnerable to global supply chain disruptions, partly due to their extensive geographic footprint. Opportunities for diversification of high-value and technology-intensive supply chains can strengthen resilience, foster the participation of technology-enabled enterprises in supply chains and optimize the participation of Africa in global supply chains.

For a private business, the scenario for a geographic diversification of supply chains or alternative, multi-source suppliers for goods, materials and services will heighten capabilities to absorb shocks related to the shortage of inputs, such as reduced access to raw materials from a conflict-affected country. Other such shocks include the soaring prices of goods (commodity price volatility due to a global crisis, for instance) and transportation restrictions, such as longer lead times for shipping and delivering products, with impacts on inventory and revenue. Moreover, the geographic diversification of supply chains and alternative, multi-source suppliers for goods, materials and services will also help lessen overdependence on a single source or supply chain market. For example, for a given economy in Africa, particularly one with little or no prior participation in global supply chains, supply chain diversification can offer new development paths. The associated development impact of global supply chain diversification includes a unique opportunity for

DIVERSIFIED GLOBAL SUPPLY CHAINS CAN UNLOCK OPPORTUNITIES AND REAP BENEFITS FROM THE AFRICA CONTINENTAL FREE TRADE AREA

Higher productivity

Employment opportunities

Integrated and competitive markets

Through:

Inclusive growth

African companies to integrate global supply chains and reap the benefits of economies of scale, integrated industries, private sector growth, productive and technological capabilities and environment sustainability. In the specific context of Africa, the diversification of supply chains can also unlock regional supply chain opportunities and draw many of the potential benefits of the African Continental Free Trade Area – higher productivity, integrated and competitive markets, employment opportunities and inclusive growth, among others.

5.2 A continent on the move

Africa offers many advantages that can drive or contribute to the diversification of global supply chains for technology-intensive industries. The roles of African countries and firms in supporting supply chain diversification can be identified through various supply chain channels and processes (procurement, production and distribution). African countries have an opportunity to integrate as suppliers of raw materials with utility in the low-carbon transition. For instance, Africa has large reserves of key metals, such as cobalt, that can be used in the production of batteries. Moreover, by taking advantage of its growing and youthful population, Africa can strike the right balance between factors of production, labour and technology, as the younger, more technology-aware and adaptable labour force will contribute to higher productivity in technology-intensive industries and supply chains. Increased employment opportunities in technology-intensive sectors, which in many countries provide higher wages than non-technology-intensive sectors, will clearly contribute to higher income levels and better welfare for consumer-based markets in Africa. A revolving cycle of job creation, improved income, higher consumer expenditure and increased demand for goods and services will communicate the value and attractiveness of African economies and societies to the world and supply chain actors. Learning from the experience of South Africa and other emerging markets, within and outside Africa, in setting cost-efficient distribution and logistics processes, and henceforth securing more investment in adequate hard and soft infrastructure, will be key steps towards leveraging the supply chain potential of Africa.

With the fastest-growing population in the world and the highest concentration of young people, as well as a great potential for e-commerce, African countries will continue to be magnets for consumer markets and products. This has deep implications for supply chains. The trade policies linkage factor in the supply chain is of particular importance, given the momentum provided by the African Continental Free Trade Area and other trade preference regimes. The continent has benefited from preferential trade agreements, such as the African Growth and Opportunity Act, established by the United States, and fostered stronger ties with other emerging and developing economies under South–South cooperation initiatives such as the grouping of States known as BRICS (Brazil, the Russian Federation, India, China and South Africa). Similarly, it is expected that the African Continental Free Trade Area will provide immense benefits for countries in Africa, including employment opportunities and increased intra-Africa trade.

Finally, the low emissions level of countries in Africa and their commitment to emissions reduction are an advantage for diversified and sustainable supply chains. The vast and economically viable green hydrogen potential of the region is an added advantage, as it can lead to lower production and distribution costs. For example, green hydrogen potential could be particularly attractive to energy-intensive industries – steel, chemical, automotive and pharmaceutical industries.

5.3 Market opportunities in dynamic, high-knowledge and technology-intensive supply chains

The role of Africa in technology-intensive global supply chains will be significant in the near future, owing to the rising demand for critical materials. The changing dynamics in technology-intensive supply chains brought about by green technologies provide impetus for African countries to achieve deeper supply chain integration. For instance, an electric car requires about six times the mineral inputs of a conventional car. Africa holds approximately 19 per cent of all the global metal reserves required to make an electric vehicle. Out of those metals, the continent accounts for 48 per cent of world reserves of cobalt and manganese, 80 per cent of phosphate and 92 per cent of platinum. It also accounts for 97 per cent of the world's exports of cobalt and 84 per cent of manganese and at least a fifth of the world's reserves in a dozen minerals that are necessary for the energy transition.

Africa's main natural resource reserves compared to the world's

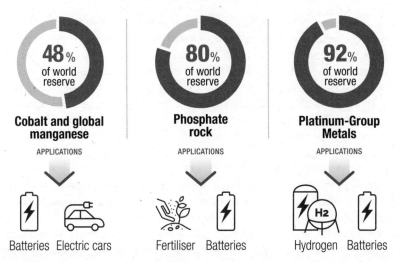

48% of world reserve

Cobalt and global manganese

APPLICATIONS

Batteries   Electric cars

80% of world reserve

Phosphate rock

APPLICATIONS

Fertiliser   Batteries

92% of world reserve

Platinum-Group Metals

APPLICATIONS

Hydrogen   Batteries

The heart of the automotive supply chain lies in the parts and component industry, but countries in Africa provide few inputs to a rising assembling industry. The landscape of various small assembly plants and a few large-scale plants in Morocco and South Africa hinders sufficiently large-scale production to attract automotive parts and component suppliers.

Investment incentives should be aimed at larger-scale or higher-return investment in value added supply chain processes, coupled with access to foreign markets and export promotion. The manufacture of non-specific automotive parts and components (so-called tier 2) is a sound target, as it is often the next processing stage based on the abundant metals in the region sought by a range of manufacturing sectors. Further, it could provide additional incentives to relocate the manufacture of tier 1 products to the continent, as vehicle production is steadily growing. The necessity of firm and harmonized used-vehicle regulations must be emphasized to allow affordability of vehicles without harming the environment or undermining regional production incentives.

There is substantial opportunity to strengthen regional supply chains in the manufacture of mobile telephones, made possible by the abundance of cobalt, manganese and nickel to make cathode precursors in electric vehicle assembly plants. For example, the Democratic Republic of the Congo, which represented about 70 per cent of global cobalt supply in 2020, recently announced plans to produce a battery precursor. Such plans can be viable only if the regional supply of other materials is supported by infrastructure investment.

In Africa, solar panel module assembly is a lucrative area for investment, given the high growth in renewable energy investment stemming from the region's vast potential for solar energy. Between 2000 and 2020, renewables investment in Africa reached an average yearly growth rate of 96 per cent. Yet, the continent still suffers from significant investment gaps, receiving about 2 per cent of global investments in renewable energy. The production of solar photovoltaics is limited, with some initial opportunities materializing in Egypt, Morocco and South Africa. Despite the rapid growth in demand for solar home systems, systems in Africa are tiny compared with their counterparts in the developed countries and require batteries and charge controllers to ensure stable output. Assembly of the solar field, which must be performed at the site, offers significant local manufacturing potential. Moreover, the need for parts, such as ball joints, bearings and cables, whose manufacture and supply do not necessarily require high-knowledge-intensive specialization, but which are used by many industries, opens up opportunities for already established companies to engage in lateral diversification and extend their customer base. For newcomers in the industry, opportunities further down the supply chain, such as project development, advisory services and installation and repair services, provide more feasible opportunities for employment creation.

Medical products and devices require a range of materials and components and could be the next transformative industry in Africa. Despite some progress, African countries recorded a trade deficit in medical devices of $2.6 billion between 2018 and 2020. For instance, South Africa maintains a strong export position as the world's largest exporter of two critical materials utilized in the medical devices sector, titanium and platinum. However, it only accounts for 5 per cent of those materials imported to Africa. Despite the large trade deficit of the sector, there is foreseeable optimism and great potential under the African Continental Free Trade Area, which can play an important part in facilitating exports to the continent by reducing tariffs and infrastructure investments.

These expected benefits will make it easier to import the necessary inputs from countries in Africa and localize production downstream the supply chain. Encouragingly, there have been strong advances in Africa in providing health care and diagnostics to people in rural areas through the implementation of technologies and innovative solutions. Apart from collaboration with multinational companies to access knowledge and technology to manufacture and supply medical products and devices, including generic medicines, attention should be given to increasing the local sourcing and manufacturing of raw materials. For example, in Egypt there are already major local research initiatives under way to produce the most needed active pharmaceutical ingredients.

5.4 Unlocking capabilities to achieve value creation in supply chains

While many factors can drive the participation of African countries in global supply chains, they could embark on a more impactful path by building upon and strengthening domestic and regional supply chains. However, the comparative advantage of African economies and supply chains can be constrained by several factors, including export concentration, inadequate infrastructure capacity and lack of technology and skills, which may negate the potential benefits of relocating parts of global supply chains to the continent. The non-diversification and non-regionalization of supply chains in Africa have the consequence of slowing down the region's economic emergence, causing supply chain disruption and heightening the vulnerability of its economy to external shocks.

In Africa, viable technology-enabled services could overcome constraints faced by supply chains by contributing to their diversification and enabling their resilience and sustainability. Such technology-enabled services include supply chain connectivity and logistics, supply chain digitization, electronic data interchange, supply chain traceability software and smart services. In particular, software supply chains, such as application and infrastructure software, can help develop and deepen supply chain networks (for example, supplier–customer relationships) by facilitating reliable and accurate information flow, effective supply chain governance and streamlined operational processes, including the production and distribution of goods and services.

In Africa, most private sector and small and medium-sized enterprises are not yet close to integrating regional and global supply chain networks. This can be partly explained by their lack of access to finance, technology and market opportunities. Low investment in technology and innovation limits the ability of African firms to tap into these opportunities for global supply chain diversification. Supply chain finance can be a solution for small and medium-sized enterprises. Supply chain finance focuses on working capital financing, bridging the payment time gap between buyers and sellers to manage the cash levels and needs of suppliers in daily operations in an efficient manner and reduce stress to the balance sheet. It facilitates their access to finance by using their accounts receivable – money due to a buyer or another supplier in the short term – as collateral or selling their accounts receivable at a discount to a finance provider. This is particularly beneficial to non-investment grade-rated small and medium-sized enterprises, as it facilitates their access to loans or advanced payments against underlying assets, such as accounts receivable and inventory.

Scaling innovative supply chain finance solutions could significantly improve the access of small and medium-sized enterprises to financing and improve their competitiveness in a well-integrated supply chain that could further increase employment, income, quality of life and economic growth. However, the level of involvement in supply chain finance remains low. In 2022, Africa contributed $2.2 trillion, or 1.9 per cent of the volume of global supply chain finance.[42] Although it remains the most underdeveloped supply chain finance market across major regions, its growth has been accelerating. The supply of supply chain finance continues to be far below continental demands. Addressing the challenges to supply chain finance growth – lack of technological infrastructure, inadequate legal and regulatory frameworks, high credit risk perception and sustainability issues – will unlock the financing capabilities of African firms and optimize their integration in regional and global supply chains.

5.5 Practical policy options for building resilient supply chains

This section provides a policy framework that will help African countries become the next frontier destination for global companies that are reassessing their geographic footprint in supply chains and devising strategies to diversify their supply chain networks to build resilience to global shocks and related economic, market and supply chain pressures and disruptions. The public and private sectors, as well as financial and regional institutions, will need to intensify their efforts in acquiring the necessary skills

---

[42] Defined solely as payables finance.

and capabilities to integrate regional and global supply chains for high-knowledge and technology-intensive industries, such as automotives, electronics, renewable energy technologies and health care. The section also provides strategic and actionable policy recommendations to leverage the potential of other drivers and enablers of supply chain diversification. These include the localization of supply chains, regional market opportunities under the African Continental Free Trade Area, technology transfer and corporate innovation, technology-enabled service provision by small and medium-sized enterprises and supply chain financing for such enterprises.

5.5.1 Automotive industry: Regional vehicle supply chain

To leverage the increasing demand for production, new vehicle-financing mechanisms that favour lower interest rates should be developed. Further, there is a need for harmonized and transparent standards to facilitate vehicle sales and promote the domestic supply of parts and components, as well as aftersales goods and services. The African Continental Free Trade Area can provide a platform to create the essential linkages between car companies and local suppliers that would enable them to access the necessary knowledge and technology to meet car-specific requirements.

Apart from niche markets, new vehicle assembly locations, such as Ghana, Kenya and Nigeria, should consider setting up multi-brand mega-factories, run by contract manufacturers, to achieve higher production volumes, which is necessary to attract parts and components production.

Despite varying motorization rates, all countries in Africa will see an increase in cars and will participate in the supply chain, especially through aftersales repair and maintenance, if not vehicle assembly. There is a need for a more coordinated automotive strategy and regional automotive development plan to avoid the duplication of efforts. For instance, in 2022, the Economic Community of West African States adopted a framework policy on the development of automotive value chains in the region. Such a regional framework could provide the base for a continental framework. The African Continental Free Trade Area has promoted several initiatives, such as the establishment of a fund to develop automotive manufacturing in Africa.

Low-income countries in Africa have lesser productive capacity and face more structural challenges than more affluent ones. They should be given priority in a regionally coordinated automotive strategy to provide fewer complex products. For example, preferential treatment under the African Continental Free Trade Area rules of origin requirements should be considered to allow them more flexibility in production and the sourcing of necessary inputs. Policy incentives designed to encourage localization or local content competitive advantage, which can take the form of a specific percentage of mining products that must be used or transformed locally, would facilitate local market linkages and strengthen the industrial capabilities of domestic firms.

Employment in the automotive industry, especially in retail and repairs, is dominated by the informal sector. However, if people are sufficiently trained, they will be able to work in a formal manner. Governments in Africa should implement strategies that identify the necessary human capital, and technical institutes should work with firms in the automotive sector to provide apprenticeships for students.

Increased automation requires gradually moving from simple engineering to more complex product development based on advanced research and development. African countries, in collaboration with the private sector, could provide funding for technical Institutes that specialize in the automotive sector and adapt curriculums to reflect new developments in technology, such as electric vehicles. For instance, the Centre of Excellence in Electric and Industrial Welding Technologies of Sunyani Technical University in Ghana is supported by the Ghana National Gas Company, which aims to build capacity in the niche area of electrical engineering for the manufacture of electric vehicles.

5.5.2 Electronics: Mobile telephone supply chain

Resource-rich countries, such as the Democratic Republic of the Congo, can leverage their cobalt reserves to promote the local assembly and manufacture of mobile telephones by setting up special economic zones and nurturing more conducive environments for foreign and domestic investment.

Addressing legacy environmental, social and governance issues, such as raw materials transparency, is important to ensure the sector's sustainable development. Strategies and mechanisms that foster the adoption of circular supply chains, which consist in recycling and remanufacturing products and components instead of discarding them, will increase supply chain sustainability and attract sustainable investments to the sector.

The enforcement of decent labour laws is necessary in an assembly industry that has a higher share of women, as they are often more vulnerable to exploitation and health risks than men. The private sector should be encouraged to be more responsible by introducing Sustainable Development Goal indicators in investment agreements and ensure readiness for jurisdictions to adopt sustainability disclosure standards set by the recently established International Sustainability Standards Board.

A one-stop joint venture partner to coordinate local investment and implementation could help reduce regulatory red tape, de-risk projects and facilitate a well-structured knowledge transfer between multinational corporations and local companies.

Investing in skills development and technical training would help create a skilled workforce for the mobile telephone industry. Countries that already engage in some mobile telephone assembly should develop research facilities to invest in next-generation battery technology.

5.5.3 Renewable energy technologies: Solar panel supply chain

Given that investment in Africa is currently low, in particular with regard to renewable energy, demand for solar panels should be stimulated, for example, through structured renewable energy procurement programmes.

A key challenge for companies in the solar panel industry concerns both financial and organizational capability. Local advisory services can help target customers' individual needs and provide guidance for the implementation of large-scale projects.

Not all African countries may be in a position to produce solar panels for their markets, but the additional employment generated by advisory, installation and repair services can be substantial and should receive greater attention. Local entrepreneurs possess a keen awareness of local needs, such as language and culture. This is also true in regard to other renewable energy technologies.

There is a need for intensified collaboration to enhance knowledge and technology transfer. This could take the form of mentoring programmes, in which more established and successful companies can share information and benefit from formal and informal intra-industry exchanges that are necessary for continuous learning.

Most funding from development finance institutions is directed towards large-scale projects, which often restricts or excludes the participation of local companies. These institutions should ensure the inclusivity of local companies and consider local content requirements in tender procedures.

With regard to training and skills development, training in solar photovoltaic projects should be provided for commercial banks, as it is important to enhance understanding of complex projects and facilitate financing.

5.5.4 Health care industry: Pharmaceutical product and medical devices supply chain

Harmonized regulation and product registration is essential to facilitate market access and economies of scale in production. The African Medicines Regulatory Harmonization programme, for example, has achieved a reduction in marketing-approval time but more effort is needed to achieve a regional certification process.

To increase demand and access to medicine, pooled procurement and financing should be further promoted through programmes, such as the Africa Medical Equipment Facility, created by the International Finance Corporation, as well as platforms, such as the Africa Medical Supplies Platform, an online portal that enables the delivery of medical supplies to Governments in Africa. The centralized pooled procurement mechanism of the African Continental Free Trade Area Pharmaceutical Initiative, launched by the United Nations, Economic Commission for Africa, is another important example.

Cluster formation can be beneficial to ensuring access to electricity, water and other key infrastructure for manufacturing activities, including pharmaceutical operations across the continent. An industrial cluster, such as Medicine City, Egypt, has been a common model of pharmaceutical sector development in many emerging economies to provide an attractive environment for investment. One of the focuses when building an industrial cluster should be on increasing the local sourcing and manufacturing of raw materials.

The limited involvement of African countries in upstream research and development, production of intermediate goods and active pharmaceutical ingredients requires the development of an innovation ecosystem. This should be promoted at the regional level through a continental-wide effort, which can create economies of scale, especially for low-income countries.

In light of the challenges of multilateral negotiations on technology transfer, countries should collaborate with companies to access knowledge and technology, as well as industrial design information. For instance, the Government of Egypt has encouraged local companies to establish partnerships and joint ventures with multinational companies to enter the domestic market, in exchange for technology transfer and intellectual property. South–South cooperation (for instance, as shown by the examples of.India–Egypt and India–Nigeria technology transfer) is also important.

5.5.5 Mining industry

Local content requirements and supplier programmes will not sufficiently promote domestic firms if the initial challenges of these firms – lack of electricity and access to finance, for example – are not tackled. Supply chain finance and targeted support to these companies can be negotiated ex-ante with mining companies before granting licences.

African countries should receive support in negotiating and renegotiating contracts to ensure fair value from the extractive industries.

The Sustainable Development Licence to Operate, a holistic multilevel and multi-stakeholder governance framework aimed at enhancing the contribution of the mining sector to sustainable development, could provide a framework for negotiations and re-negotiations.

A regionally coordinated mining policy could ensure that disadvantaged countries can also supply other inputs, for example, one that provides a common fund covering the additional cost of transporting inputs from countries with weak transport infrastructure to where the activity is taking place. This example can be found in the Regional Mining Vision of the Southern African Development Community. In addition, it is recommended that the implementation of the Africa Mining Vision be stepped up and enhanced.

Governments, private companies and development partners in Africa should encourage recycling and circular economy practices to minimize environmental impact and reduce the demand for virgin materials. More research and development is necessary to tailor the investment needs relating to materials and industries.

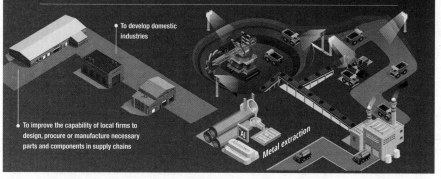

BETTER MINING CONTRACTS AND EXPLORATION LICENSES FOR METALS USED IN HIGH-TECHNOLOGY PRODUCTS AND SUPPLY CHAINS ARE NEEDED

• To develop domestic industries

• To improve the capability of local firms to design, procure or manufacture necessary parts and components in supply chains

AI

Metal extraction

5.5.6 Localization of supply chains

The future of supply chain transformation in Africa, especially in technology-intensive industries such as automotives, electronics, renewable energy and pharmaceuticals, will require viable options for creating domestic supply chains that are reliant and resilient. This can be achieved through localized supply chains, supplier development programmes and local procurement requirements. The following policy and operational practices are recommended:

- As inconsistency within local content requirements or the lack of sound implementation can introduce unnecessary rigidities when sourcing inputs, other requirements, such as those relating to export performance, transfer of knowledge and technology to local firms, and employment and skills creation, should be favoured.

- Industrial policies relating to science and technology, human capital development, infrastructure, capacity-building and marketing tools should prioritize local sourcing.

- Domestic companies should be given structured support, with a view to increasing their supply to the mining industry, access to technology and structured finance, and technical mentorship.

- Governments in Africa should work with foreign investors and other partners on innovative supplier development programmes. Such programmes can be beneficial, as they can help firms obtain relevant international certifications, link small and medium-sized firms to lead firms, provide consultancy, establish a forum for lead firms to disclose sourcing needs and develop links for technology transfer to small and medium-sized enterprises.

- Targeted public procurement programmes should be reserved for local suppliers, based on a thorough assessment of goods and services.

- To create incentives for large companies to partner with local enterprises, investment promotion agencies could set up vendor development programmes and create linkages between foreign firms and local suppliers, for which the Singapore Economic Development Board is a good model.

- Active localization strategies should be coupled with corporate social responsibility practices. For example, the Global Reporting Initiative states that multinational enterprises should report on how much they buy locally. Similarly, corporate social responsibility guidelines issued by the Organisation for Economic Co-operation and Development recommend human capital formation and encourage local capacity-building through close collaboration with local communities.

5.5.7 Regional market opportunities offered by the African Continental Free Trade Area

The implementation of the African Continental Free Trade Area provides momentum to draw greater attention towards more high-technology sectors that create local value addition and employment opportunities. As it also aims to strengthen national and regional competitiveness by facilitating regional economic performance and industrial innovation, the African Continental Free Trade Area will help enhance regional supply chain capabilities and contribute to the economic development of supply chain hubs on the continent. To leverage such opportunities, the following policy and operational practices are recommended:

- National and regional development plans should factor in and focus on sectors they would like to target. For instance, national implementation plans under the African Continental Free Trade Area focus on key strategic sectors that can provide maximum benefits through participation in the continental trade agreement.

- While there are private sector strategies in place throughout Africa for the automotive and pharmaceutical industries, the African Continental Free Trade Area Secretariat may consider developing similar strategies for mobile telephone assembly, renewable energy technologies and medical devices, owing to the local linkages of these sectors and their importance for environmental and social development.

- African countries should receive support from international organizations to identify their individual potential and niche areas in these technology-intensive supply chains.

5.5.8 A push for technology and innovation in supply chain transformation

The use of new technologies and digital solutions can provide comprehensive supply chain visibility and transparency and facilitate the ability of companies participating in supply chains to respond more effectively to shifting global market dynamics. Identifying the potential of individual countries in technology-intensive supply chains; assessing the technology and digital readiness of African firms; facilitating technology transfer, reverse engineering and domestic innovation; and developing and increasing the use of digital technology in supply chain processes and interactions, will be important for transforming supply chains in Africa. The following policy and operational practices are recommended:

- Better data and information sharing would attract international investors to more countries in Africa, as multinational companies also require supply chain information to be agile and to comply with environmental, social and governance regulations.

- The use of digital solutions, such as the Africa Medical Supplies Platform and the Green Token blockchain solution offered by the company System Analysis Programme Development, also known as SAP, and electronic data interchange technology in general, can facilitate linkages and help obtain supply chain information.

- Automated product identification, for instance, through electromagnetic fields, also helps identify and track objects, and can, for instance, reduce trade in counterfeit and imitated drugs.

- Corporate social responsibility practices should be fostered to facilitate technology transfer, research and development and access to production knowledge.

- Along with sound legal frameworks, good political stability and low corruption levels, the implementation of strong intellectual property rights can attract foreign investment in high-technology- and research-and-development-intensive supply chains and promote innovation to provide products tailored to meet the needs of Africa.

- The Protocol on Intellectual Property Rights for the African Continental Free Trade Area promises to overcome divergent and overlapping regional regulations relating to such rights. Two intellectual property organizations in Africa, namely the African Intellectual Property Organization and the African Regional Intellectual Property Organization, can be leveraged to implement a robust continental regime.

- There is a need to strengthen investment facilitation services through the streamlining and digitization of administrative processes, making them transparent and accessible to all investors.

- Few investment promotion agencies have concrete road maps for the promotion of investment in the Sustainable Development Goals (SDGs or Goals). Development partners should support investment promotion agencies on how to mainstream the SDGs into their investment promotion work. Costa Rica offers the example of a country whose investment promotion agency has identified priority Goals and reports routinely on these.

5.5.9 Technology-enabled service provision by small and medium-sized enterprises and supply chain financing for such enterprises

Small and medium-sized enterprises can be strategic sources and key drivers of global supply chain diversification and supply chain transformation in Africa. Adopting digital solutions and models to their business performance, operating in a conducive technology-based supply chain environment and tapping into novel finance tools to increase the participation of small and medium-sized enterprises in supply chains will be necessary for those sector enterprises seeking to expand their markets and integrate supply chains. These enterprises could also reinforce their collaboration with larger firms or supply chain participating companies by creating complementary businesses (vertical integration) or creating similar businesses in other locations (horizontal integration). Large companies should seek to integrate, whether vertically or horizontally, start-ups and small and medium-sized enterprises to diversify and regionalize their supply chains. This is particularly important to enhance regional integration by means of the African Continental Free Trade Area. The following policy and operational practices are recommended:

- The adoption of digital technologies could facilitate the participation of small and medium-sized enterprises in supply chains and linkages with firms that already belong to global supply chains. The integration of technological services through supply chain digitization enhances the visibility of small and medium-sized enterprises throughout the world, thus attracting large companies to work with them.

- New technologies, such as digital invoicing, are particularly important to improve supply chain transparency, enable real-time data capture to facilitate know-your-customer due diligence on buyers and suppliers, lower financing risks and prevent fraud.

- There is a need for technology-led solutions, especially for payments systems. Digitization will serve as a new enabler to reconceiving and developing trade finance ecosystems, such as electronic invoicing, application programming interfaces, blockchain, cloud-based solutions and software as a service, to improve supply chain efficiency and transparency. Vertical and horizontal integration, supported by viable technology-enabled services, can lead to supply chain diversification and regionalization. Collaboration and vertical or horizontal integration cannot perform effectively without good coordination, requiring smart currencies and factories, real-time data and the Internet of things.

- Countries in Africa should consider building an enabling environment for a well-functioning, technology-enabled supply chain finance market by improving and enforcing legal and regulatory frameworks. This requires greater homogeneity of legal frameworks to facilitate financial investment across borders. Standards of the regulatory framework should be aligned with supply chain finance prerequisites, such as ensuring the application of laws related to contract enforcement and dematerialization for digital invoicing, signatures and accounting.

- The public and private sectors should play a leading role in educating potential market players across the public, financial, corporate and entrepreneurial sectors, presenting supply chain finance solutions to manage cash flow and deal effectively with late payments, long payment terms and working capital liquidity squeeze.

- Innovative and custom-made credit assessment and financing tools for African firms could help manage and change the risk perception of potential market players. Owing to the disproportionately high-risk perception of African firms, Governments could take part in the guaranteed schemes for pre-shipment loans and sales order advances for small and medium-sized enterprises. Other possibilities include sustainable supply chain finance, which includes working capital loans with environmental, social and governance demands on products sold, and asset financing loans bridging order deposits with environmental, social and governance requirements on equipment procurement.

5.5.10 How UNCTAD can support the implementation of these policy recommendations

To leverage and benefit from supply chain opportunities provided by recent global disruptions and emerging challenges, Governments in Africa can count on the research and policy analysis, technical cooperation and consensus-building support of UNCTAD. As the focal point of the United Nations for the integrated treatment of trade and development and interrelated issues in the areas of finance, investment, technology and sustainable development, UNCTAD provides ahead-of-the-curve and innovative analysis on tailored policy and frameworks that could help Governments in Africa and their stakeholders develop improved capabilities for accelerated industrialization and enhanced participation in global markets and supply chains.

Building upon its expertise and of experience providing on-the-ground technical assistance and innovative capacity-building tools, UNCTAD could develop, jointly with Governments in Africa and other relevant stakeholders, bespoke training programmes and tools that can assist industry leaders and small and medium-sized enterprises in understanding the opportunities to integrate global supply chains through increased access to new technologies, financing and re-skilling programmes. Such technical assistance and training programmes will also strengthen the ability of small and medium-sized enterprises to better mitigate some of the risks that come with access to new markets and potential exposure to external shocks. By providing a forum for open and constructive dialogue for policymakers, financiers and development partners, UNCTAD could work with Governments in Africa, domestic and global industry leaders, and domestic and foreign investors to facilitate, streamline and increase visibility, transparency and impact in overall supply chain processes, from adopting policies and standards that would encourage more local content requirements, to strengthening local capabilities for innovating, producing and delivering goods and services across regional and global supply chains.

References

Abdelgafar B, Thorsteinsdóttir H, Quach U, Singer, PA and Daar, AS (2004). The emergence of Egyptian biotechnology from generics. Nature Biotechnology. 22(12):CD25–DC30. Supplement.

Achilles (2014). The role of customers in the supply chain. Available at www.achilles.com/industry-insights/the-role-of-customers-in-the-supply-chain/ (accessed 4 May 2023).

Ackah-Baidoo P (2020). Implementing local content under the Africa Mining Vision: An achievable outcome? *Canadian Journal of Development Studies/Revue Canadienne d'études du Développement*. 41:486–503.

Adobor H and McMullen R (2007). Supplier diversity and supply chain management: A strategic approach. *Business Horizons*. 50(3):219–229.

Africa Centre for Energy Policy (2020). Reviving the sleepy vision: An evaluation of the implementation status of the Africa Mining Vision. Available at www.jstor.org/stable/pdf/resrep31231.pdf.

African Continental Free Trade Area (2023). The automotive fund. Available at https://au-afcfta.org/operational-instruments/the-automotive-fund (accessed 11 June 2023).

African Development Bank (2011). The Middle of the Pyramid: Dynamics of the Middle Class in Africa. Market Brief. April 20, 2011. Available at www.afdb.org.

African Development Bank (2020). Trade finance in Africa: Trends over the past decade and opportunities ahead. Policy Research Document 3. Available at www.afdb.org/en/documents/trade-finance-africa-trends-over-past-decade-and-opportunities-ahead (accessed 30 June 2023).

African Development Bank (2022a). A new frontier for [the] African pharmaceutical manufacturing industry. 15 April.

African Development Bank (2022b). African Development Bank's Board approves landmark institution: Establishment of African Pharmaceutical Technology Foundation to transform Africa's pharmaceutical industry. 27 June.

African Development Bank (2023). African Development Bank Group —Projects and operations—Financial products. Available at www.afdb.org/en/projects-and-operations/financial-products/african-development-bank (accessed 4 May 2023).

African Export–Import Bank (n.d.). Trade finance programmes. Available at www.afreximbank.com/products-services/our-key-services/trade-project-financing/trade-finance-programs/ (accessed 4 May 2023).

African Export–Import Bank (2017). *Contemporary Issues in African Trade and Trade Finance*. 3(1). Cairo.

African Export–Import Bank (2021). Afreximbank [African Export–Import Bank] supports ARSO [African Organisation for Standardization] in the harmonization of African automotive standards. 6 August.

African Union (2009). Africa Mining Vision. February 2009. Available at https://au.int/sites/default/files/documents/30995-doc-africa_mining_vision_english_1.pdf.

African Union (2012). Decisions, resolution and declarations. Assembly of the Union. Eighteenth Ordinary Session, 29–30 January 2012, Addis Ababa. Available at https://au.int/sites/default/files/decisions/9649-assembly_au_dec_391_-_415_xviii_e.pdf (accessed 4 May 2023).

African Union (2022). High-Level Forum on Financing Energy Transition in Africa at COP27 [Conference of the Parties on its twenty-seventh session, Sharm el-Sheikh, Egypt, 6–20 November 2022]. 14 November

African Union Commission and Organisation for Economic Co-operation and Development (2022). *Africa's Development Dynamics 2022: Regional Value Chains for a Sustainable Recovery*. African Union Commission, Addis Ababa and Organisation for Economic Co-operation and Development Publishing, Paris.

Agarwal P, Black A, Lemma A, Mkhabela V and Stuart J (2022). The African Continental Free Trade Area and the automotive value chain. Briefing Report. Overseas Development Institute.

Agiba AM (2022). Localization of pharmaceutical manufacturing in Egypt after the outbreak of COVID-19: Part one. The Pharma Letter. 8 August.

Alami A (2021). How Morocco went big on solar energy. British Broadcasting Corporation. 19 November.

Albaladejo M, Altenburg T, Fokeer S, Wenck N and Schwager P (2022). Green hydrogen: Fuelling industrial development for a clean and sustainable future. Industrial Analytics Platform. United Nations Industrial Development Organization.

Allied Market Research (2022). *Supply Chain Finance Market Research, 2031*. Available at www.alliedmarketresearch.com/supply-chain-finance-market-A08187 (accessed 1 July 2023).

Alpert A and Turlakova M (2014). Scoring for access: Emerging evidence on the impact of credit scoring on SME[small and medium-sized enterprise] lending. Innovations for Poverty Action.

Altenburg T and Assmann C, eds. (2017). *Green Industrial Policy: Concept, Policies, Country Experiences*. United Nations Environment Programme and German Development Institute. Geneva and Bonn.

Altman S and Bastian CR (2022). DHL Global Connectedness Index 2020. DHL.

Andreoni A and Torreggiani S (2020). Mining equipment industry in South Africa: Global context, industrial ecosystem and pathways for feasible sectoral reform. Centre for Competition, Regulation and Economic Development Report for Masterplan. Centre for Competition, Regulation and Economic Development Working Paper 3/2020. University of Johannesburg, South Africa.

Andreoni A, Kaziboni L and Roberts S (2021). Metals, machinery, and mining equipment industries in South Africa: The relationship between power, governance and technological capabilities. In: Andreoni A, Mondliwa P, Roberts S and Tregenna F, eds. *Structural Transformation in South Africa: The Challenges of Inclusive Industrial Development in a Middle-Income Country*. Oxford University Press. Oxford, United Kingdom: 53–77.

Argus Media (2022). Central Africa calls for battery value chain creation. 17 May.

Arima A (2022). Titanium: The metal of choice for medical devices. *Medical Device News Magazine*. 9 November.

Asian Development Bank (n.d.). Gender Action Plan. Available at www.adb.org/sites/default/files/project-documents/46920/46920-015-gap-en.pdf (accessed 5 May 2023).

Asian Development Bank (2023). What trade policy and aid for trade support for Cambodia after LDC [least development country] graduation? National Research and Policy Dialogue Workshop. 15 and 16 March. Phnom Penh.

Asian Development Bank (2023). Trade and Supply Chain Finance Programme. Available at www.adb.org/what-we-do/trade-supply-chain-finance-program/main (accessed 27 June 2023).

Auboin M, Smythe H and Teh R (2016). Supply chain finance and SMEs [small and medium-sized enterprises]: Evidence from international factoring data. Centre for Economic Studies and Leibniz Institute for Economic Research at the University of Munich Working Paper No. 6039.

Auktor G (2022). The opportunities and challenges of industry 4.0 for industrial development: A case study of Morocco's automotive and garment sectors. Discussion Paper 2/2022. German Development Institute.

Automotive News Europe (2020). VW [Volkswagen], Nissan chase African new-car market where financing is rare. 13 January.

Automotive News Europe (2022). Stellantis to double production capacity in Morocco, adds new small cars. 10 November.

Avenyo EK and Tregenna F (2022). Greening manufacturing: Technology intensity and carbon dioxide emissions in developing countries. Applied Energy, 324:119726.

Baldock D (2022). Designing the perfect supply chain: Is regionalization the answer? Escatec. 24 March.

Bam W and De Bruyne K (2019). Improving industrial policy Intervention: The Case of steel in South Africa. The Journal of Development Studies. 55(11):2460–2475.

Bam W, De Bruyne K and Laing M (2021). The IO–PS [input–output product space] in the context of GVC [global value chain]-related policymaking: The case of the South African automotive industry. Journal of International Business Policy. 4:410–432.

Barnes J, Black A and Techakanont K (2017). Industrial policy, multinational strategy and domestic capability: A comparative analysis of the development of South Africa's and Thailand's automotive industries. The European Journal of Development Research. 29(1):37–53.

Barroso AP, Machado VH, Barros AR and Cruz Machado V (2010). Toward a resilient supply chain with supply disturbances. *2010 IEEE [Institute of Electrical and Electronics Engineers] International Conference on Industrial Engineering and Engineering Management.* Macao, China, 7–10 December 2010. IEEE Computer Society. 245–249.

Barton J (2021). Mobile phones to be assembled in DRC [the Democratic Republic of the Congo] for first time. Developing Telecoms. 17 November.

BCR (2019). *World Supply Chain Finance Report 2019.* BCR Publishing. Bromley, Kent, United Kingdom.

BCR (2022). *World Supply Chain Finance Report 2022.* BCR Publishing. Bromley, Kent, United Kingdom.

BCR (2023). *World Supply Chain Finance Report 2023.* BCR Publishing. Bromley, Kent, United Kingdom.

Berlemann M and Wesselhöft JE (2014). Estimating aggregate capital stocks using the perpetual inventory method: A survey of previous implementations and new empirical evidence for 103 countries. *Review of Economics.* 65(1):1–34.

Besherati N and MacFeely S (2019). Defining and quantifying South–South cooperation. Research Paper No. 30. UNCTAD.

BFSI Network (2021). Supply Chain Finance: Outlook 2021 and Trends 2022. Elets BFSI. Available at https://bfsi.eletsonline.com/supply-chain-finance-outlook-2021-and-trends-2022/

Bhorat H, Kimani ME, Lappeman J and Egan P (2023). Characterization, definition and measurement issues of the middle class in sub-Saharan Africa. *Development Southern Africa.* 40(1):39–56.

Black A and McLennan T (2016). The last frontier: Prospects and policies for the automotive industry in Africa. *International Journal of Automotive Technology and Management.* 16(2):193–220.

bladi.net. 2023. Fabriquée au Maroc, la Citroën Ami est la plus vendue en Espagne en 2022. 7 January.

Bloomberg Finance (2021). *The Cost of Producing Battery Precursors in the DRC [Democratic Republic of the Congo].*

Boyadzhieva Y (2021). Africell pilots feature phone production in DRC [the Democratic Republic of the Congo]. Mobile World Live. 18 November.

Brandon-Jones E, Squire B, Autry CW and Petersen KJ (2014). A contingent resource-based perspective of supply chain resilience and robustness. *Journal of Supply Chain Management*. 50(3):55–73.

Buck G (2019). Africa's costly hedges prompt alternative solutions. EuroFinance. *The Economist Newspaper*. 19 March.

Business Insider Africa (2023). High expectations for Dangote Sinotruck as the company boasts a production capacity of 10,000 units per year. 10 February.

Business Today Egypt (2021). EDA [Egyptian Drug Authority] supports local pharma industry with new export subsidy initiative. 10 February.

Capgemini (2021). The value of a blockchain-enabled supply chain. Available at www.capgemini.com/se-en/wp-content/uploads/sites/20/2022/11/The-value-of-a-blockchain-enabled-supply-chain-2.pdf.

Carrière-Swallow Y, Deb P, Furceri D, Jiménez D and Ostry JD (2022). Shipping costs and inflation. International Monetary Fund Working Papers. WP/22/61.

Carvalho H, Duarte S and Cruz-Machado V (2011). Lean, agile, resilient and green: divergencies and synergies. *International Journal of Lean Six Sigma*. 2(2):151–179.

Castell H (2021). African risks become harder to read. EuroFinance. *The Economist Newspaper*. 15 March.

Chauffour J-P and Maur J-C, eds. (2011). *Preferential Trade Agreement Policies for Development: A Handbook*. World Bank. Washington, D.C.

Christensen CM, Dillon K and Ojomo E (2019). *The Prosperity Paradox: How Innovation Can Lift Nations Out of Poverty*. Harper Business. New York.

Christopher M and Peck H (2004). Building the resilient supply chain. *The International Journal of Logistics Management*. 15(2):1–14.

Christopher PM and Rutherford C (2004). Creating supply chain resilience through Agile Six Sigma. June–August. Criticaleye.net.

Cirera X, Comin D, Cruz M and Lee KM (2021). Firm-level adoption of technologies in Senegal. Policy Research Working Paper No. 9657. World Bank Group.

Colling A (2021). Socioeconomic issues threaten South Africa's supply chain. Crisis24. 24 August.

Conzade J, Engel H, Kendall A and Pais G (2022). Power to move: Accelerating the electric transport transition in sub-Saharan Africa. McKinsey and Company. 23 February.

Credit Rating Analytics (2023). Available at www.creditratinganalytics.co.za/ (accessed 8 May 2023).

Cunningham (2021). It's time to take the tech out of technology. Digit News. 25 June.

Dahir AL (2018). A low-profile, Chinese handset maker has taken over Africa's mobile market. Quartz. 30 August.

Daly T (2021). CATL [Contemporary Amperex Technology] takes stake in China Moly cobalt mine for $137.5 million. Reuters. 11 April.

Deloitte (2017b). Supply chain's role in M and A [mergers and acquisitions]: Achieving value creating through supply chain.

Deloitte (2017a). Using blockchain to drive supply chain innovation.

Deloitte (2021). *2021 Global Automotive Supplier Study. Navigating Disruption in the Supply Chain*. Deloitte.

Edrawsoft (2023). Value Chain vs. Supply Chain: Explained with Examples. Available at www.edrawmax.com

Egypt (2016). Sustainable Development Strategy: Egypt's Vision 2030. Ministry of Planning, Monitoring and Administrative Reform. Available at www.mped.gov.eg/en.

Egypt (2021a). Pharmaceutical and medical industries. General Authority for Investment and Free Zones. Available at www.investinegypt.gov.eg/english/pages/sector. aspx?SectorId=96#:~:text=The%20Egyptian%20pharmaceutical%20market%20 is,in%20addition%20to%20local%20companies (accessed 3 July 2023).

Egypt (2021b). President El-Sisi inaugurates Gypto Pharma in Khanka. 1 April. Available at /www.presidency.eg/en

El Fihri S, Omary O, Nielsen J, Dupoux P and Bour A (2021). What's new and next for M and A [mergers and acquisitions] in Africa. Boston Consulting Group. 12 Janaury.

El Mataoui R, Abail M and Lahjouji F (2019). L'intégration du secteur automobile dans le tissu productif marocain: Analyse input–output. In: Chatri A, ed. *Ouverture, productivité et croissance économique au Maroc*. Laboratoire d'Économie Appliquée and Policy Centre for the New South. Rabat:105–116.

Elshaarawy R and Ezzat RA (2022). Global value chains, financial constraints and innovation. *Small Business Economics*. Article not assigned to an issue.

Erol O, Sauser BJ and Mansouri M (2010). A framework for investigation into extended enterprise resilience. *Enterprise Information Systems*. 4(2):111–136.

European Investment Bank (2022). New study confirms €1 trillion Africa's extraordinary green hydrogen potential. 21 December.

Eyewitness News (2021). DR [Democratic Republic of the] Congo seeks $58 billion to rebuild industry. 27 August.

Factors Chain International [FCI] (2022). *FCI [Factors Chain International] Annual Review* 2022. Amsterdam. Available at https://fci.nl/en/media/29926/download#:~:text=Factoring%20volumes%20grew%20in%20CEE,2021%2C%20representing%2018%25%20growth (accessed 8 May 2023).

fDi Markets database. Available at www.fDimarkets.com.

fDi Intelligence Magazine (2021). Global Free Zones of the Year awards 2021: Winners. *Financial Times*. 14 October. Available at www.fdiintelligence.com.

Financial Times (2023). Apple's manufacturing shift to India hits stumbling blocks. 14 February.

Fofaria A (2020). The emerging wave of local content regulations in the African mining sector. Pinset Masons. 29 October. Available at www.pinsentmasons.com/out-law/analysis/the-emerging-wave-of-local-content-regulations-in-the-african-mining-sector (accessed 3 July 2023).

Fortune Business Insights (2020). Electric Vehicle Market Size, Share and COVID-19 Impact Analysis, by Vehicle Type (Passenger Car and Commercial Vehicle), by Type

(Battery Electric Vehicle, Plug-in Hybrid Electric Vehicle and Hybrid Electric Vehicle) and Regional Forecasts, 2021–2028.

Gandhi S (2022). Leveraging new tech[nology] to boost supply chain resilience. *Harvard Business Review*. 26 October.

Garcia MH (2022). Egypt outpacing Middle East and Africa's top markets. Pharma Boardroom. 11 May.

Garnizova E and Khorana S (2021). What's the impact of investing in trade and supply chain finance? British International Investment. Insight Series: Evidence Review. Impact Study No. 023. Available at https://assets.bii.co.uk/wp-content/uploads/2021/09/27154905/Whats-the-impact-of-investing-in-TSCF.pdf.

Gaur V and Gaiha A (2020). Building a transparent supply chain: Blockchain can enhance trust, efficiency and speed. *Harvard Business Review*. May–June 2020. Available at https://hbr.org/2020/05/building-a-transparent-supply-chain (accessed 27 June 2023).

Ghana News Agency (2023). Government to roll out new vehicle financing scheme for "ordinary" Ghanians. 12 January.

Goering K, Kelly R and Mellors N (2018). The next horizon for industrial manufacturing: Adopting disruptive digital technologies in making and delivering. McKinsey and Company. 15 November.

Grossman GM and Helpman E (2005). Outsourcing in a global economy. *The Review of Economic Studies*. 72(1):135–159.

GSM [Global System for Mobile Communications] Association (2019). 618 active tech hubs: The backbone of Africa's tech ecosystem. Mobile for development. 10 July.

Gupta P (2022). India seizes opportunities in African health care. British Broadcasting Corporation. 2 December.

Hahn T and Vidican-Auktor G (2017). The effectiveness of Morocco's industrial policy in promoting a national automotive industry. Discussion Paper 27/2017. German Development Institute. Bonn.

Hayes A (2022). Vertical integration explained: How it works, with types and examples. Investopedia. 26 August.

Hendricks IN (2015). Africa: A hub for innovation in medical diagnostic solutions. 21 October. Africa Business.

Hendriwardani M and Ramdoo I (2022). Critical minerals: A primer. Intergovernmental Forum on Mining, Minerals, Metals and Sustainable Development.

Herath G (2015). Supply-chain finance: The emergence of a new competitive landscape. McKinsey on Payments. 8(22):10–16.

Hoberg, K. and Alicke, K. (2014). 5 Lessons for Supply Chains from the Financial Crisis. McKinsey & Company.

Honke J and Skender L (2022). Cobalt as a 'conflict mineral'? On the opportunities and limits of new supply chain laws. Infraglob. 20 December. Available at https://infraglob.eu/2022/12/20/cobalt-as-conflict-mineral-on-the-opportunities-and-limits-of-new-supply-chain-laws/ (accessed 3 July 2023).

Horigoshi A, Custer S, Burgess B, Marshall K, Choo V, Andrzejewski K and Dumont E (2022). *Delivering the Belt and Road: Decoding the Supply of and Demand for Chinese Overseas Development Projects*. AidData at William and Mary. Williamsburg, Virginia, United States.

Ing LY and Losari JJ (2022). Local content requirements: Assessment from investment law. Economic Research Institute for the Association of Southeast Asian Nations and East Asia Discussion Paper No. 416. Jakarta.

International Centre for Research on Women and Kenya Association of Manufacturers (2020). Women in Manufacturing: Mainstreaming Gender and Inclusion. Nairobi.

International Chamber of Commerce, Bankers Association for Finance and Trade, Euro Banking Association, Factors Chain International and International Trade and Forfaiting Association (2016). Standard definitions for techniques of supply chain finance. Global Supply Chain Finance Forum. 9 January.

International Diabetes Federation (2021). Diabetes atlas. Available at https://diabetesatlas.org/data/en/ (accessed 13 June 2023).

International Energy Agency (2019). Morocco renewable energy target 2030. 10 October.

International Energy Agency (2022a). *The Role of Critical Minerals in Clean Energy Transitions*. World Energy Outlook Special Report. France.

International Energy Agency (2022b). *Special Report on Solar PV [Photovoltaic] Global Supply Chains*. Available at https://iea.blob.core.windows.net/assets/2d18437f-211d-4504-beeb-570c4d139e25/SpecialReportonSolarPVGlobalSupplyChains.pdf.

International Finance Corporation (2014). *Supply Chain Finance: Knowledge Guide*. Washington, D.C. Available at www.ifc.org/wps/wcm/connect/254277bc-86bd-420e-b390-94a13b19ca36/SCF+Knowledge+Guide+FINAL.pdf?MOD=AJPERES&CVID=mYOre4A (accessed 9 May 2023).

International Finance Corporation (2017). *MSME [Micro, Small and Medium Enterprises] Finance Gap: Assessment of the Shortfalls and Opportunities in Financing Micro, Small and Medium Enterprises in Emerging Markets*. World Bank. Washington, D.C.

International Finance Corporation (2020). *Technology and Digitization in Supply Chain Finance*. Handbook. Washington, D.C.

International Finance Corporation (2021a). Demand for Digital Skills in Sub-Saharan Africa: Key Findings from a Five-Country Study: Côte d'Ivoire, Kenya, Mozambique, Nigeria and Rwanda.

International Finance Corporation (2021b). *Supply Chain Finance by Development Banks and Public Entities*. Guidebook. World Bank. Washington, D.C.

International Finance Corporation (2022a). Supply Chain Finance Market Assessment: Kenya. International Finance Corporation Financial Institutions Group Advisory Services Africa.

International Finance Corporation (2022b). Supply Chain Finance Market Assessment: Nigeria. International Finance Corporation Financial Institutions Group Advisory Services Africa.

International Finance Corporation (2022c). Supply Chain Finance Market Assessment: Côte d'Ivoire. International Finance Corporation Financial Institutions Group Advisory Services Africa.

International Institute for Sustainable Development and Intergovernmental Forum on Mining, Minerals, Metals and Sustainable Development (2019). Local *Content Policies in the Mining Sector: Scaling up Local Procurement*. Available at www.iisd.org/system/files/publications/local-content-policies-mining.pdf.

International Insulin Foundation (n.d.). Fact sheet on diabetes in sub-Saharan Africa. Available at www.access2insulin.org/uploads/4/9/1/0/4910107/factsheet.pdf.

International Labour Organization (2019). Child labour in mining and global supply chains. Available at www.ilo.org/wcmsp5/groups/public/---asia/---ro-bangkok/---ilo-manila/documents/publication/wcms_720743.pdf.

International Labour Organization (2020). Global Wage Report 2020-2021: Wages and minimum wages in the time of COVID-19. International Labor Office - Geneva: ILO 2020.

International Labour Organization (2021). *Women in Mining: Towards Gender Equality*. Geneva.

International Monetary Fund (2022a). *World Economic Outlook [Report October] 2022: Countering the Cost-of-Living Crisis*. Washington, D.C.

International Monetary Fund (2022b). IMF [International Monetary Fund] Executive Board concludes 2022 Article IV consultation with the Republic of Mozambique and approves US$456 million extended credit facility arrangement. Press Release No. 22/145. 9 May.

International Renewable Energy Agency (2016). Solar PV in Africa: Costs and markets. Available at https://www.irena.org/-/media/Files/IRENA/Agency/Publication/2016/IRENA_Solar_PV_Costs_Africa_2016.pdf?rev=d3f8f61a82f14186ab6f8c20e7fa9e44

International Renewable Energy Agency and African Development Bank (2022). *Renewable Energy Market Analysis: Africa and Its Regions*. Abu Dhabi and Abidjan.

International Telecommunication Union (2021). *Digital Trends in Africa: Information and Communication Technology Trends and Developments in the Africa Region 2017–2020*. Geneva.

International Trade Administration (2021). South Africa. Information technology. Available at www.trade.gov/knowledge-product/south-africa-information-technology (accessed 3 July 2023).

International Trade Centre (2022). *Made by Africa: Creating Value through Integration*. Geneva.

International Trade Centre and UNCTAD (2021). Unlocking regional trade opportunities in Africa for a more sustainable and inclusive future. 6 December.

IPCC (2022). Climate Change 2022: Impacts, Adaptation, and Vulnerability. Contribution of Working Group II to the Sixth Assessment Report of the Intergovernmental Panel on Climate Change. Cambridge University Press. Cambridge University Press, Cambridge, UK and New York, NY, USA, 3056 pp., doi:10.1017/9781009325844.

Iqvia (2022). Localization of pharmaceutical manufacturing in Middle East and North Africa region: An evolving landscape of the health-care ecosystem. White Paper. Available at www.iqvia.com/-/media/iqvia/pdfs/mea/white-paper/localization-of-pharmaceutical-manufacturing-in-middle-east-and-north-africa-region.pdf.

Jabil (2022). Global supply chain readiness report: The pandemic and beyond. Jabil Industry Week.

Japan International Cooperation Agency and Boston Consulting Group (2022). *Study for the promotion of the African automotive industry: Post-COVID-19 supply chain and mobility reform*. ED-JR-22-049.

Jenkins A (2021). Just-in-time vs just-in-case: Choosing the right strategy. Oracle Netsuite. 3 May.

Jia F, Zhang T and Chen L (2020). Sustainable supply chain finance: Towards a research agenda. *Journal of Cleaner Production*. 243:118680.

Johnson E (2022). Shipper focus yields revenue growth for DP [Dubai Port] World. *Journal of Commerce*. 10 March.

Kabeer N (2012). Women's economic empowerment and inclusive growth: Labour markets and enterprise development. SIG Working Paper 2012/1.

Karingi SN, Pesce O, and Mevel S (2016). Preferential trade agreements in Africa: Lessons from the tripartite free trade agreements and an African continent-wide FTA [free trade area]. In: Low P, Osakwe C and Oshikawa M, eds. *African Perspectives on Trade and the WTO: Domestic Reforms, Structural Transformation and Global Economic Integration*. World Trade Organization. Cambridge University Press. Cambridge, United Kingdom:230–268.

Kasraoui S (2022). China's XEV to produce electric cars for the Italian market in Morocco. *Morocco World News*. 28 December.

Kassa W and Coulibaly S (2019). Revisiting the trade impact of the African Growth and Opportunity Act: A synthetic control approach. Policy Research Working Paper 8993. World Bank.

Kaur K and Kau I (2022). *Global Value Chain*. Conestoga College. Kitchener, Ontario, Canada.

Kearney (2022). Buying resilience: How M and A [mergers and acquisitions] can future-proof your supply chain. 20 December.

Kemp D, Owen JR, Gotzmann N and Bond CJ (2011). Just relations and company: Community conflict in mining. *Journal of Business Ethics*. 101(1):93–109.

Kenton W (2022). What is horizontal integration? Definition and examples. Investopedia. 27 August.

Kharas H (2010). The emerging middle class in developing countries. Working Paper No. 285. Organisation for Economic Co-operation and Development. Paris.

Khattabi A (2023). À Rabat, Ryad Mezzour roule en électrique, une voiturette fabriquee à Kénitra. *Le 360*. 11 January.

Kilpatrick J (2022). Supply chain implications of the Russia [Russian Federation]–Ukraine conflict. Deloitte Insights. 25 March.

Klapper L (2006). The role of factoring for financing small and medium enterprises. *Journal of Banking and Finance*. 30(11):3111–3130.

Klonner S and Nolen P (2008). Does ICT [information and communications technology] benefit the poor? Evidence from South Africa. Verein für Socialpolitik. Research Committee Development Economics. Proceedings of the German Development Economics Conference, Hannover 2010.

Korinek J and Ramdoo I (2017). Local content policies in mineral-exporting countries. Organisation for Economic Co-operation and Development Trade Policy Paper No. 209. Organisation for Economic Co-operation and Development Publishing. Paris.

Kuteyi D and Winkler H (2022). Logistics challenges in sub-Saharan Africa and opportunities for digitalization. *Sustainability*. 14(4):2399.

Le Derf Y (2022). Is regionalization the answer to supply chain risk mitigation? Jabil.

Jabil (2020). Special Report: Supply Chain Resilience in a Post-Pandemic World: A Survey of Supply Chain Decision-Makers. Jabil.

Lee J, Gereffi G and Nathan D (2013). Mobile phones: Who benefits in shifting global value chains? Capturing the Gains. Revised Summit Briefing No. 6.1. Available at file:///C:/Users/delbl/Downloads/SSRN-id2265845.pdf.

Lee, N. and Clarke, S. (2019). Do low-skilled workers gain from high-tech employment growth?: High -technology multipliers, employment and wages in Britain. Research Policy 48 (2019) 103803. Available at https://www.sciencedirect.com/journal/research-policy.

Lema R and Rabellotti R (2023). The green and digital transition in manufacturing global value chains in latecomer countries. UNCTAD Background Paper. Available at https://unctad.org/system/files/non-official-document/tir2023_background1_en.pdf.

Lilly (2022). Lilly and Eva Pharma announce collaboration to enhance sustainable access to affordable insulin in Africa. 14 December.

Lin Y, Fan D, Shi X and Fu M (2021). The effects of supply chain diversification during the COVID-19 crisis: Evidence from Chinese manufacturers. *Transportation Research. Part E: Logistics and Transportation Review*. 155:102493.

Loannou I and Demirel G (2022). Blockchain and supply chain finance: A critical literature review at the intersection of operations, finance and law. *Journal of Banking and Financial Technology* 6:83–107.

Lombe WC (2020). Local content in Zambia: A faltering experience? In: Page J and Tarp F, eds. *Mining for Change: Natural Resources and Industry in Africa*. United Nations University World Institute for Development Economics Research. Oxford University Press. Oxford, United Kingdom:422–446.

Manufacturing Chemist (2014). Zambia and IBM [International Business Machines] improve access to life saving drugs. 23 May.

Marin A and Goya D (2021). Mining: The dark side of the energy transition. *Environmental Innovation and Social Transitions*. 41:86–88.

Markowitz C and Black A (2019). The prospects for regional value chains in the automotive sector in Southern Africa. In: Scholvin S, Black A, Revilla Diez J and Turok I. *Value Chains in Sub-Saharan Africa: Challenges of Integration into the Global Economy*. Advances in African Economic, Social and Political Development Series. Springer International Publishing. Cham, Switzerland:27–41.

Mashilo AM (2019). Auto production in South Africa and components manufacturing in Gauteng province. Global Labour University Working Paper No. 58. International Labour Office.

Maximize Market Research (2022). Supply chain finance market: Supply chain finance is becoming increasingly popular in emerging economies. December.

Mbodiam BR (2021). Slow at first, sales of Arthur Zang's Cardiopad is rising at an exponential rate in Cameroon. Business in Cameroon. 18 October.

McIntyre A, Li MX, Wang K and Yun H (2018). Economic benefits of export diversification in small States. International Monetary Fund Working Paper No. WP/18/86. International Monetary Fund.

McKinsey and Company. (2010). Lions on the move: The progress and potential of African economies.

McKinsey and Company (2020). *Risk, Resilience and Rebalancing in Global Value Chains*. Available at www.mckinsey.com/~/media/McKinsey/Business%20Functions/Operations/Our%20Insights/Risk%20resilience%20and%20rebalancing%20in%20global%20value%20chains/Risk-resilience-and-rebalancing-in-global-value-chains-full-report-vH.pdf.

McMillan M and Zeufack A (2022). Labour productivity growth and industrialization in Africa. *Journal of Economic Perspectives*. 36(1):3–32.

McMillan MS and Rodrik D (2011). Globalization, structural change and productivity growth. National Bureau of Economic Research Working Paper No. 17143. National Bureau of Economic Research. Cambridge, Massachusetts, United States.

Mefford, R. (2009). The Financial Crisis and Global Supply Chains. University of San Francisco.

Melber H (2022). Africa's middle classes. *Africa Spectrum*. 57(2):204–219.

Mining Review Africa (2023). Partnership will improve battery recycling in South Africa. 2 January.

Moneim DA (2019). FRA [Financial Regulatory Authority] allows credit rating companies to start activities in Egypt. Ahram Online. 2 September.

Mordor Intelligence (2022). South Africa Battery Market: Growth, Trends, COVID-19 Impact and Forecasts (2023–2028).

Moretto A, Grassi L, Caniato F, Giorgino M and Ronchi S (2019). Supply chain finance: From traditional to supply chain credit rating. *Journal of Purchasing and Supply Management*. 25(2):197–217.

Moretti, E. and Thulin, P. (2013). Local multipliers and human capital in the US and Sweden. Ind. Corp. Chang. 22 (1), 339–362.

Morley M (2022). How IoT [Internet of things], AI [artificial intelligence] and blockchain will enable tomorrow's autonomous supply chain. Opentext. 27 May.

Mosley P (2018). Why has export diversification been so hard to achieve in Africa? *The World Economy*. 41(4):1025–1044.

Motari M, Nikiema J-B, Kasilo OMJ, Kniazkov S, Loua A, Sougou A and Prosper T (2021). The role of intellectual property rights on access to medicines in the WHO [World Health Organization] African region: 25 years after the TRIPS [Trade-Related Aspects of Intellectual Property Rights] Agreement. *BMC Public Health*. 21:490.

Mukherjee S and Padhi SS (2022). Sourcing decision under interconnected risks: An application of mean–variance preferences approach. *Annals of Operations Research*. 313(2):1243–1268.

Naji A (2020). Morocco automotive production: Exports and attractiveness of Investments. *Meer*. 17 February.

National Association of Automobile Manufacturers of South Africa (2023). The SA [South African] labour force remains a backbone for the automotive industrial capacity. Press Release. 2 May.

Natsuda K and Thoburn J (2021). *Automotive Industrialization: Industrial Policy and Development in Southeast Asia*. Routledge. Oxon, United Kingdom and New York, United States.

Natural Resource Governance Institute (2022). Triple win: How mining can benefit Africa's citizens, their environment and the energy transition. Available at https://resourcegovernance.org/sites/default/files/documents/triple-win_how-mining-can-benefit-africas-citizens-their-environment-the-energy-transition.pdf.

Ncube M and Shimeles A (2013). The making of middle class in Africa: Evidence from DHS [Demographic and Health Surveys] data. Institute for the Study of Labour Discussion Paper No. 7352. Bonn, Germany.

Neu Group (2022). FASB [Financial Accounting Standards Board] has issued new disclosure rules for supply chain finance. What do they mean for corporates? 17 November.

Nielsen (2020). Overcoming online shopping obstacles amid lockdowns in Africa and the Middle East is not only retailer driven.

Observatory of Economic Complexity (2022). Available at https://oec.world/en (accessed 1 July 2023).

Office of the United States Trade Representative (2022). *2022 Biennial Report on the Implementation of the African Growth and Opportunity Act*. Washington, D.C.

Office of the United States Trade Representative (2023). AGOA [African Growth and Opportunity Act] Eligible and ineligible countries – 2023. Available at https://ustr.gov/sites/default/files/files/gsp/2023AGOA.pdf.

Oke A, Boso N and Marfo JS (2022). Out of Africa. *Supply Chain Management Review*. 5 January.

Oliver Wyman (2020). Making supply chains more resilient: How manufacturers can solve the supply chain dilemma while remaining flexible and competitive.

Open Capital (2021). A review of the trade finance landscape in East Africa and the Horn of Africa: Barriers, opportunities and potential interventions to drive uptake. Available at www.fsdafrica.org/wp-content/uploads/2021/04/21-04-23-Review-of-the-Trade-Financial-Landscape-in-EA-and-HA.pdf (accessed 9 May 2023).

Organisation for Economic Co-operation and Development (2022a). *Africa's Development Dynamics 2022: Regional Value Chains for a Sustainable Recovery.* Organisation for Economic Co-operation and Development Publications. Paris.

Organisation for Economic Co-operation and Development (2022b). *Financing SMEs [Small and Medium-sized Enterprises] and Entrepreneurs 2022: An OECD [Organisation for Economic Co-operation and Development] Scoreboard.* Organisation for Economic Co-operation and Development Publications. Paris.

Oxfam (2017). From Aspiration to Reality. Unpacking the Africa Mining Vision. Available at www-cdn.oxfam.org/s3fs-public/bp-africamining-vision-090317-en.pdf.

Pedro A (2021). Critical materials and sustainable development in Africa. *One Earth.* 4(3):346–349.

Perrin C, Ewen M and Beran D (2017). The role of biosimilar manufacturers in improving access to insulin globally. *The Lancet.* Correspondence. (5)8:578.

Pickard J, Plimmer G and Smith R (2021). How Lex Greensill helped sow the seeds of Carillion crisis. *Financial Times.* 10 May.

Pitchbook (2022). Private equity's opportunity in supply chain technology: An introduction to a burgeoning vertical in technology. 22 June.

PriceWaterhouseCooper (2017). Sizing the prize: What's the real value of AI [artificial intelligence] for your business and how can you capitalize?

PriceWaterhouseCooper (2018). Shipping and ports. Available at www.pwc.com/ua/en/industry/transportation-and-logistics/shipping-and-ports.html (accessed 9 May 2023).

Priya Datta P, Christopher M and Allen PM (2007). Agent-based modelling of complex production/distribution systems to improve resilience. *International Journal of Logistics Research and Applications.* 10(3):187–203.

Ravallion M (2009). The developing world's bulging (but vulnerable) "middle class". Policy Research Working Paper 4816. World Bank.

Research Network Sustainable Global Supply Chains (2022). *Sustainable Global Supply Chains Report 2022*. German Development Institute. Bonn, Germany.

Reuters (2019). Maroc Telecom signs $1 billion investment deal with Moroccan Government. 26 August.

Reuters (2021). Ivory Coast [Côte d'Ivoire] rubber output expected to rise 16% in 2021. 8 April.

Roberts, B. and Wolf, M. (2018). "High-tech industries: an analysis of employment, wages, and output," Beyond the Numbers: Employment & Unemployment, vol. 7, no. 7 (U.S. Bureau of Labor Statistics, May 2018), https://www.bls.gov/opub/btn/volume-7/high-tech-industries-an-analysis-of-employment-wages-and-output.htm.

Roland Berger (2018). Recent development paradigms to support women's empowerment. 28 September.

Ross M, Lujala P and Rustad SA (2012). Horizontal inequality, decentralizing the distribution of natural resource revenues and peace. In: Rustad SA and Lujala P, eds. *High-value Natural Resources and Post-conflict Peacebuilding*. Environmental Law Institute and United Nations Environment Programme. Earthscan. Oxon, United Kingdom: 251–259.

Saidi T and Douglas T (2019). Medical device regulation in Africa. In: Douglas T, ed. *Biomedical Engineering for Africa*. University of Cape Town Libraries. Cape Town:175–185.

Salah F (2022). Egypt's FRA [Financial Regulatory Authority] is working on developing credit rating system for unbanked categories. Zawya. 29 March

Samuel M (2021). Boko Haram teams up with bandits in Nigeria. Institute for Security Study Africa. 3 March.

Sanon S and Slany A (2023). Identifying African countries' potential in the African automotive industry: A continental supply chain mapping approach. UNCTAD.

Savoy CM and Ramanujam SR (2022). Diversifying supply chains: The role of development assistance and other official finance. Centre for Strategic and International Studies Brief. Centre for Strategic and International Studies.

Scott K (2017). Is Africa's $30 smartphone a game changer? Cable News Network. 5 May.

ShipBob (2022). Value Chain vs. Supply Chain: Understanding the Differences to Grow Your Business. Available at www.shipbob.com.

Shrivastava P, Punatar P, Stefanski S and Yaworsky K (2019). How digitized supply chain finance can help small merchants grow. Accion. 16 January.

Signé L (2018). *Africa's Consumer Market Potential: Trends, Drivers, Opportunities and Strategies*. Africa Growth Initiative. Brookings Institution.

Simchi-Levi, D. and Haren, P. (2021). How the war in Ukraine is further disrupting global supply chains. Harvard Business School.

Singh R, Bakshi M and Prashant Mishra P (2015). Corporate social responsibility: Linking bottom of the pyramid to market development? *Journal of Business Ethics*. 131(2):361-373.

Siripurapu A (2021). What happened to supply chains in 2021? Council on Foreign Relations. 13 December.

Sodhi MS, Son B-G and Tang CS (2012). Researchers' perspectives on supply chain risk management. *Production and Operations Management*. 21(1):1–13.

South Africa (2023). Renewable independent power producer programme. Available at www.gov.za/about-government/government-programmes/renewable-independent-power-producer-programme (accessed 9 June 2023).

Spiller P (2021). Making supply-chain decarbonization happen. McKinsey and Company.

Statista (2023). Available at www.statista.com/ (accessed 6 June 2023).

Stellantis (2023). Available at www.stellantis.com/fr (accessed 6 June 2023).

Subban (2022) Africa: Bringing supply chains to life across the continent. Baker McKenzie. 7 February.

Supply Chain Brain (2018). How intelligent business networks will empower tomorrow's autonomous supply chains. 9 April.

Supply Chain Junction (n.d). A perspective on BRICS [Brazil, Russian Federation, China and South Africa] and the South African supply chain.

SustainAbility, United Nations Environment Programme and United Nations Global Compact (2008). *Unchaining Value: Innovative Approaches to Sustainable Supply.* Pensord Press. Blackwood, United Kingdom.

Tanchum M. (2022a). Germany's expanding partnership with Morocco: Strengthening supply chain resilience is the driving factor. Middle East Institute. Available at www.mipa.institute/en/9329.

Tanchum M (2022b). Morocco's green mobility revolution: The geo-economic factors driving its rise as an electric vehicle manufacturing hub. Middle East Institute. Available at www.mei.edu/sites/default/files/2022-08/Tanchum%20-%20 Morocco%20Green%20Mobility%20Revolution.pdf.

Tarver, E. (2022). Value Chain vs. Supply Chain: What's the Difference? Investopedia. Available at https://www.investopedia.com.

Tech Insights (2023). The DRAM [dynamic random access memory] crash of 2008. The Chip History Centre. Available at www.chiphistory.org/720-the-dram-crash-of-2008 (accessed 4 May 2023).

Techtarget Network (2021). What is a supply chain? Definition, Models and Best Practices. June.

The North Africa Post (2018). Germany's Kromberg and Schubert boosts Morocco's car industry cluster. 14 November.

Trade and Industrial Policy Strategies (2021). Opportunities to develop the lithium-ion battery value chain in South Africa. Available at www.tips.org.za/images/Battery_ Manufacturing_value_chain_study_main_report_March_2021.pdf.

Trade Finance Global (2023). Supply chain finance. 2023 supply chain finance guide. Available at www.tradefinanceglobal.com/supply-chain-finance/ (accessed 30 June 2023).

Trade Law Centre (2021). AfCFTA [African Continental Free Trade Area] rules of origin. Available at www.tralac.org/documents/resources/infographics/4328-afcfta-rules-of-origin-fact-sheet-may-2021/file.html (accessed 22 June 2023).

Tukamuhabwa BR, Stevenson M, Busby J and Zorzini M (2015). Supply chain resilience: Definition, review and theoretical foundations for further study. *International Journal of Production Research*. 53(18):5592–5623.

UNCTAD (1999). *Investment Policy Review: Egypt* (United Nations publication. Sales No. E.99.II.D.20. Geneva).

UNCTAD (2003). *Foreign Direct Investment and Performance Requirements: New Evidence from Selected Countries* (United Nations publication. Sales No. E.03.II.D.32. New York and Geneva).

UNCTAD (2005). *Developing Countries in International Trade: Trade and Development Index* (United Nations publication. New York and Geneva).

UNCTAD (2018). *Trade and Development Report 2018: Trade and Power, Platforms and the Free Trade Delusion* (United Nations publication. Sales No. E.18.II.D.7. New York and Geneva).

UNCTAD (2020a). *World Investment Report 2020: International Production beyond the Pandemic* (United Nations publication. Sales No. E.20.II.D.23. Geneva).

UNCTAD (2020b). *Commodities at a Glance: Special Issue on Strategic Battery Raw Materials*. No. 13 (United Nations publication. Geneva).

UNCTAD (2020c). *Economic Development in Africa Report 2020: Tackling Illicit Financial Flows for Sustainable Development in Africa* (United Nations publication. Sales No. E.20.II.D.21. Geneva).

UNCTAD (2021a). *The Least Developed Countries Report 2021: The Least Developed Countries in the Post-COVID World: Learning from 50 years of Experience* (United Nations publication. Sales No. E.21.II.D.4. Geneva).

UNCTAD (2021b). *Economic Development in Africa Report 2021: Reaping the Potential Benefits of the African Continental Free Trade Area for Inclusive Growth* (United Nations publication. Sales No. E.21.II.D.3. Geneva).

UNCTAD (2021c). Promoting investment in health post-pandemic: A global trend? *The IPA Observer*. No. 11.

UNCTAD (2021d). *Technology and Innovation Report 2021: Catching Technological Waves – Innovation with Equity* (United Nations publication. Sales No. E.21.II.D.8. Geneva).

UNCTAD (2022a). *Review of Maritime Transport 2022: Navigating Stormy Waters* (United Nations publication. Sales No. E.22.II.D.42. Geneva).

UNCTAD (2022b). Maritime trade disrupted: The war in Ukraine and its effects on maritime trade logistics. 28 June 2022.

UNCTAD (2022c). *The Least Developed Countries Report 2022: The Low-carbon Transition and Its Daunting Implications for Structural Transformation* (United Nations publication. Sales No. E.22.II.D.40. Geneva).

UNCTAD (2022d). *Economic Development in Africa Report 2022: Rethinking the Foundations of Export Diversification in Africa – The Catalytic Role of Business and Financial Services* (United Nations publication. Sales No. E.22.II.D.31. Geneva).

UNCTAD (2022e). *World Investment Report 2022: International Tax Reforms and Sustainable Investment* (United Nations publication. Sales No. E.22.II.D.20. Geneva).

UNCTAD (2022f). *The New Frontier in Entrepreneurship: Entrepreneurship and Innovation in the New Health Economy*. Series No. 2. (United Nations publication).

UNCTAD (2023). *Technology and Innovation Report 2023: Opening Green Windows – Technological Opportunities for a Low-carbon World* (United Nations publication. Sales No. E.22.II.D.53. Geneva).

UNCTAD and Common Market for Eastern and Southern Africa (2023). *The Utilization of Trade Preferences by COMESA [Common Market for Eastern and Southern Africa] Member States: Intra-regional Trade and North–South Trade* (United Nations publication. Sales No.: E.22.II.D.12. Geneva).

United Nations (2015). *Paris Agreement*. Available at https://unfccc.int/files/essential_background/convention/application/pdf/english_paris_agreement.pdf

United Nations (2022). *2022 Revision of World Population Prospects*. Available at https://population.un.org/wpp/ (accessed 18 May 2023).

United Nations (2023) *World Economic Situation and Prospects 2023* (United Nations publication. Sales No. E.23.II.C.1). Available at www.un.org/development/desa/dpad/publication/world-economic-situation-and-prospects-2023/ (accessed 12 May 2023).

United Nations, Economic Commission for Africa (2014). *A Country Mining Vision Guidebook: Domesticating the Africa Mining Vision*. Addis Ababa.

United Nations, Economic Commission for Africa (2015). *Economic Report on Africa 2015: Industrializing Through Trade*. Addis Ababa.

United Nations, Economic Commission for Africa (2018). *The Potential for the Creation of Regional Value Chains in North Africa: A Sector-Based Mapping*. Addis Ababa.

United Nations, Economic Commission for Africa (2020a). COVID-19 and beyond: Solar energy in Africa – Powering responses, accelerating inclusive and sustainable development. Available at www.uneca.org/sites/default/files/AEC/2020/presentations/covid_19_and_beyond_-_solar_energy_in_africa_-_powering_responses_accelerating_inclusive_and_sustainable_development_.pdf.

United Nations, Economic Commission for Africa (2020b). Economic Report on Africa 2020: Finance for Private Sector Development in Africa. United Nations. Addis Ababa.

United Nations, Economic Commission for Africa (2021). *COVID-19 Impact on E-commerce: Africa*. Addis Ababa.

United Nations, Economic Commission for Africa (2023). ECA [Economic Commission for Africa] and Afreximbank [African Export–Import Bank] sign framework agreement to establish special economic zones for the production of battery electric vehicles in DRC [the Democratic Republic of the Congo] and Zambia. 27 March.

United Nations, General Assembly (2022). State of South–South cooperation. Report of the Secretary-General. A/77/297. New York. 17 August.

United Nations Development Programme (2017). Accelerating pico-solar photovoltaic lighting market in Kenya. Policy Brief.

United Nations Development Programme (2022). *Crime and Terror Nexus: The Intersections between Terror and Criminal Groups in the Lake Chad Basin.* N'Djamena.

United Nations Environment Programme (2020). *Mineral Resource Governance in the 21st Century: Gearing Extractive Industries towards Sustainable Development.* United Nations Educational, Scientific and Cultural Organization. Paris.

United Nations Environment Programme (2021). *Local Value Capture from the Energy Transition: Insights from the Solar PV [Photovoltaic] Industry in Kenya.* United Nations Environment Programme DTU Partnership. Copenhagen. Available at https://unepccc.org/wp-content/uploads/2021/08/local-value-capture-from-the-energy-transition-insights-from-the-solar-pv-industry-in-kenya-web.pdf.

United Nations Industrial Development Organization (2019). *Industrial Development Report 2020: Industrializing in the Digital Age.* Vienna.

United States Agency for International Development (2023). *Global Health Supply Chain Programme: Technical Assistance South Africa – Year Five Annual Report.* Available at www.ghsupplychain.org/sites/default/files/2023-02/GHSC-TA%20_Year%20 5%20Annual%20Report_vF%20no%20fin%20%282%29.pdf.

United We Care (2022). The pros and cons of just in time vs just in case inventory management strategies. 4 June.

University of Cambridge (2021). What is a value chain? Definitions and characteristics. Available at https://www.cisl.cam.ac.uk/education/graduate-study/pgcerts/value-chain-defs.

Vakil V (2022). Regionalized supply chains: The key to resilience. *Supply Chain Quarterly.* 15 May.

Van Blerk H (2018). African lions: Who are Africa's rising middle class? Ipsos Views. No. 15.

van Zyl G (2013). Congo's [Republic of the Congo] VMK Tech building Brazzaville factory. 4 November.

Volkswagen Group (2023). Available at www.volkswagenag.com/en/group/brands-and-models.html (accessed 6 June 2023).

Vu TL, Nguyen DN, Luong TA, Nguyen TTX, Nguyen TTT and Doan TDU (2022). The impact of supply chain financing on SMEs [small and medium-sized enterprises] performance in global supply chain. *Uncertain Supply Chain Management*. 10(1):255–270.

Wallstreetmojo Team (2021). WallStreetMojo. Available at https://www.wallstreetmojo.com/supply-chain-vs-value-chain/ (accessed 21 March 2023).

Wass S (2018). Standard Chartered and Huawei develop IoT [Internet of things]-led smart financing solution. *Global Trade Review*. 17 October.

Wass S (2022). Banks risk widening trade finance gap as they push for green label. Standard and Poor's Global Market Intelligence. 29 September.

Webb H (2022). The global supply chain of a mobile phone. Ethical Consumer Research Association. 16 November.

Wolters Kluwer (2021). The value in supply chain flexibility. 12 February.

Wood M (2019). Major Chinese bank, pharma wholesaler in supply chain finance blockchain. Ledger Insights. 20 November.

World Bank (2016). Connectivity, logistics and trade facilitation: Facilitating trade at the border, behind the border and beyond. Brief. 21 June.

World Bank (2017). *The Growing Role of Minerals and Metals for a Low-Carbon Future*. Washington, D.C.

World Bank (2018). Morocco energy policy MRV [Measurement, Reporting and Verification]: Emission reductions from energy subsidies reform and renewable energy policy.

World Bank (2019a). *Global Economic Prospects: Heightened Tensions, Subdued Investments*. June. Washington, D.C.

World Bank (2019b). Achieving broadband access for all in Africa comes with a $100 billion price tag. 17 October.

World Bank (2019c). Global horizontal irradiation, photovoltaic power potential: Kenya. Global Solar Atlas. Available at https://globalsolaratlas.info/download/kenya (accessed 3 July 2023).

World Bank (2020). Enforcing contracts. Subnational Studies. Measuring Business Regulations. Available at https://subnational.doingbusiness.org/en/data/exploretopics/enforcing-contracts/score (accessed 11 May 2023).

World Bank (2023a). *Women, Business and the Law 2023*. Washington, D.C.

World Bank (2023b). *Digital Africa: Technological Transformation for Jobs*. Washington, D.C.

World Business Council for Sustainable Development (2021). Reaching net zero: Incentives for supply chain decarbonization.

World Economic Forum (2016). Manufacturing our future cases on the future of manufacturing. White Paper. Geneva. Available at www3.weforum.org/docs/GAC16_The_Future_of_Manufacturing_report.pdf.

World Economic Forum (2019). Rwanda pioneers first "made in Africa" smartphones. 16 October.

World Economic Forum (2022). The art and science of eliminating hepatitis: Egypt's experience. White Paper. Geneva.

World Health Organization (2022). African region tops world in undiagnosed diabetes: WHO [World Health Organization] analysis. 14 November.

World Trade Organization (2020a). An economic analysis of the US [United States]–China trade conflict. Staff Working Paper ERSD-2020-04. 19 March.

World Trade Organization (2020b). Waiver from certain provisions of the TRIPS Agreement [Agreement on Trade-related Aspects of Intellectual Property Rights] for the prevention, containment and treatment of COVID-19: Communication from India and South Africa. Council for Trade-related Aspects of Intellectual Property Rights. IP/C/W/669. 2 October.

World Trade Organization (2021). Waiver from certain provisions of the Trips Agreement [Agreement on Trade-related Aspects of Intellectual Property Rights] for the prevention, containment and treatment of COVID-19. IP/C/W/669/Rev. 1. 25 May.

Wuttke T (2022). The automotive industry in developing countries and its contribution to economic development. Centre of African Economies Working Paper 2021:2. Roskilde University, Denmark.

Yin W and Ran W (2022). Supply chain diversification, digital transformation, and supply chain resilience: Configuration analysis based on fsQCA [fuzzy set qualitative comparative analysis]. *Sustainability*. 14(13):7690.

Yoshino N and Taghizadeh-Hesary F (2015). Analysis of credit ratings for small and medium-sized enterprises: Evidence from Asia. *Asian Development Review*. 32(2):18–37.

Yoshino N, Taghizadeh-Hesary F, Charoensivakorn P and Niraula B (2015). SME [small and medium-sized enterprise] credit risk analysis using bank lending data: An analysis of Thai SMEs [small and medium-sized enterprises]. Asian Development Bank Institute Working Paper 536. Tokyo.

Youssef H (2021). Egypt's GYPTO Pharma partners with Japanese Otsuka to produce, export medical products. 3 June. Ahram Online.

Yuan Y and Li W (2022). The effects of supply chain risk information processing capability and supply chain finance on supply chain resilience: A moderated and mediated model. *Journal of Enterprise Information Management*. 35(6):1592–1612.

Zeng K (2021). Chinese supply chains prove resilient to global shocks and pressure. East Asia Forum. 27 May.

Zhang G (2021). AfCFTA [African Continental Free Trade Area]: A more Integrated Africa in the global supply chain. 17 February. Upply.

Zhang LY (2012). Does climate change make industrialization an obsolete development strategy for cities in the South? In: Hoornweg D, Frieire M, Lee JM, Bpada-Tata P and and Yueh B, eds. *Cities and Climate Change: Responding to an Urgent Agenda*. Volume 2. World Bank. Washington, D.C.:564–582.

Zhao L and Huchzermeier A (2018). *Supply Chain Finance: Integrating Operations and Finance in Global Supply Chains*. Springer. Cham, Switzerland.

Zoeller J-F (2022). Supply chain regionalization not a binary decision. Flex. 19 September.